D1563760

Credit Derivatives: Instruments, Applications, and Pricing

THE FRANK J. FABOZZI SERIES

Credit Derivatives:
Instruments, Applications, and Pricing

MARK J.P. ANSON

FRANK J. FABOZZI

MOORAD CHOUDHRY

REN-RAW CHEN

WILEY

John Wiley & Sons, Inc.

MJPA

To my wife, Mary, and to my children, Madeleine and Marcus, for their enduring patience

FJF

To my sister, Lucy

MC

To Yves Gaillard, respect, and an inspiration to us all

RRC

To my wife, Hsing-Yao

Contents

Preface

The credit derivative market has grown from a few customized trades in the early 1990s to a large, organized market that trades billions of dollars each year. This market has expanded to reflect the growing demand from asset managers, corporations, insurance companies, fixed income trading desks, and other credit-sensitive users to buy and sell credit exposure.

In this book we provide a comprehensive examination of the credit derivatives market. As the title of the book indicates, we cover the practical applications of credit derivatives as well as the most current pricing models applied by asset managers and traders. We also discuss investment strategies that may be applied using these tools.

Our soup to nuts approach begins with an overview of credit risk. In many cases, credit is the predominant, if not overwhelming, economic exposure associated with a note, bond, or other fixed-income instrument. We discuss the nature of credit risk, discuss its economic impact, and provide graphical descriptions of its properties.

We next discuss some of the basic building blocks in the credit derivative market: credit default swaps, asset swaps, and total return swaps. These chapters are descriptive in nature to introduce the reader to the credit derivatives market.

The following chapters provide numerous examples of credit derivative applications. Specifically, we describe the credit-linked note market as well as synthetic collateralized debt obligations. Credit derivatives are used to provide the underlying credit exposure embedded within these fixed-income instruments. These chapters demonstrate how credit derivatives are efficient conduits of economic exposure that would otherwise be difficult to acquire in the cash markets.

The next group of chapters provides the mechanics for the modeling and pricing of credit risk. These chapters are more quantitative in nature as is necessary to provide a thorough review of current credit pricing models. However, our goal is not to dazzle the reader with out knowledge of rigorous mathematics, but rather, to provide a comprehensive framework in which credit derivative contracts can be efficiently priced.

Finally, we provide a discussion on the accounting and tax treatment of credit derivatives. Throughout the book, we provide numerous examples of credit derivatives, their practical applications, and where pricing information can be found through *Bloomberg* and other sources. Our ultimate goal is to provide the reader with a complete guide to credit derivatives, whether it be for reference purposes, day to day use, or strategy implementation.

We would like to thank Abukar Ali of Bloomberg L.P. in London for his assistance with the chapter on credit-linked notes (Chapter 6) and help with Bloomberg screens. We benefited from insightful discussions regarding credit default swap pricing with Dominic O'Kane of Lehman Brothers in London.

The views, thoughts, and opinions expressed in this book represent those of the authors in their individual private capacity. They do not represent those of Mark Anson's employer, the California Public Employees' Retirement System, nor KBC Financial Products (UK) Limited or KBC Bank N.V. or of Moorad Choudhry as an employee, representative or officer of KBC Financial Products (UK) Limited or KBC Bank N.V.

Mark J.P. Anson
Frank J. Fabozzi
Moorad Choudhry
Ren-Raw Chen

About the Authors

Mark Anson is the Chief Investment Officer for the California Public Employees' Retirement System (CalPERS). He has complete responsibility for all asset classes in which CalPERS invests. Dr. Anson earned his law degree from the Northwestern University School of Law in Chicago where he graduated as the Executive/Production Editor of the Law Review, and his Ph.D. and Masters in Finance from the Columbia University Graduate School of Business in New York City where he graduated with honors as Beta Gamma Sigma. Dr. Anson is a member of the New York and Illinois State Bar Associations. He has also earned the Chartered Financial Analyst, Certified Public Accountant, Certified Management Accountant, and Certified Internal Auditor degrees. Dr. Anson is the author of three other books on the financial markets and is the author of over 60 published articles.

Frank J. Fabozzi, Ph.D., CFA, CPA is the Frederick Frank Adjunct Professor of Finance in the School of Management at Yale University. Prior to joining the Yale faculty, he was a Visiting Professor of Finance in the Sloan School at MIT. Professor Fabozzi is a Fellow of the International Center for Finance at Yale University and the editor of the *Journal of Portfolio Management*. He earned a doctorate in economics from the City University of New York in 1972. In 1994 he received an honorary doctorate of Humane Letters from Nova Southeastern University and in 2002 was inducted into the Fixed Income Analysts Society's Hall of Fame.

Moorad Choudhry is Head of Treasury at KBC Financial Products (U.K.) Limited in London. He previously worked as a government bond trader and Treasury trader at ABN Amro Hoare Govett Limited and Hambros Bank Limited, and in structured finance services at JPMorgan Chase Bank. Mr. Choudhry is a Fellow of the Centre for Mathematical Trading and Finance, CASS Business School, and a Fellow of the Securities Institute. He is author of *The Bond and Money Markets: Strategy, Trading, Analysis*, and a member of the Education Advisory Board, ISMA Centre, University of Reading.

Ren-Raw Chen is an associate professor at the Rutgers Business School of Rutgers, The State University of New Jersey. He received his doctoral degree from the University of Illinois at Champaign-Urbana in 1990. Professor Chen is the author of *Understanding and ManagingInterest Rate Risks* and a coauthor of *Managing Dual Risk Risks* (in Chinese). He is an associate editor of the *Review of Derivatives Research, Taiwan Academy of Management Journal,* and *Financial Analysis and Risk Management.* Dr. Chen's articles have been published in numerous journals, including *Review of Financial Studies, Journal of Financial and Quantitative Analysis, Journal of Futures Markets, Journal of Derivatives, Journal of Fixed Income,* and *Review of Derivatives Research.*

CHAPTER 1

Introduction

Derivatives are financial instruments designed to efficiently transfer some form of risk between two or more parties. Derivatives can be classified based on the form of risk that is being transferred: interest rate risk (interest rate derivatives), credit risk (credit derivatives), currency risk (foreign exchange derivatives), commodity price risk (commodity derivatives), and equity prices (equity derivatives). Our focus in this book is on credit derivatives, the newest entrant to the world of derivatives.

Credit derivatives are financial instruments that are designed to transfer the credit exposure of an underlying asset or assets between two parties. With credit derivatives, an asset manager can either acquire or reduce credit risk exposure. Many asset managers have portfolios that are highly sensitive to changes in the credit spread between a default-free asset and credit-risky assets and credit derivatives are an efficient way to manage this exposure. Conversely, other asset managers may use credit derivatives to target specific credit exposures as a way to enhance portfolio returns. In each case, the ability to transfer credit risk and return provides a new tool for asset managers to improve performance. Moreover, as will be explained, corporate treasurers can use credit derivatives to transfer the risk associated with an increase in credit spreads.

Credit derivatives include credit default swaps, asset swaps, total return swaps, credit-linked notes, credit spread options, and credit spread forwards. In addition, there are index-type products that are sponsored by banks that link the payoff to the investor to a specified credit exposure such as emerging or high yield markets. By far the most popular credit derivatives is the credit default swap. Credit default swaps include single-name credit default swaps and basket default swaps. Credit default swaps have a number of applications and are used extensively for flow trading of single reference name credit risks or, in *portfolio swap form*, for trading a basket of reference credits. Credit default swaps and credit-linked notes are used in structured credit products, in various combinations, and their flexibility has been behind the growth and wide application of the synthetic collateralized debt obligation and other credit hybrid products.

Credit derivatives are grouped into funded and unfunded instruments. In a *funded credit derivative*, typified by a credit-linked note, the investor in the note is the credit protection seller and is making an upfront payment to the protection buyer when buying the note. In an *unfunded credit derivative*, typified by a credit default swap, the protection seller does not make an upfront payment to the protection buyer. In a funded credit derivative, the protection seller is in effect making the credit insurance payment upfront and must find the cash at the start of the transaction; whereas in an unfunded credit derivative the protection, payment is made on termination of the trade (if there is a credit event).

Unlike the other types of derivatives, where there are both exchange-traded and over-the-counter (OTC) or dealer products, as of this writing credit derivatives are only OTC products. That is, they are individually negotiated financial contracts. As with other derivatives, they can take the form of options, swaps, and forwards. Futures products are exchange-traded and, as of this writing as well, there are no credit derivative futures contracts.

Moreover, there are derivative-type payoffs that are embedded in debt instruments. Callable bonds, convertible bonds, dual currency bonds, and commodity-linked bonds are examples of bonds with embedded options. A callable bond has an embedded interest rate derivative, a convertible bond has an embedded equity derivative, a dual currency bond has an embedded foreign exchange derivative, and a commodity-linked bond has an embedded commodity derivative. Derivatives have made it possible to create many more debt instruments with complex derivative-type payoffs that may be sought by asset managers. These debt instruments are in the form of medium-term notes and referred to as structured products.

Credit derivatives are also used to create debt instruments with structures whose payoffs are linked to or derived from the credit characteristics of a reference asset (reference obligation), an issuer (reference entity), or a basket of reference assets or entities. Credit-linked notes (CLNs) and synthetic collateralized debt obligations (CDOs) are the two most prominent examples. In fact, the fastest growing sector of the market is the synthetic CDO market. Credit derivatives are the key to the creation of synthetic CDOs.

ROLE OF CREDIT DERIVATIVES IN FINANCIAL MARKETS

In discussing the role of credit derivatives in the U.S. financial market, Alan Greenspan, Chairman of the Federal Reserve Board, in a speech in September 2002 stated:

> More generally, such instruments appear to have effectively spread losses from defaults by Enron, Global Crossing, Railtrack, World-Com, and Swissair in recent months from financial institutions with largely short-term leverage to insurance firms, pension funds, or others with diffuse long-term liabilities or no liabilities at all. In particular, the still relatively small but rapidly growing market in credit derivatives has to date functioned well, with payouts proceeding smoothly for the most part. Obviously, this market is still too new to have been tested in a widespread down-cycle for credit. But so far, so good.[1]

There have been and continue to be mechanisms for protecting against credit risk but these mechanisms have been embedded within bond structures and loan agreements and not traded separately. Examples in bond structures are private mortgage insurance in residential mortgage-backed securities, insurance wraps provided by monoline insurance companies for municipal bonds and asset-backed securities, and letters of credit. The issuance of bonds backed by collateral in the structured finance market has required the transfer of assets. In the case of collateralized loan obligations, loans have to be transferred to a special purpose vehicle. This is a disadvantage for legal reasons—in some countries the borrower must approve the assignment of a loan—and business reasons—potential impairment of banking client relationships. The growth of the market for synthetic CDOs is a testament to this desire not to transfer assets.

Credit derivatives are a natural extension of the long-term trend of shifting credit risk from banks to nonbank investors who are willing to accept credit risk for the potential of an enhanced yield. Consider, for example, the public market for bonds. This debt instrument is simply a substitute for bank borrowing. In the United States, the typical publicly traded bond was one that at issuance had an investment-grade rating. Thus, credit risk of investment-grade corporate borrowers was shared by banks and nonbank investors via bond issuance. This is a relatively new economic phenomena in many non-U.S. countries where bond markets

---

[1] "World Finance and Risk Management," speech presented at Lancaster House, London, U.K., September 25, 2002.

are developing. In the 1980s, noninvestment grade rated issuers whose primary funding source was commercial loans were able to access the public bond markets. Since the early 1990s, there was the rapid growth of the asset-backed securities market in which the credit risk of various loans was shifted from bank portfolios to the portfolios of nonbank investors. The syndicated loan market has provided the same transference of credit risk. In each of these cases, however, a nonbank investor has had to obtain the necessary funding to obtain credit exposure. With the arrival of credit derivatives, a nonbank entity can obtain credit exposure but need only make a payment if a credit event occurs.

Surveys of capital market participants have identified the usage of these instruments. A summer 2001 survey by Greenwich Associates of 230 North American financial entities (banks, insurance companies, and fund managers) and corporations about their credit derivatives trading activities found that 150 indicated that they currently used derivatives and 80 were nonusers.[2] However, of the nonusers, 40% indicated that they planned to use credit derivatives in the future.

Understanding of credit derivatives is critical even for those who wish not to use these instruments. As Chairman Greenspan stated:

> The growing prominence of the market for credit derivatives is attributable not only to its ability to disperse risk but also to the information it contributes to enhanced risk management by banks and other financial intermediaries. Credit default swaps, for example, are priced to reflect the probability of net loss from the default of an ever broadening array of borrowers, both financial and nonfinancial.
>
> As the market for credit default swaps expands and deepens, the collective knowledge held by market participants is exactly reflected in the prices of these derivative instruments. They offer significant supplementary information about credit risk to a bank's loan officer, for example, who heretofore had to rely mainly on in-house credit analysis. To be sure, loan officers have always looked to the market prices of the stocks and bonds of a potential borrower for guidance, but none directly answered the key question for any prospective loan: What is the probable net loss in a given time frame? Credit default swaps, of course, do just that and presumably in the process embody all relevant market prices of the financial instruments issued by potential borrowers.

---

[2] Peter B. D'Amario, *North American Credit Derivatives Market Develops Rapidly*, Greenwich Associates, January 9, 2002.

MARKET PARTICIPANTS

The credit derivatives market consists of three groups of players:

- End-buyers of protection
- End-sellers of protection
- Intermediaries[3]

End-buyers of protection are entities that seek to hedge credit risk taken in other parts of their business. The predominate entity in this group are commercial banks. For the reasons explained later in this chapter, there are also insurance, pension funds, and mutual funds that seek protection for credits held in their portfolio. End-sellers of protection are entities that seek to diversify their current portfolio and can do so more efficiently with credit derivatives. An entity that provides protection is seeking exposure to a specific credit or a basket of credits.

Intermediaries include investment banking arms of commercial banks and securities houses. Their key role in the credit derivatives market is to provide liquidity to end-users. They trade for their own account looking for "arbitrage" and other opportunities. In addition, some will assemble using credit derivatives structured products which, in turn, they may or may not manage.

TYPES OF CREDIT RISK

To appreciate the various types of credit derivatives, we must review the underlying risk which these new financial instruments transfer and hedge. They include:

- Default risk
- Downgrade risk
- Credit spread risk

Default risk is the risk that the issuer of a bond or the debtor on a loan will not repay the outstanding debt in full. Default risk can be complete in that no amount of the bond or loan will be repaid, or it can be partial in that some portion of the original debt will be recovered.

---

[3] David Rule, "The Credit Derivatives Market: Its Development and Possible Implications For Financial Stability," G10 Financial Surveillance Division, Bank of England.

Downgrade risk is the risk that a nationally recognized statistical rating organization such as Standard & Poor's, Moody's Investors Services, or Fitch Ratings reduces its outstanding credit rating for an issuer based on an evaluation of that issuer's current earning power versus its capacity to pay its debt obligations as they become due.

Credit spread risk is the risk that the spread over a reference rate will increase for an outstanding debt obligation. Credit spread risk and downgrade risk differ in that the latter pertains to a specific, formal credit review by an independent rating agency, while the former is the financial markets' reaction to perceived credit deterioration.

In this section we provide a short discussion on the importance of credit risk. In particular, we provide a review of the credit risks inherent in three important sectors of the debt market: high-yield bonds, highly leveraged bank loans, and sovereign debt. Each of these markets is especially attuned to the nature and amount of credit risk undertaken with each investment. Indeed, most of the discussion and examples provided in this book will focus on these three sectors of the debt market.

Credit Risk and the High-Yield Bond Market

A fixed-income debt instrument represents a basket of risks. There is the risk from changes in interest rates (interest rate risk as measured by an instrument's duration and convexity), the risk that the issuer will refinance the debt issue (call risk), and the risk of defaults, downgrades, and widening credit spreads (credit risk). The total return from a fixed-income investment such as a corporate bond is the compensation for assuming all of these risks. Depending upon the rating on the underlying debt instrument, the return from credit risk can be a significant part of a bond's total return.

However, the default rate on credit-risky bonds can be quite high. Estimates of the average default rates for high-yield bonds range from 3.17% to 6.25%.[4] In fact, default rates have been as high as 11% for high-yield bonds in any one year.[5] Three factors have been demonstrated to influence default rates in the high-yield bond market. First, because defaults are most likely to occur three years after bond issuance, the length of time that high-yield bonds have been outstanding will influence the default rate. This factor is known as the "aging

---

[4] See Edward Altman, "Measuring Corporate Bond Mortality and Performance," *The Journal of Finance* (June 1991), pp. 909–922; and Gabriella Petrucci, "High-Yield Review—First-Half 1997," Salomon Brothers Corporate Bond Research (August 1997).
[5] See Jean Helwege and Paul Kleiman, "Understanding the Aggregate Default Rates of High-Yield Bonds," *The Journal of Fixed Income* (June 1997), pp. 55–61.

affect." Second, the state of the economy affects the high-yield default rate. A recession reduces the economic prospects of corporations. As profits decline, companies have less cash to pay their bondholders. Finally, changes in credit quality affects default rates. Studies that will be discussed in Chapter 2 have demonstrated that credit quality is the most important determinant of default rates, followed by macroeconomic conditions. The aging factor plays only a small role in determining default rates.[6]

Credit derivatives, therefore, appeal to asset managers who invest in high-yield or junk bonds, real estate, or other credit-dependent assets. The possibility of default is a significant risk for asset managers, and one that can be effectively hedged by shifting the credit exposure.

In addition to default risk for noninvestment grade bonds, there is the risk of downgrades for investment-grade bonds and the risk of increased credit spreads. For instance, in the year 2002, S&P had 272 rating changes for investment-grade issues: 231 were rating downgrades and 41 were rating upgrades. For Moody's for the same year, there were 244 upgrades and 46 downgrades for the 290 rating changes by that rating agency.[7]

With respect to credit spread risk, in the United States, corporate bonds are typically priced at a spread to comparable U.S. Treasury bonds. Should this spread widen after purchase of the corporate bond, the asset manager would suffer a diminution of value in his portfolio. Credit spreads can widen based on macroeconomic events such as volatility in the financial markets.

As an example, in October of 1997, a rapid decline in Asian stock markets spilled over into the U.S. stock markets, causing a significant decline in financial stocks.[8] The turbulence in the financial markets, both domestically and worldwide, resulted in a flight to safety of investment capital. In other words, investors sought safer havens for their investments in order to avoid further losses and volatility. This flight to safety resulted in a significant increase in credit spreads of corporate bonds relative to U.S. Treasuries.

For instance, at June 30, 1997, corporate bonds rated BB by Standard & Poor's were trading at an average spread over U.S. Treasuries of 215 bps.[9] However, by October 31, 1997, this spread had increased to

---

[6] Helwege and Kleiman, "Understanding the Aggregate Default Rates of High-Yield Bonds," p. 57.

[7] *Global Relative Value*, Lehman Brothers, Fixed Income Research, July 21, 2003, p. 135.

[8] For instance, the Dow Jones Industrial Average suffered a one-day decline of value of 554 points on October 27, 1997.

[9] See Chase Securities Inc., "High-Yield Research Weekly Update," *Chase High-Yield Research*, November 4, 1997, p. 43.

319 bps. For a $1,000 market value BB rated corporate bond with a duration of five, this resulted in a loss of value of about $52.50 per bond.

In their simplest form, credit derivatives may be nothing more than the purchase of credit protection. The ability to isolate credit risk and manage it independently of underlying bond positions is the key benefit of credit derivatives. Prior to the introduction of credit derivatives, the only way to manage credit exposure was to buy and sell the underlying assets. Because of transaction costs and tax issues, this was an inefficient way to hedge or gain exposure.

Credit derivatives, therefore, represent a natural extension of the financial markets to unbundle the risk and return buckets associated with a particular financial asset, such as credit risk. They offer an important method for asset managers to hedge their exposure to credit risk because they permit the transfer of the exposure from one party to another. Credit derivatives allow for an efficient exchange of credit exposure in return for credit protection.

However, credit risk is not all one-sided. There are at least three reasons why an asset manager may be willing to assume the credit risk of an underlying corporate bond or issuer. First, there are credit upgrades as well as downgrades. For example, in the year 1999, S&P had 207 rating changes for investment-grade issues: 85 were rating upgrades and 122 were rating downgrades. For the same year, of the 202 rating changes for investment-grade issues by Moody's, there were 88 upgrades and 114 downgrades.[10] A factor affecting credit rating upgrades is a strong stock market which encourages public offerings of stock by credit-risky companies. Often, a large portion of these equity financings are used to reduce outstanding costly debt, resulting in improved balance sheets and credit ratings for the issuers.

A second reason why an asset manager may be willing to sell corporate credit protection is that there is an expectation of other credit events which have a positive effect on an issuer. Mergers and acquisitions, for instance, have historically been a frequent occurrence in the high-yield corporate bond market. Even though a credit-risky issuer may have a low debt rating, it may have valuable technology worth acquiring. High-yield issuers tend to be small- to mid-cap companies with viable products but nascent cash flows. Consequently, they make attractive takeover candidates for financially mature companies.

The third reason is that with a growing economy, banks are willing to provide term loans to companies that have issued high-yield bonds at more attractive rates than the bond markets. Consequently, it has been

---

[10] *Global Relative Value*, p. 135.

advantageous for companies to redeem their high-yield bonds and replace the bonds with a lower cost term loan from a bank. The resulting premium for redemption of high-yield bonds is a positive credit event which enhances portfolio returns for an asset manager.

Credit Risk and the Bank Loan Market

Similar to high-yield corporate bonds, a commercial loan investment represents a basket of risks. There is the risk from changes in interest rates (interest rate risk), the risk that the borrower will refinance or pay down the loan balance (call risk), and the risk of defaults, downgrades, and widening credit spreads (credit risk). The total return from a commercial loan is the compensation for assuming all of these risks. Once again, the credit rating of the borrower is a key determinant in the pricing of the bank loan.

The corporate bank loan market typically consists of syndicated loans to large- and mid-sized corporations. They are floating-rate instruments, often priced in relation to LIBOR. Corporate loans may be either revolving credits (known as "revolvers") that are legally committed lines of credit, or term loans that are fully funded commitments with fixed amortization schedules. Term loans tend to be concentrated in the lower-credit-rated corporations because revolvers usually serve as backstops for commercial paper programs of fiscally sound companies. Therefore, we will primarily focus on the application of credit derivatives to term bank loans.

Term bank loans are repriced periodically. Because of their floating interest rate nature, they have reduced market risk resulting from fluctuating interest rates. Consequently, credit risk takes on greater importance in determining a commercial loan's total return.

Since the mid-1990s, the bank loan market and the high-yield bond market have begun to converge. This is due partly to the relaxing of commercial banking regulations which have allowed many banks to increase their product offerings, including high-yield bonds. Contemporaneously, investment banks and brokerage firms have established loan trading and syndication desks. The credit implications from this "one-stop" shopping are twofold.

First, the debt capital markets have become less segmented as commercial banks and investment firms compete in the bank loan, high-yield bond, and private placement debt markets. This has led to more flexible, less stringent bank loan constraints. This increased competition for business in the commercial loan market has resulted in more favorable terms for debtors and less credit protection for investors.

Second, hybrid debt instruments with both bank loan and high-yield bond characteristics are now available in the capital markets. These hybrid commercial loans typically have a higher prepayment penalty than standard commercial loans, but only a second lien (or no lien) on assets instead of the traditional first claim. Additionally, several commercial loan tranches may now be offered as part of a financing package, where the first tranche of the bank loan is fully collateralized and has a regular amortization schedule, but the last tranche has no security interest and only a final bullet payment at maturity. These new commercial loans have the structure of high-yield bonds, but have the floating rate requirement of a bank loan. Consequently, the very structure of these hybrid bank loans make them more susceptible to credit risk.

Just like the high-yield bond market, bank loans are also susceptible to the risk of credit downgrades (downgrade risk) and the risk of increased credit spreads (credit spread risk). As an example of credit spread risk during the U.S. economic recession of 1990–1991, the credit spread for B rated bank loans increased on average from 250 bps over LIBOR to 325 bps, as default rates climbed to 10%.[11] Not surprisingly, over this time period the total return to B rated bank loans underperformed the total return to BBB and BB rated bank loans by 6.41% and 8.64%, respectively. Conversely, during the economic expansion years of 1993–1994, the total return to B rated bank loans outperformed the total return to BBB and BB rated bank loans by 3.43% and 1.15% as the default rate for B rated loans declined in 1993 and 1994 to 1.1% and 1.45%, respectively.[12]

In the event of a default, commercial bank loans generally have a higher recovery rate than that for defaulted high-yield bonds due to a combination of collateral protection and senior capital structure. Nonetheless, estimates of lost value given a commercial bank loan default are about 35% of the loan value.[13] Even for asset-backed loans, which are highly collateralized and tightly monitored commercial loans, where the bank controls the cash receipts against the collateralized assets, the average loss of value in the event of default is about 13%.[14]

---

[11] See Elliot Asarnow, "Corporate Loans as an Asset Class," *The Journal of Portfolio Management* (Summer 1996), pp. 92–103; and Edward Altman and Joseph Bencivenga, "A Yield Premium Model for the High-Yield Debt Market," *Financial Analysts Journal* (September–October 1995), pp. 49–56.

[12] See Asarnow, "Corporate Loans as an Asset Class," p. 96, and Altman and Bencivenga, "A Yield Premium Model for the High-Yield Debt Market," p. 51.

[13] See Asarnow, "Corporate Loans as an Asset Class," p. 94; and Barnish, Miller and Rushmore, "The New Leveraged Loan Syndication Market," p. 85.

[14] See Asarnow, "Corporate Loans as an Asset Class," p. 95.

The loss in value due to a default can have a significant impact on the total return of a bank loan. For a commercial bank loan the total return comes from two sources: The spread over the reference rate (LIBOR plus) and the return from price appreciation/depreciation. As might be expected, B rated bank loans are priced on average at higher rates than BBB rated bank loans—an average 250–300 bps over LIBOR compared to 50 bps over LIBOR for BBB rated loans. Yet, over the time period 1988–1994, the cumulative return to B rated bank loans was 10 percentage points less than that for BBB rated loans.[15] The lower total return to B rated loans was due to a price return of −10.26%. Simply put, changes in credit quality reduced the total return to lower-rated bank loans despite their higher coupon rates.

Credit risk, however, can also provide opportunities for gain. Over the same time period, the cumulative total return to BB rated bank loans exceeded that of BBB bank loans by 11.6%.[16] Part of this higher return was due to higher interest payments offered to induce investors to purchase the lower rated BB bank loans, but a significant portion, over 5%, was due to enhanced credit quality. Consequently, over this time period, asset managers had ample opportunity to target specific credit risks and improve portfolio returns.

Similar to the high-yield corporate bond market, the ability to isolate credit risk and manage it independently of underlying investment positions is the key benefit of credit derivatives. Prior to the introduction of credit derivatives, the only way to manage credit exposure was to buy and sell bank loans or restrict lending policies. Because of transaction costs, tax issues, and client relationships, this was an inefficient way to hedge or gain exposure.

Furthermore, credit derivatives offer an attractive method for hedging credit risk in lieu of liquidating the underlying collateral in a bank loan. Despite the security interest of a fully collateralized bank loan, there may be several reasons why a bank manager or asset manager may be reluctant to liquidate the collateral.

From a bank manager's perspective, the decision to liquidate the collateral will undoubtedly sour the customer relationship. Most banks consider loans as part of a broader client relationship that includes other noncredit business. Preserving the broader relationship may make a bank reluctant to foreclose.

Conversely, institutional investors focus on commercial loans as standalone investments and consider the economic risks and benefits of foreclosure. From their perspective, seizure of collateral may provoke a

---

[15] See Asarnow, "Corporate Loans as an Asset Class," p. 95.
[16] See Asarnow, "Corporate Loans as an Asset Class," p. 95.

litigation defense by the debtor. The attempt to foreclose on collateral may result in dragging the investor into protracted litigation on issues and in forums that the institutional investor may wish to avoid. Additionally, foreclosure by one creditor/investor may trigger similar responses from other investors leading to a feeding frenzy on the debtor's assets. The debtor may have no choice but to seek the protection of the bankruptcy laws which would effectively stop all seizures of collateral and extend the time for collateral liquidation. Lastly, there may be possible collateral deficiencies such as unperfected security interests which could make collateral liquidation problematic.[17]

The seizure, holding, and liquidation of collateral is also an expensive course of action. The most obvious costs are the legal fees incurred in seizing and liquidating the collateral. Additional costs include storage costs, appraisal fees, brokerage or auction costs, insurance, and property taxes. Hidden costs include the time spent by the investor and its personnel in managing and monitoring the liquidation process.

In sum, there are many reasons why the seizure and liquidation of collateral may not be a feasible solution for bank loan credit protection. Credit derivatives can solve these problems through the efficient exchange of credit risk. Furthermore, credit derivatives avoid the inevitable disruption of client relationships.

Credit Risk in the Sovereign Debt Market

Credit risk is not unique to the domestic U.S. financial markets. When investing in the sovereign debt of a foreign country, an investor must consider two crucial risks. One is *political risk*—the risk that even though the central government of the foreign country has the financial ability to pay its debts as they come due, for political reasons (e.g. revolution, new government regime, trade sanctions), the sovereign entity decides to forfeit (default) payment.[18] The second type of risk is default risk—the same old inability to pay one's debts as they become due.

A sovereign government relies on two forms of cash flows to finance its government programs and to pay its debts: taxes and revenues from state-owned enterprises. Taxes can come from personal income taxes, corporate taxes, import duties, and other excise taxes. State-owned enterprises can be

---

[17] A security interest is effective between a lender and a borrower without any perfection. Perfection is the legal term for properly identifying an asset as collateral for a bank loan such that other lenders and creditors will not attach their security interests to the identified collateral except in a subordinated role.

[18] This raises the interesting idea of whether such a construct as a political derivative could be developed. While this may currently seem farfetched, it is no less implausible than credit derivatives once appeared.

EXHIBIT 1.1 JPMorgan Chase EMBI Index

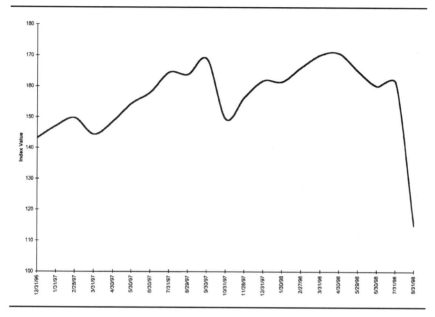

oil companies, telephone companies, national airlines and railroads, and other manufacturing enterprises.

In times of economic turmoil such as a recession, cash flows from state-owned enterprises decline along with the general malaise of the economy. Additionally, tax revenues decline as corporations earn less, as unemployment rises, and as personal incomes decline. Lastly, with a declining foreign currency value, imports decline, reducing revenue from import taxes.

The extreme vicissitudes of the sovereign debt market are no more apparent than in the emerging market arena. Here, the "Asian Tigers"—Hong Kong, Taiwan, Korea, and Singapore—enjoyed a real average growth rate over the 1986–1996 period of about 8% per year. During this period, investors could have earned an average of 14% by investing in the public (or quasi-public) debt of these countries.

However, as the "Asian Contagion" demonstrated, the fortunes of the emerging market countries can deteriorate rapidly. Exhibit 1.1 presents the monthly price chart for JPMorgan Chase's Emerging Bond Index (EMBI) from December 31, 1996 to March 2003. EMBI is a weighted average of the returns to sovereign bonds for 15 emerging market countries from Latin America, Eastern Europe, and Asia.

As Exhibit 1.1 demonstrates, the performance of the EMBI index was generally positive for most of 1997, with a total return of more than 18% for the first three quarters of 1997. However, this good performance soured dramatically in the month of October. From a high of almost 172 on October 7, the index tumbled to 144 by November 10, a decline of over 16%. In the space of about one month, the declining fortunes of a broad sample of emerging market sovereigns wiped out most of the gains which had been earned over the nine previous months.

Once again, we point out that credit risk is not all one sided. Even though there was a rapid decline in the credit quality of emerging market sovereign debt in 1997, such a steep retreat presented opportunities for credit quality improvement. For instance, from its low point of 144 in November 1997, the EMBI index rebounded to a value of 172 by the end of March 1998, a gain of over 19%. Those investors who chose to include emerging market debt in their portfolios in the first quarter of 1998 earned excellent returns. In fact, the returns to the EMBI for the first quarter of 1998 outperformed U.S. Treasury bonds.

Even so, this recovery was short lived. Unfortunately, history often repeats itself. In August 1998 the Russian government defaulted on its outstanding bonds, sending the emerging bond market into another tailspin. This resulted in a one month decline of the EMBI Index of over 27% in August 1998.

For example, consider the Russian 10% government bond due in 2007. In July 1997 when this bond was issued, its credit spread over a comparable U.S. Treasury bond was 350 bps. As of July 1998, this credit spread had increased to 925 bps, an increase of 575 bps. In fact, the change in credit spread was so large, it was even greater than the current effective yield of a 30-year U.S. Treasury bond in July 1998!

The Russian bond was sold with a coupon of 10% in July 1997. In July 1998, the credit spread was 925 bps. The Russian bond had nine remaining annual coupon payments and a final balloon payment of $1,000 at maturity. The rate on a 9-year U.S Treasury bond was 5.8%. Therefore, the current value of the bond in 1998 was about $759.46. This represented a decline of $240.53, or 24% of the Russian bond's face value in one year's time.

If you think that the above example may be extreme, consider that in August 1998 the Russian economy suffered a total collapse and the credit spread for Russian debt increased to 5,300 bps over comparable U.S. Treasury bonds! This tremendous widening of credit spreads led to billions of dollars of losses by banks, brokerage houses, and hedge funds, as Russian investments were written down to 10 cents on the dollar.

VISUALIZING CREDIT RISK

The discussion in the previous section demonstrates that emerging market debt is subject to considerable credit risk. Sudden drops of the JPMorgan Chase EMBI index indicate the extent to which credit events can hit quickly and harshly in emerging market debt. A default in one emerging country can lead to widening credit spreads across all emerging markets. In addition, as the Russian bond example demonstrates, emerging market debt is subject to considerable default risk.

The same is true for high-yield corporate bonds. Credit events can have a devastating impact on the value of the bonds. To analyze this risk, we graphed the frequency distribution of the Salomon Smith Barney High Yield Index and the JPMorgan Chase EMBI index. The frequency distribution of returns provides a graphical depiction of the range and likelihood of returns associated with credit-risky bonds. From such a distribution, we can calculate the mean return, the standard deviation, the skew, and the kurtosis of the return distribution.

Return distributions can be described by what are known as "moments" of the distribution. Most market participants understand the first two moments of a distribution: they identify the mean and variance of the distribution. Often in finance, it is assumed that the returns to financial assets follow a normal, or bell-shaped, distribution. However, this is not the case for credit-risky assets.

Credit-risky assets are typically exposed to significant downside risk associated with credit downgrades, defaults, and bankruptcies. This downside risk can be described in terms of kurtosis and skewness. *Kurtosis* is a term used to describe the general condition that the probability mass associated with the tails of a return distribution, otherwise known as "outlier events," is different from that of a normal distribution. The condition of large tails in the distribution is known as *leptokurtosis*.[19] This means that the tails of the distribution have a greater concentration of mass (more outlier events) than what would be expected if the returns were symmetrically distributed under a normal distribution.

The skew of a distribution is also measured relative to a normal distribution. A normal distribution has no skew—its returns are symmetrically distributed around the mean return. A negative skew to a distribution indicates a bias towards downside exposure. This means that there are more frequent large negative outliers than there are large positive outliers. This indicates a return profile biased towards large negative returns.

---

[19] The converse of leptokurtosis is *platykurtosis*—the condition where the tails of the distribution are thinner than that of a normal distribution.

EXHIBIT 1.2 Return Distribution on the Salomon Smith Barney High-Yield Index, 1990–2000

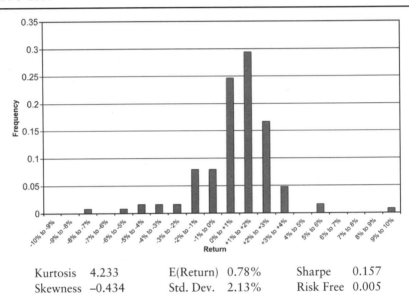

| Kurtosis | 4.233 | E(Return) | 0.78% | Sharpe | 0.157 |
| Skewness | −0.434 | Std. Dev. | 2.13% | Risk Free | 0.005 |

In Exhibit 1.2 we present the frequency return distribution for high-yield bonds over the time period 1990–2000. Over this time period, high-yield bonds had a negative skew value of −0.434 as well as a large positive value of kurtosis of 4.233. This distribution demonstrates significant leptokurtosis. Specifically, the distribution of returns to high-yield bonds demonstrates a significant downside tail. This "fat" tail reflects the credit event risk of downgrades, defaults, and bankruptcies.

Emerging market fares even worse. Exhibit 1.3 presents the frequency distribution of the returns for emerging market bonds. Emerging market debt has an even larger negative skew value as well as a larger value of kurtosis compared to high-yield bonds. Once again, the negative skew combined with large tails leads to considerable exposure to downside credit risk. Emerging market debt has a "fatter" tail than high-yield bonds. The "fat" negative tail associated with emerging market bonds reflects the risk of downgrades, defaults, and widening credit spreads.

RISKS OF CREDIT DERIVATIVES

While credit derivatives offer investors alternative strategies to access credit-risky assets, they come with specialized risks.

EXHIBIT 1.3   Return Distribution on the JPMorgan Chase Emerging Market Composite, 1990–2000

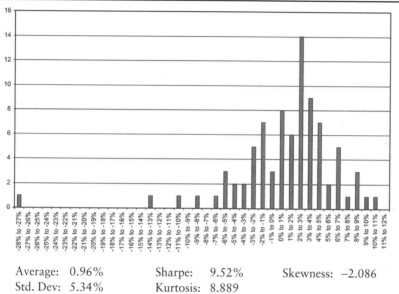

Average:	0.96%	Sharpe:	9.52%	Skewness:	−2.086
Std. Dev:	5.34%	Kurtosis:	8.889		

First, there is *operational risk*. This is the risk that traders or asset managers could imprudently use credit derivatives. Since these are off-balance sheet contractual agreements, excessive credit exposures can be achieved without appearing on an investor's balance sheet. Without proper accounting systems and other back-office operations, an investor may not be fully cognizant of the total credit risk it bears.

Second, there is *counterparty risk*. This is the risk that the counterparty to a credit derivative will default on its obligations. It is ironic that a credit protection buyer, for example, can introduce a new form of credit risk into a portfolio (counterparty risk) from the purchase of a credit derivative. For a credit protection buyer to suffer a loss, two things must happen: (1) there must be a credit event on the underlying credit-risky asset; and (2) the credit protection seller must default on its obligations to the credit protection buyer.

Another source of risk is *liquidity risk*. As noted in this chapter, currently there are no exchange-traded credit derivatives. Instead they are traded over the counter as customized contractual agreements between two parties. The very nature of this customization makes them illiquid. Credit derivatives will not suit all parties in the marketplace, and a party to a custom-tailored credit derivative contract may find it hard to obtain the "fair value" of the contract when trying to sell it.

Finally, there is *pricing risk*. As the credit derivative market has matured, the mathematical models used to price derivative contracts have become increasingly complex. These models, described in later chapters of this book, are dependent upon sophisticated assumptions regarding underlying economic parameters. Consequently, the prices of credit derivatives are very sensitive to the assumptions of the model employed.

FUTURE GROWTH OF THE CREDIT DERIVATIVES MARKET

The British Bankers Association (BBA) estimated that the global credit derivatives market (excluding asset swaps) was about $1.2 trillion by the end of 2001. Expectations are that the credit derivatives market will grow rapidly in the next few years. The BBA projects that without considering asset swaps the global credit derivatives market will grow to $4.8 trillion by 2004; the market is projected to exceed $5 trillion if asset swaps are included.[20]

As with every financial innovation, there will be setbacks in the market. As discussed in later chapters, several have already occurred in the credit derivatives market. These have provided critics of credit derivatives with ammunition. The criticisms are the same as those advanced for all derivative products and several cash market products such as high-yield bonds and asset-backed securities.

While the market will grow, the impediments to growth are the following:

- Documentation of the transactions
- Liquidity and transparency
- Counterparty risk
- Complexity of pricing
- Hedging difficulty
- Information asymmetries
- Lack of understanding by end users

We will discuss documentation of a credit derivative transaction in 3. What is important to understand is that the documentation a credit event is. This definition is obviously crucial since it the credit protection buyer is to receive one or more payredit protection seller. Market participants are structurbe more specific about what constitutes a credit event.

ciation, *Credit Derivatives Report 2002.*

Credit derivatives have limited liquidity. There are only a few dealers in the market. Exhibit 1.4 provides a list of the 25 commercial banks and trust companies in the United States as of March 2002 with the most exposure to derivatives. Note the following. First, relative to their exposure to derivatives in general, credit derivatives rarely exceed 2%, and in most instances are less than 1%. Second, and most important for our point here, is that there are only seven major commercial banks/trust companies involved in the market. As a result, there are concerns with liquidity. Since the transactions are over-the-counter trades, transparency is an issue. Market transparency has improved as a few firms specializing in credit derivatives have provided internet trading platforms. Two examples are *creditex* and *CreditTrade*.[21]

Due to the limited number of dealers in the credit derivatives area, counterparty risk is more pronounced than for other types derivatives. Thus, a credit protection buyer is exposed to the credit risk of the dealer. Since market participants seek to reduce their counterparty risk, a credit protection buyer may have to limit its exposure to credit derivatives because of overexposure to the limited number of acceptable dealers.

When the array of interest rate derivatives were first introduced, their pricing was viewed to be the province of the financial engineer. Today, the pricing of basic interest rate derivatives is well understood by market participants. Pricing is not so simple for most credit derivative products. We will discuss the general principles of the valuation of credit derivatives in later chapters. The complexity of pricing them has made some investors who could benefit from participating in the credit derivatives market cautious about doing so. Moreover, because of their complexity it is difficult for dealers to hedge their positions, thereby reducing the number of potential dealers.[22]

A major concern in the market is the information asymmetry between the buyers of protection and the sellers of protection. This results in two adverse consequences to protection sellers. The first is that when banks buy protection based on credits in their loan portfolio, they often have access to information about those credits that are not readily available to the public. In fact, it could be that such information is the very reason why a bank would want to purchase credit protection. This consequence is referred to as *adverse selection*. The second consequence of information asymmetry occurs when the protection buyer has the ability to influence the likelihood that a credit event will occur. For example, suppose a credit event includes the restructuring of a loan. If

---

[21] Their web sites are www.creditex.com and www.credittrade.com.
[22] Moreover, the capital charges associated with hedging have made making markets in credit derivatives less profitable.

EXHIBIT 1.4   Notional Amount of Derivatives Contracts of the 25 Commercial Banks and Trust Companies with the Most Derivative Contracts: March 31, 2002 ($ millions)

Rank	Bank Name	Total Derivatives	Total Credit Derivatives (OTC)	Percent Credit Derivatives
1	JPMorgan Chase Bank	$23,480,417	$268,429	1.1
2	Bank of America NA	9,820,528	65,733	0.7
3	Citibank National Assn.	6,683,260	77,158	1.2
4	First Union National Bank	2,304,420	4,113	0.2
5	Bank One National Assn.	957,097	5,091	0.5
6	Wells Fargo Bank NA	728,524	2,131	0.3
7	Bank of New York	425,493	1,920	0.5
8	HSBC Bank USA	368,185	801	0.2
9	Fleet National Bank	311,760	7,209	2.3
10	State Street Bank & Trust Co.	182,866	0	0.0
11	National City Bank	122,668	176	0.1
12	Keybank National Assn	78,410	0	0.0
13	Lasalle Bank National Assn.	67,817	0	0.0
14	Standard Federal Bank NA	65,936	0	0.0
15	Mellon Bank National Assn.	66,390	471	0.7
16	National City Bank of Indiana	63,544	0	0.0
17	Suntrust Bank	63,724	245	0.4
18	Bankers Trust Co.	59,604	189	0.3
19	PNC Bank National Assn.	48,627	169	0.3
20	Wachovia Bank National Assn.	41,689	96	0.2
21	Merrill Lynch Bank USA	30,992	890	2.9
22	U S Bank National Assn.	28,551	0	0.0
23	First Tennessee Bank NA	27,736	217	0.8
24	Comerica Bank	21,070	11	0.1
25	Northern Trust Co.	18,236	53	0.3
	Top 25 commercial banks & TCs with derivatives	$46,067,544	$435,100	
	Other 354 commercial banks & TCs with derivatives	$263,741	$2,431	
	Total amounts for all 379 BKS & TCs with derivatives	$46,331,285	$437,532	

Data source: *Call Report*, schedule RC-L.
Source: Office of the Comptroller of the Currency.

the credit protection buyer is a bank that made the loan and the bank has the authorization to restructure the loan, then the bank can cause a credit event to occur and realize a payoff by restructuring loan. Another example would be where a credit event includes a specified deterioration of the cash flows of a borrower. If the borrowing entity's cash flows are affected by the extension of credit from the bank that is buying protection, then the bank can trigger a credit event and receive a payoff from the protection seller.

Finally, as with all new markets, an understanding of the product and its application by potential market participants is critical. Credit derivatives are perceived as complex products. Potential end users frequently read in the popular press about fiascoes with new financial products. That is what sells newspapers and magazines. It is not very interesting for journalists to report on how derivatives may have prevented an end user from a financial disaster.

The purpose of this book is provide the basic features and applications of credit derivatives so that the reader will understand how he or she may be able to benefit from participating in this new sector of the derivatives market.

CHAPTER 2

Types of Credit Risk

In Chapter 1 we discussed the three types of credit risk: credit default risk, credit spread risk, and downgrade risk. Credit default risk is the risk that the issuer will fail to satisfy the terms of the obligation with respect to the timely payment of interest and repayment of the amount borrowed. To gauge the default risk, investors rely on analysis performed by nationally recognized statistical rating organizations that perform credit analysis of issues and issuers and express their conclusions in the form of a credit rating. Credit spread risk is the loss or underperformance of an issue or issues due to an increase in the credit spread. Downgrade risk is the risk that an issue or issuer will be downgraded, resulting in an increase in the credit spread. In this chapter we take a closer look at each type of credit risk.

CREDIT DEFAULT RISK

We begin our discussion of credit default risk with an explanation of credit ratings and the factors used by rating agencies in assigning a credit rating. We then discuss the rights of creditors in a bankruptcy in the United States and why the actual outcome of a bankruptcy typically differs from credit protection afforded under the bankruptcy laws. Finally, we will look at corporate bond default rates and recovery rates in the United States. In Chapter 10, we review methodologies for estimating defaults for a basket of credit-risky bonds.

Credit Ratings

The prospectus or offer document for an issue provides investors with information about the issuer so that credit analysis can be performed on the issuer before the bonds are placed. Credit assessments take time, however, and also require the specialist skills of credit analysts. Large institutional investors do in fact employ such specialists to carry out credit analysis; however, often it is too costly and time-consuming to assess every issuer in every debt market. Therefore investors commonly employ two other methods when making a decision on the credit default risk of debt securities: name recognition and formal credit ratings.

Name recognition is when the investor relies on the good name and reputation of the issuer and accepts that the issuer is of such good financial standing, or sufficient financial standing, that a default on interest and principal payments is highly unlikely. An investor may feel this way about say, Microsoft or British Petroleum plc. However the experience of Barings in 1995 suggested to many investors that it may not be wise to rely on name recognition alone in today's marketplace. The tradition and reputation behind the Barings name allowed the bank to borrow at LIBOR or occasionally at sub-LIBOR interest rates in the money markets, which put it on a par with the highest-quality banks in terms of credit rating. However name recognition needs to be augmented by other methods to reduce the risk against unforeseen events, as happened with Barings.

A credit rating is a formal opinion given by a rating agency of the credit default risk faced by investing in a particular issue of debt securities. For long-term debt obligations, a credit rating is a forward-looking assessment of the probability of default and the relative magnitude of the loss should a default occur. For short-term debt obligations, a credit rating is a forward-looking assessment of the probability of default.

Credit ratings are provided by specialist companies referred to as *rating agencies*. They include Moody's Investors Service, Standard & Poor's Corporation, and Fitch Ratings. On receipt of a formal request, the rating agencies will carry out a rating exercise on a specific issue of debt capital. The request for a rating comes from the organization planning the issuance of bonds. Although ratings are provided for the benefit of investors, the issuer must bear the cost. However, it is in the issuer's interest to request a rating as it raises the profile of the bonds, and investors may refuse to buy a bond that is not accompanied with a recognized rating.

Although the rating exercise involves credit analysis of the issuer, the rating is applied to a specific debt issue. This means that in theory the credit rating is applied not to an organization itself, but to specific debt securities that the organization has issued or is planning to issue. In practice it is common for the market to refer to the creditworthiness of organizations themselves in terms of the rating of their debt. A highly rated company, for example, may be referred to as a "triple-A rated" company, although it is the company's debt issues that are rated as triple A.

The rating systems of the rating agencies use similar symbols. Separate categories are used by each rating agency for short-term debt (with original maturity of 12 months or less) and long-term debt (over one year original maturity). Exhibit 2.1 shows the long-term debt ratings. In all rating systems the term "high grade" means low credit risk or, conversely, high probability of future payments. The highest-grade bonds are designated by Moody's by the letters Aaa, and by the others as AAA. The next highest grade is Aa (Moody's), and by the others as AA; for the third grade all rating agencies use A. The next three grades are Baa (Moody's) or BBB, Ba (Moody's) or BB, and B, respectively. There are also C grades. S&P and Fitch use plus or minus signs to provide a narrower credit quality breakdown within each class. Moody's uses 1, 2, or 3 for the same purpose. Bonds rated triple A (AAA or Aaa) are said to be "prime"; double A (AA or Aa) are of high quality; single A issues are called "upper medium grade"; and triple B are "medium grade." Lower-rated bonds are said to have "speculative" elements or be" distinctly speculative."

Bond issues that are assigned a rating in the top four categories are referred to as *investment-grade bonds*. Bond issues that carry a rating below the top four categories are referred to as *noninvestment grade bonds* or more popularly as *high-yield bonds* or *junk bonds*. Thus, the bond market can be divided into two sectors: the investment grade sector and the noninvestment grade sector. Distressed debt is a subcategory of noninvestment grade bonds. These bonds may be in bankruptcy proceedings, may be in default of coupon payments, or may be in some other form of distress.

Factors Considered in Rating Corporate Bond Issues

In conducting its examination of corporate bond issues, the rating agencies consider the four Cs of credit: character, capacity, collateral, and covenants.

The first of the Cs stands for *character* of management, the foundation of sound credit. This includes the ethical reputation as well as the business qualifications and operating record of the board of directors, management, and executives responsible for the use of the borrowed funds and repayment of those funds. The next C is *capacity* or the ability of an issuer to repay its obligations. The third C, *collateral*, is looked at not only in the traditional sense of assets pledged to secure the debt, but also to the quality and value of those unpledged assets controlled by the issuer. In both senses the collateral is capable of supplying additional aid, comfort, and support to the debt and the debt holder. Assets form the basis for the generation of cash flow which services the debt in good times as well as bad. The final C is for *covenants*, the terms and

EXHIBIT 2.1   Summary of Long-Term Bond Rating Systems and Symbols

Fitch	Moody's	S&P	Summary Description
Investment Grade			
AAA	Aaa	AAA	Gilt edged, prime, maximum safety, lowest risk, and when sovereign borrower considered "default-free"
AA+	Aa1	AA+	
AA	Aa2	AA	High-grade, high credit quality
AA-	Aa3	AA-	
A+	A1	A+	
A	A2	A	Upper-medium grade
A-	A3	A-	
BBB+	Baa1	BBB+	
BBB	Baa2	BBB	Lower-medium grade
BBB-	Baa3	BBB-	
Speculative Grade			
BB+	Ba1	BB+	
BB	Ba2	BB	Low grade; speculative
BB-	Ba3	BB-	
B+	B1		
B	B	B	Highly speculative
B-	B3		
Predominantly speculative, Substantial Risk or in Default			
CCC+		CCC+	
CCC	Caa	CCC	Substantial risk, in poor standing
CC	Ca	CC	May be in default, very speculative
C	C	C	Extremely speculative
		CI	Income bonds—no interest being paid
DDD			
DD			Default
D		D	

conditions of the lending agreement. Covenants lay down restrictions on how management operates the company and conducts its financial affairs. Covenants can restrict management's discretion. A default or violation of any covenant may provide a meaningful early warning alarm enabling investors to take positive and corrective action before the situation deteriorates further. Covenants have value as they play an important part in minimizing risk to creditors. They help prevent the unconscionable transfer of wealth from debt holders to equity holders.

Character analysis involves the analysis of the quality of management. In discussing the factors it considers in assigning a credit rating, Moody's Investors Service notes the following regarding the quality of management:

> Although difficult to quantify, management quality is one of the most important factors supporting an issuer's credit strength. When the unexpected occurs, it is a management's ability to react appropriately that will sustain the company's performance.[1]

In assessing management quality, the analysts at Moody's, for example, try to understand the business strategies and policies formulated by management. Following are factors that are considered: (1) strategic direction, (2) financial philosophy, (3) conservatism, (4) track record, (5) succession planning, and (6) control systems.[2]

In assessing the ability of an issuer to pay, an analysis of the financial statements is undertaken. In addition to management quality, the factors examined by Moody's, for example, are (1) industry trends, (2) the regulatory environment, (3) basic operating and competitive position, (4) financial position and sources of liquidity, (5) company structure (including structural subordination and priority of claim), (6) parent company support agreements, and (7) special event risk.[3]

In considering industry trends, the rating agencies look at the vulnerability of the company to economic cycles, the barriers to entry, and the exposure of the company to technological changes. For firms in regulated industries, proposed changes in regulations are analyzed to assess their impact on future cash flows. At the company level, diversification of the product line and the cost structure are examined in assessing the basic operating position of the firm.

---

[1] "Industrial Company Rating Methodology," *Moody's Investor Service: Global Credit Research* (July 1998), p. 6.
[2] "Industrial Company Rating Methodology," p. 7.
[3] "Industrial Company Rating Methodology," p. 3.

The rating agencies look at the capacity of a firm to obtain additional financing and backup credit facilities. There are various forms of backup facilities. The strongest forms of backup credit facilities are those that are contractually binding and do not include provisions that permit the lender to refuse to provide funds. An example of such a provision is one that allows the bank to refuse funding if the bank feels that the borrower's financial condition or operating position has deteriorated significantly. (Such a provision is called a *material adverse change clause*.) Noncontractual facilities such as lines of credit that make it easy for a bank to refuse funding should be of concern to the rating agency. The rating agency also examines the quality of the bank providing the backup facility. Other sources of liquidity for a company may be third-party guarantees, the most common being a contractual agreement with its parent company. When such a financial guarantee exists, the analyst must undertake a credit analysis of the parent company.

A corporate debt obligation can be secured or unsecured. In our discussion of creditor rights in a bankruptcy discussed later, we will see that in the case of a liquidation, proceeds from a bankruptcy are distributed to creditors based on the absolute priority rule. However, in the case of a reorganization, the absolute priority rule rarely holds. That is, an unsecured creditor may receive distributions for the entire amount of his or her claim and common stockholders may receive something, while a secured creditor may receive only a portion of its claim. The reason is that a reorganization requires approval of all the parties. Consequently, secured creditors are willing to negotiate with both unsecured creditors and stockholders in order to obtain approval of the plan of reorganization.

The question is then, what does a secured position mean in the case of a reorganization if the absolute priority rule is not followed in a reorganization? The claim position of a secured creditor is important in terms of the negotiation process. However, because absolute priority is not followed and the final distribution in a reorganization depends on the bargaining ability of the parties, some analysts place less emphasis on collateral compared to the other factors discussed earlier and covenants discussed later.

Covenants deal with limitations and restrictions on the borrower's activities. Affirmative covenants call upon the debtor to make promises to do certain things. Negative covenants are those which require the borrower not to take certain actions. Negative covenants are usually negotiated between the borrower and the lender or their agents. Borrowers want the least restrictive loan agreement available, while lenders should want the most restrictive, consistent with sound business practices. But lenders should not try to restrain borrowers from accepted business activities and conduct. A borrower might be willing to include additional restrictions (up to a point) if it can get a lower interest rate on the debt obligation. When borrowers seek to weaken restrictions in their favor, they are often willing to pay more interest or give other consideration.

Factors Considered in Rating Sovereign Debt

While U.S. government debt is not rated by any nationally recognized statistical rating organization, the debt of other national governments is rated. These ratings are referred to as *sovereign ratings*. Standard & Poor's and Moody's rate sovereign debt.

The two general categories used by S&P in deriving their ratings are economic risk and political risk. The former category is an assessment of the ability of a government to satisfy its obligations. Both quantitative and qualitative analyses are used in assessing economic risk. Political risk is an assessment of the willingness of a government to satisfy its obligations. A government may have the ability to pay but may be unwilling to pay. Political risk is assessed based on qualitative analysis of the economic and political factors that influence a government's economic policies.

There are two ratings assigned to each national government. The first is a local currency debt rating and the second is a foreign currency debt rating. The reason for distinguishing between the two types of debt is that historically, the default frequency differs by the currency denomination of the debt. Specifically, defaults have been greater on foreign currency-denominated debt.[4]

The reason for the difference in default rates for local currency debt and foreign currency debt is that if a government is willing to raise taxes and control its domestic financial system, it can generate sufficient local currency to meet its local currency debt obligation. This is not the case with foreign currency-denominated debt. A national government must purchase foreign currency to meet a debt obligation in that foreign currency and therefore has less control with respect to its exchange rate. Thus, a significant depreciation of the local currency relative to a foreign currency in which a debt obligation is denominated will impair a national government's ability to satisfy such obligation.

The implication of this is that the factors both rating agencies analyze in assessing the creditworthiness of a national government's local currency debt and foreign currency debt will differ to some extent. In assessing the credit quality of local currency debt, for example, S&P emphasizes domestic government policies that foster or impede timely debt service. The key factors looked at by S&P are:

---

[4] David T. Beers, "Standard & Poor's Sovereign Ratings Criteria," Chapter 24 in Frank J. Fabozzi (ed.), *The Handbook of Fixed Income Securities: Fifth Edition* (Burr Ridge, IL: Irwin Professional Publishing, 1997).

- Stability of political institutions and degree of popular participation in the political process.
- Economic system and structure.
- Living standards and degree of social and economic cohesion.
- Fiscal policy and budgetary flexibility.
- Public debt burden and debt service track record.
- Monetary policy and inflation pressures.[5]

The single most important leading indicator according to S&P is the rate of inflation.

For foreign currency debt, credit analysis by S&P focuses on the interaction of domestic and foreign government policies. S&P analyzes a country's balance of payments and the structure of its external balance sheet. The area of analysis with respect to its external balance sheet are the net public debt, total net external debt, and net external liabilities.

Bankruptcy and Creditor Rights in the United States

The holder of a corporate debt instrument has priority over the equity owners in the case of bankruptcy of a corporation. There are creditors who have priority over other creditors. Here we will provide an overview of the bankruptcy process and then look at what actually happens to creditors in bankruptcies.

The Bankruptcy Process

The law governing bankruptcy in the United States is the Bankruptcy Reform Act of 1978 as amended.[6] One purpose of the act is to set forth the rules for a corporation to be either liquidated or reorganized. The *liquidation* of a corporation means that all the assets will be distributed to the holders of claims of the corporation and no corporate entity will survive. In a *reorganization*, a new corporate entity will result. Some holders of the claim of the bankrupt corporation will receive cash in exchange for their claims, others may receive new securities in the corporation that results from the reorganization, and others may receive a combination of both cash and new securities in the resulting corporation.

Another purpose of the Bankruptcy Act is to give a corporation time to decide whether to reorganize or liquidate and then the necessary time to formulate a plan to accomplish either a reorganization or liquidation.

---

[5] Beers, "Standard & Poor's Sovereign Ratings Criteria."

[6] For a discussion of the Bankruptcy Reform Act of 1978 and a nontechnical description of its principal features, see Jane Tripp Howe, "Investing in Chapter 11 and Other Distressed Companies," Chapter 18 in Frank J. Fabozzi (ed.), *Handbook of Corporate Debt Instruments* (New Hope, PA: Frank J. Fabozzi Associates, 1998).

This is achieved because when a corporation files for bankruptcy, the Act grants the corporation protection from creditors who seek to collect their claims. The petition for bankruptcy can be filed either by the company itself, in which case it is called a *voluntary bankruptcy*, or be filed by its creditors, in which case it is called an *involuntary bankruptcy*. A company that files for protection under the bankruptcy act generally becomes a "debtor-in-possession" (DIP), and continues to operate its business under the supervision of the court.

The Bankruptcy Act is comprised of 15 chapters, each chapter covering a particular type of bankruptcy. Of particular interest to us are two of the chapters, Chapter 7 and Chapter 11. Chapter 7 deals with the liquidation of a company; Chapter 11 deals with the reorganization of a company.

Absolute Priority: Theory and Practice

When a company is liquidated, creditors receive distributions based on the "absolute priority rule" to the extent assets are available. The absolute priority rule is the principle that senior creditors are paid in full before junior creditors are paid anything. For secured creditors and unsecured creditors, the absolute priority rule guarantees their seniority to equity holders.

In liquidations, the absolute priority rule generally holds, In contrast, there is a good body of literature that argues that strict absolute priority has not been upheld by the courts or the SEC.[7] Studies of actual reorganizations under Chapter 11 have found that the violation of absolute priority is the rule rather the exception.[8]

There are several hypotheses that have been suggested as to why in a reorganization the distribution made to claim holders will diverge from that required by the absolute priority principle.

The *incentive hypothesis* argues that the longer the negotiation process among the parties, the greater the bankruptcy costs and the smaller

---

[7] See, for example, William H. Meckling, "Financial Markets, Default, and Bankruptcy," *Law and Contemporary Problems*, 41 (1977), pp. 124–177; Merton H. Miller, "The Wealth Transfers of Bankruptcy: Some Illustrative Examples," *Law and Contemporary Problems*, 41 (1977), pp. 39–46; Jerold B. Warner, "Bankruptcy, Absolute Priority, and the Pricing of Risky Debt Claims," *Journal of Financial Economics*, 4 (1977), pp. 239–276; and, Thomas H. Jackson, "Of Liquidation, Continuation, and Delay: An Analysis of Bankruptcy Policy and Nonbankruptcy Rules," *American Bankruptcy Law Journal*, 60 (1986), pp. 399–428.

[8] See: Julian R. Franks and Walter N. Torous, "An Empirical Investigation of U.S. Firms in Reorganization," *Journal of Finance* (July 1989), pp. 747–769; Lawrence A. Weiss, "Bankruptcy Resolution: Direct Costs and Violation of Priority of Claims," *Journal of Financial Economics* (1990), pp. 285–314; and Frank J. Fabozzi, Jane Tripp Howe, Takashi Makabe, and Toshihide Sudo, "Recent Evidence on the Distribution Patterns in Chapter 11 Reorganizations," *Journal of Fixed Income* (Spring 1993), pp. 6–23.

the amount to be distributed to all parties. This is because in a reorganization, a committee representing the various claim holders is appointed with the purpose of formulating a plan of reorganization. To be accepted, a plan of reorganization must be approved by at least two-thirds of the amount and a majority of the number of claims voting and at least two-thirds of the outstanding shares of each class of interests. Consequently, a long-lasting bargaining process is expected. The longer the negotiation process among the parties, the more likely that the company will be operated in a manner that is not in the best interest of the creditors and, as a result, the smaller the amount to be distributed to all parties. Since all impaired classes including equity holders generally must approve the plan of reorganization, creditors often convince equity holders to accept the plan by offering to distribute some value to them.

The *recontracting process hypothesis* argues that the violation of absolute priority reflects a recontracting process between stockholders and senior creditors that gives recognition to the ability of management to preserve value on behalf of stockholders.[9] According to the *stockholders' influence on reorganization plan hypothesis,* creditors are less informed about the true economic operating conditions of the firm than management. As the distribution to creditors in the plan of reorganization is based on the valuation by the firm, creditors without perfect information easily suffer the loss.[10] According to Wruck, managers generally have a better understanding than creditors or stockholders about a firm's internal operations while creditors and stockholders can have better information about industry trends. Management may therefore use its superior knowledge to present the data in a manner which reinforces its position.[11]

The essence of the *strategic bargaining process hypothesis* is that the increasing complexity of firms which declare bankruptcy will accentuate the negotiating process and result in an even higher incidence of violation of the absolute priority rule. The likely outcome is further supported by the increased number of official committees in the reorganization process as well as the increased number of financial and legal advisors.

There are some who argue that creditors will receive a higher value in reorganization than they would in liquidation in part because of the

---

[9] Douglas G. Baird and Thomas H. Jackson, "Bargaining After the Fall and the Contours of the Absolute Priority Rule," *University of Chicago Law Review,* 55 (1988), pp. 738–789.

[10] L.A. Bebchuk, "A New Approach to Corporate Reorganizations," *Harvard Law Review,* 101 (1988), pp. 775–804.

[11] Karen Hooper Wruck, "Financial Distress, Reorganization, and Organizational Efficiency," *Journal of Financial Economics,* 27 (1990), pp. 419–444.

costs associated with liquidation.[12] Finally, the lack of symmetry in the tax system (negative taxes are not permitted, although loss deductions may be carried forward) results in situations in which the only way to use all current loss deductions is to merge.[13] The tax system may encourage continuance or merger and discourage bankruptcy.

Consequently, while investors in the debt of a corporation may feel that they have priority over the equity owners and priority over other classes of debtors, the actual outcome of a bankruptcy may be far different from what the terms of the debt agreement state.

One study examined the extent of violation of the absolute priority rule among three broad groups: secured creditors, unsecured creditors and equity holders, and also among various types of debt and equity securities.[14] The study also provided evidence on which asset class bears the cost of violations of absolute priority and an initial estimate of total distributed value relative to liquidation value. The findings of this study suggest that unsecured creditors bear a disproportionate cost of reorganization, and that more senior unsecured creditors may bear a disproportionate cost relative to the junior unsecured creditors while equity holders often benefit from violations of absolute priority.

U.S. Default and Recovery Statistics

There is a good deal of research published on default rates by both rating agencies and academicians. From an investment perspective, default rates by themselves are not of paramount significance: it is perfectly possible for a portfolio of corporate bonds to suffer defaults and to outperform Treasuries at the same time, provided the yield spread of the portfolio is sufficiently high to offset the losses from defaults. Furthermore, because holders of defaulted bonds typically recover a percentage of the face amount of their investment, the *default loss rate* can be substantially lower than the default rate. The default loss rate is defined as follows:

Default loss rate = Default rate × (100% − Recovery rate)

---

[12] Michael C. Jensen, "Eclipse of the Public Corporation," *Harvard Business Review*, 89 (1989), pp. 61–62; and Wruck, "Financial Distress, Reorganization, and Organizational Efficiency."

[13] J.I. Bulow and J.B. Shoven, "The Bankruptcy Decision," *Bell Journal of Economics*, 1978. For a further discussion of the importance of net operating losses and the current tax law, see Fabozzi, *et al* "Recent Evidence on the Distribution Patterns in Chapter 11 Reorganizations."

[14] Fabozzi, Howe, Makabe, and Sudo, "Recent Evidence on the Distribution Patterns in Chapter 11 Reorganizations."

For instance, a default rate of 5% and a recovery rate of 30% means a default loss rate of only 3.5% (70% of 5%).

Therefore, focusing exclusively on default rates merely highlights the worst possible outcome that a diversified portfolio of corporate bonds would suffer, assuming all defaulted bonds would be totally worthless.

Default Rates

There have been several studies of default rates and the reported findings are at times significantly different. The reason is due to the different approaches used by researchers to measure default rates. Three metrics have been used to compute default rates.

In several studies of high-yield corporate bond default rates, Altman defines the default rate as the par value of all high-yield bonds that defaulted in a given calendar year, divided by the total par value outstanding during the year.[15] Altman's estimates are simple averages of the annual default rates over a number of years.

Studies by the defunct investment banking firm of Drexel Burnham Lambert (DLB), the largest underwriter of high-yield corporate bonds in its days, investigated default rates.[16] The methodology used by DBL was to compute the cumulative dollar value of all defaulted high-yield bonds, divided by the cumulative dollar value of all high-yield issuance, and further divided by the weighted average number of years outstanding to obtain an average annual default rate.

Asquith, Mullins, and Wolff use a cumulative default statistic.[17] For all bonds issued in a given year, the default rate is the total par value of defaulted issues as of the date of their study, divided by the total par amount originally issued to obtain a cumulative default rate. Their result is not normalized by the number of years outstanding.

Although all three measures are useful indicators of bond default propensity, they are not directly comparable. Even when restated on an annualized basis, they do not all measure the same quantity. The default statistics from all studies, however, are surprisingly similar once cumulative rates have been annualized.

The rating agencies as well as Edward Altman and his colleagues publish information on default rates. These statistics are updated annu-

---

[15] Edward I. Altman, "Measuring Corporate Bond Mortality and Performance," *Journal of Finance* (September 1989), pp. 909–922 and Edward I. Altman and Scott A. Nammacher, *Investing in Junk Bonds* (New York: John Wiley, 1987).

[16] See the 1984–1989 issues of *High Yield Market Report: Financing America's Futures* (New York and Beverly Hills: Drexel Burnham Lambert, Inc.).

[17] Paul Asquith, David W. Mullins, Jr., and Eric D. Wolff, "Original Issue High Yield Bonds: Aging Analysis of Defaults, Exchanges, and Calls," *Journal of Finance* (September 1989), pp. 923–952.

ally.[18] In this section we report the default rates prepared using the Altman methodology by Kender and Petrucci of Salomon Smith Barney.[19] Exhibit 2.2 provides information about defaults or restructuring under distressed conditions from 1978–2002 for high-yield bonds in the United States and Canada. The information shown is the par value outstanding for the year, the amount defaulted, and the default rate. The annual default rate reported in the exhibit is measured by the par value of the high-yield corporate bonds that have defaulted in a given calendar year divided by the total par value outstanding of high-yield corporate bonds during the year.

The weighted average default rate for the entire period was 5.49%. One can see the increase in credit risk in recent years by looking at the default rates in 2001 and 2002. The default rate of 12.8% in 2002 was greater than the default rate in 2001 (9.8%), the previous record default rate in the 1978–2001 period (1991, 10.3%), and the weighted average default rate for the 1978–2002 period (5.49%).

Default Loss Rates/Recovery Rates

Next let's look at the historical loss rate that was realized by investors in high-yield corporate bonds. This rate, referred to earlier as the default loss rate, is reported in the last column of Exhibit 2.2. from 1978 to 2002. The methodology for computing the default loss rate is as follows. First, the default loss of principal is computed by multiplying the default rate for the year by the average loss of principal. The average loss of principal is computed by first determining the recovery per $100 of par value. The recovery per $100 of par value uses the weighted average price of all issues after default. The difference between par value of $100 and the recovery of principal is the default loss of principal. Next the default loss of coupon is computed. This is found by multiplying the default rate by the weighted average coupon rate divided by two (because the coupon payments are semiannual). The default loss rate is then the sum of the default loss of principal and the default loss of coupon.

For example, the calculation of the default loss rate for 2002 of 10.15% in Exhibit 2.2 was computed by the authors of the study as follows:[20]

---

[18] A comparison of the default rates and default loss rates among the rating agencies, as well the Altman studies, is that different universes of bonds are sometimes used.
[19] The most recent statistics at the time of this writing are reported in Michael T. Kender and Gabriella Petrucci, *Altman Report on Defaults and Returns on High Yield Bonds: 2002 in Review and Market Outlook*, Salomon Smith Barney (February 5, 2003).
[20] Kender and Petrucci, *Altman Report on Defaults and Returns on High Yield Bonds: 2002 in Review and Market Outlook*, Figure 13, p. 15.

EXHIBIT 2.2   Historical Default Rates and Default Loss Rates for High-Yield Corporate Bonds: 1978–2002 ($ millions)[a]

Year	Par Value Outstanding[a]	Par Value of Default	Default Rate (%)	Weighted Price After Default	Weighted Coupon (%)	Default Loss (%)
2002	$757,000	$96,858	12.79	25.3	9.37	10.15[b]
2001	649,000	63,609	9.80	25.5	9.18	7.76
2000	597,200	30,295	5.07	26.4	8.54	3.95
1999	567,400	23,532	4.15	27.9	10.55	3.21
1998	465,500	7,464	1.60	35.9	9.46	1.10
1997	335,400	4,200	1.25	54.2	11.87	0.65
1996	271,000	3,336	1.23	51.9	8.92	0.65
1995	240,000	4,551	1.90	40.6	11.83	1.24
1994	235,000	3,418	1.45	39.4	10.25	0.96
1993	206,907	2,287	1.11	56.6	12.98	0.56
1992	163,000	5,545	3.40	50.1	12.32	1.91
1991	183,600	18,862	10.27	36.0	11.59	7.16
1990	181,000	18,354	10.14	23.4	12.94	8.42
1989	189,258	8,110	4.29	38.3	13.40	2.93
1988	148,187	3,944	2.66	43.6	11.91	1.66
1987	129,557	7,486	5.78	75.9	12.07	1.74
1986	90,243	3,156	3.50	34.5	10.61	2.48
1985	58,088	992	1.71	45.9	13.69	1.04
1984	40,939	344	0.84	48.6	12.23	0.48
1983	27,492	301	1.09	55.7	10.11	0.54
1982	18,109	577	3.19	38.6	9.61	2.11
1981	17,115	27	0.16	72.0	15.75	0.15
1980	14,935	224	1.50	21.1	8.43	1.25
1979	10,356	20	0.19	31.0	10.63	0.14
1978	8,946	119	1.33	60.0	8.38	0.59
Arithmetic average, 1978–2002			3.62	42.3	11.06	2.51
Weighted average, 1978–2002			5.49			4.10

[a] Excludes defaulted issues.
[b] Default loss rate adjusted for fallen angels is 9.256% in 2002.
Source: Figure 25, p. 29 in Michael T. Kender and Gabriella Petrucci, *Altman Report on Defaults and Returns on High Yield Bonds: 2002 in Review and Market Outlook*, Salomon Smith Barney, February 5, 2003.

Background Data:	
Average default rate	12.795%
Average price at default	25.317
Average price at downgrade	59.792
Average recovery	25.317
Average loss of principal	74.683
Average coupon payment	9.369
Default loss computation:	
Default rate	12.795%
× Loss of principal	74.683
Default loss of principal	9.556
Default rate	12.795%
× Loss of coupon	4.684
Default loss of coupon	0.599
Default loss of principal and coupon	10.155%

The weighted average default loss rate for the entire period as reported in Exhibit 2.2 was 4.10%. This indicates that the weighted average recovery rate is 95.9%. In the last two years in the study period, the weighted average default rate was considerably higher than the average rate.

Several studies have found that the recovery rate is closely related to the bond's seniority. Exhibit 2.3 shows the weighted average recovery rate for bond issues that defaulted between 1978 and 2002 for the following bond classes: (1) senior secured, (2) senior unsecured, (3) senior subordinated, (4) subordinated, and (5) discount and zero coupon.

Seniority is not the only factor that affects recovery values. In general, recovery values will vary with the types of assets and competitive conditions of the firm, as well as the economic environment at the time of bankruptcy. In addition, recovery rates will also vary across industries. For example, some manufacturing companies, such as petroleum and chemical companies, have assets with a high tangible value, such as plant, equipment, and land. These assets usually have a significant market value, even in the event of bankruptcy. In other industries, however, a company's assets have less tangible value, and bondholders should expect low recovery rates.

To understand why recovery rates might vary across industries, consider two extreme examples: a software company and an electric utility. In the event of bankruptcy, the assets of a software company will probably have little tangible value. The company's products will have a low liquidation value because of the highly competitive and dynamic nature of the industry. The company's major intangible asset, its software developers, may literally disappear as employees move to jobs at other

EXHIBIT 2.3   Weighted Average Recovery Rates on Defaulted Debt by Seniority per $100 Face Amount (1978–2003)

Default Year	Senior Secured		Senior Unsecured		Senior Subordinated		Subordinated		Discount and Zero-Coupon		All Seniorities	
	No.	$	No.	$	No.	$	No.	$	No.	$	No.	$
2002	37	52.81	254	21.82	21	32.79	0	0.00	28	26.47	340	25.32
2001	9	40.95	187	28.84	48	18.37	0	0.00	37	15.05	281	25.48
2000	13	39.58	47	25.40	61	25.96	26	26.62	17	23.61	164	25.83
1999	14	26.90	60	42.54	40	23.56	2	13.88	11	17.30	127	31.14
1998	6	70.38	21	39.57	6	17.54	0	0.00	1	17.00	34	37.27
1997	4	74.90	12	70.94	6	31.89	1	60.00	2	19.00	25	53.89
1996	4	59.08	4	50.11	9	48.99	4	44.23	3	11.99	24	51.91
1995	5	44.64	9	50.50	17	39.01	1	20.00	1	17.50	33	41.77
1994	5	48.66	8	51.14	5	19.81	3	37.04	1	5.00	22	39.44
1993	2	55.75	7	33.38	10	51.50	9	28.38	4	31.75	32	38.83
1992	15	59.85	8	35.61	17	58.20	22	49.13	5	19.82	67	50.03
1991	4	44.12	69	55.84	37	31.91	38	24.30	9	27.89	157	40.67
1990	12	32.18	31	29.02	38	25.01	24	18.83	11	15.63	116	24.66
1989	9	82.69	16	53.70	21	19.60	30	23.95			76	35.97
1988	13	67.96	19	41.99	10	30.70	20	35.27			62	43.45
1987	4	90.68	17	72.02	6	56.24	4	35.25			31	66.63
1986	8	48.32	11	37.72	7	35.20	30	33.39			56	36.60
1985	2	74.25	3	34.81	7	36.18	15	41.45			27	41.78
1984	4	53.42	1	50.50	2	65.88	7	44.68			14	50.62
1983	1	71.00	3	67.72			4	41.79			8	55.17
1982			16	39.31			4	32.91			20	38.03
1981	1	72.00									1	72.00
1980			2	26.71			2	16.63			4	21.67
1979							1	31.00			1	31.00
1978			1	60.00							1	60.00
Total/Average	172	52.86	806	33.62	368	29.67	247	31.03	130	20.40	1,723	33.16
Median		55.75		41.99		31.91		31.00		17.50		39.44

Source: Figure 16 in Michael T. Kender and Gabriella Petrucci, *Altman Report on Defaults and Returns on High Yield Bonds: 2002 in Review and Market Outlook,* Salomon Smith Barney (February 5, 2003), p. 18.

companies. In general, in industries which spend heavily on research and development and in which technological changes are rapid, a company's liquidation value will decline sharply when its products lose their competitive edge. In these industries, bondholders can expect to recover little in the event of default.

At the other extreme, electric utility bonds will likely have relatively high recovery values. The assets of an electric company (e.g., generation, transmission, and distribution), usually continue to generate a stream of revenues even after a bankruptcy. In most cases, a bankruptcy of a utility can be solved by changing the company's capital structure, rather than by liquidating its assets. In addition, regulators have a vested interest in maintaining the company as a going concern—no one likes to see the lights turned off.

We caution that the historical recovery rates should be viewed as rough estimates, rather than guaranteed prices, because recovery rates can vary significantly from company to company even within a particular industry. In addition, the recovery rates are based on a small sample of defaults for some industries, such as paper companies and commercial banks. More importantly, recovery rates in the future may differ significantly from the past experience.

This note of caution is particularly important for bonds issued by banks and bank holding companies.[21] In the event of a bank insolvency, the claim of investors in holding company securities is generally subordinate to the claims of the bank's creditors, including its depositors, its general creditors, and its subordinated creditors. Essentially, investors in holding company securities have no claim until the claims of bank level creditors are satisfied. Also, under Federal Reserve Board policy, a bank holding company is expected to act as a "source of strength" to each subsidiary bank and to commit resources to support a subsidiary bank when it might not do so absent such policy. As a result, in the event of a bank holding company bankruptcy, we would expect low recovery values for all bank holding company bonds, regardless of whether the bonds are senior, subordinated, or deeply subordinated deferrable bonds.[22]

---

[21] Leland E. Crabbe and Frank J. Fabozzi, *Managing a Corporate Bond Portfolio* (Hoboken, NJ: John Wiley & Sons, 2002), pp. 173–174.

[22] As a result of the Financial Institutions Reform, Recovery, and Enforcement Act of 1989, any subsidiary bank of a bank holding company can generally be held liable for any expected loss incurred by the FDIC in connection with the appointment of a conservator or receiver of any other subsidiary bank of the bank holding company. Therefore, any losses to the FDIC may result in losses to the bank holding company's other subsidiary banks or a reduction in the ability of subsidiary banks to transfer funds to the holding company to service holding company bonds.

Under the Federal Deposit Insurance Corporation Improvement Act of 1991, a bank holding company is required to guarantee a capital restoration plan of an undercapitalized subsidiary bank up to certain limits. In addition, under the Crime Control Act of 1990, in the event of a bank holding company's bankruptcy, any commitment by the bank holding company to a federal bank regulatory agency to maintain the capital of a subsidiary bank will be assumed by the bankruptcy trustee and entitled to a priority of payment.

EXHIBIT 2.4   U.S. Dollar Bond Yield Curves, January 2003

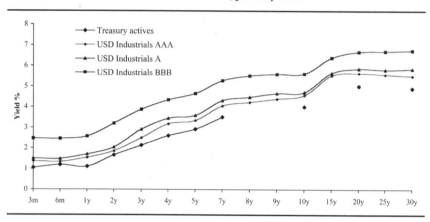

Source: Bloomberg.

CREDIT SPREAD RISK

The credit spread is the excess premium over the government or risk-free rate required by the market for taking on a certain assumed credit exposure. Exhibit 2.4 shows the credit spread in January 2003 for industrial corporate bonds with different ratings (AAA, A, and BBB). The benchmark is the on-the-run or "active" U.S. Treasury issue for the given maturity.

Notice that the higher the credit rating, the smaller the credit spread. Credit spread risk is the risk of financial loss resulting from changes in the level of credit spreads used in the marking-to-market of a product. It is exhibited by a portfolio for which the credit spread is traded and marked. Changes in observed credit spreads affect the value of the portfolio and can lead to losses for traders or underperformance relative to a benchmark for portfolio managers.

Duration is a measure of the change in the value of a bond when interest rates change. A useful way of thinking of duration is that it is the approximate percentage change in the value of a bond for a 100 bp change in "interest rates." The interest rate that is assumed to change is the Treasury rate. For credit-risky bonds, the yield is equal to the Treasury yield plus the credit spread. A measure of how a credit-risky bond's price will change if the credit spread sought by the market changes is called *spread duration*. For example, a spread duration of 2 for a credit-risky bond means that for a 100 bp increase in the credit spread (holding the Treasury rate constant), the bond's price will change by approximately 2%.

The spread duration for a portfolio is found by computing a market weighted average of the spread duration for each bond. The same is true for a bond market index. Note, however, that the spread duration reported for a bond market index is not the same as the spread duration for estimating the credit spread risk of an index. For example, on April 17, 2003, the spread duration reported for the Lehman Brothers Aggregate Bond Index was 3. However, the spread duration for the index is computed by Lehman Brothers based on all non-Treasury securities. Some of these sectors offer a spread to Treasuries that encompasses more than just credit risk. For example, the mortgage sector in the index offers a spread due to prepayment risk. The same is true for some subsectors within the ABS sector. Lehman Brothers does a have Credit Sector for the index. For that sector, the spread duration reflects the exposure to credit spreads in general. It was 1.48 on April 17, 2003 and is interpreted as follows: If credit spreads increase by 100 bps, the approximate decline in the value of the index will be 1.48%.

Fundamental Factors that Affect Credit Spreads

To understand credit spread risk it is necessary to understand the fundamental factors that affect credit spreads. These factors can be classified as macro and micro.

Macro Fundamentals

The ability of a corporation to meet its obligations on its debt depends on its expected cash flows. During prosperous economic times, investors expect that corporate cash flows will improve. In contrast, in an economic recession, investors expect that corporate cash flows will deteriorate, making it more difficult to satisfy its bond obligations. Consequently, it is reasonable to assume that credit spreads are tied to the business cycle.[23]

The empirical evidence supports the view that the economic cycle has an effect on credit spreads. Exhibit 2.5 shows the yield spread between Baa rated and Aaa rated corporate bonds over business cycles dating back to 1919. Using the National Bureau of Economic Research's definition of economic cycles, economic recessions are shaded in the exhibit. The evidence suggests that, in general, spreads tightened during the early stages of economic expansion, and spreads widened sharply during economic recessions.

---

[23] For a more detailed discussion of macro fundamental factors that affect credit spreads, see Chapter 10 in Crabbe and Fabozzi, *Managing a Corporate Bond Portfolio*.

EXHIBIT 2.5   Yield Spread Between Baa and Aaa Bonds

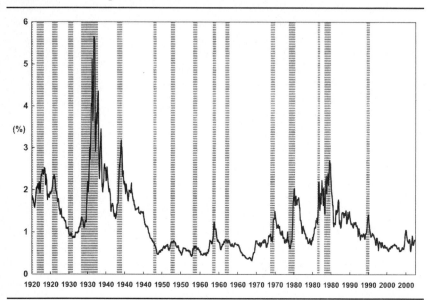

Source: Exhibit 1 in Chapter 10 of Leland E. Crabbe and Frank J. Fabozzi, *Managing a Corporate Bond Portfolio* (Hoboken, NJ: John Wiley & Sons, 2002).

Investors tend to be forward looking and therefore credit spreads react to anticipated changes in the economic cycle. For example, typically credit spreads begin to widen before the official end of an economic expansion. Consequently credit spreads can change based on an anticipated change in the economic cycle that does not materialize.

Anticipating changes in economic cycles is, therefore, important in assessing an adverse change in credit spreads. There has been extensive research by economists to identify economic indicators that lead economic cycles, referred to as "leading economic indicators." Exhibit 2.6 shows the 10 U.S. leading economic indicators used by The Conference Board.[24] From the 10 leading economic indicators a leading index is constructed. The weighting used for each leading economic indicator to obtain the leading index is shown in the exhibit.

Moreover, some industries within the economy exhibit strong economic cycle patterns. As a result, credit spreads for industries can be expected to be affected by economic cycles. For example, the auto

---

[24] The Conference Board constructs a leading index for other countries, namely, Germany, Japan, Australia, France, Spain, and Korea.

EXHIBIT 2.6   The Conference Board's Components of the Leading Index for the United States

Leading Economic Indicator	Factor
Average weekly hours, manufacturing	0.1946
Average weekly initial claims for unemployment insurance	0.0268
Manufacturers' new orders, consumer goods and materials	0.0504
Vendor performance, slower deliveries diffusion index	0.0296
Manufacturers' new orders, nondefense capital goods	0.0139
Building permits, new private housing units	0.0205
Stock prices, 500 common stocks	0.0309
Money supply, M2	0.2775
Interest rate spread, 10-year Treasury bonds less federal funds	0.3364
Index of consumer expectations	0.0193

Source: The Conference Board, www.tcb-indicators.org/us/LatestReleases/.

industry is more adversely impacted by a recession than other industries such as consumer staples.

Micro Fundamentals

At the micro level, the analysis of a potential change in the credit spread focuses on the fundamental factors that may alter the individual corporation's ability to meet its debt obligations. These are the same factors that the rating agencies use to assess the credit default risk of a corporation that we discussed earlier in this chapter.

DOWNGRADE RISK

As explained in the previous section, market participants gauge the credit default risk of an issue by looking at the credit ratings assigned to issues by the rating agencies. Once a credit rating is assigned to a debt obligation, a rating agency monitors the credit quality of the issuer and can reassign a different credit rating. An improvement in the credit quality of an issue or issuer is rewarded with a better credit rating, referred to as an *upgrade*; a deterioration in the credit rating of an issue or issuer is penalized by the assignment of an inferior credit rating, referred to as a *downgrade*. The actual or anticipated downgrading of an issue or issuer increases the credit spread and results in a decline in the price of the issue or the issuer's bonds. This risk is referred to as *downgrade risk* and is closely related to credit spread risk.

EXHIBIT 2.7 Hypothetical 1-Year Rating Migration Table

Rating at Start of Year	Rating at End of Year								
	AAA	AA	A	BBB	BB	B	CCC	D	Total
AAA	93.20	6.00	0.60	0.12	0.08	0.00	0.00	0.00	100
AA	1.60	92.75	5.07	0.36	0.11	0.07	0.03	0.01	100
A	0.18	2.65	91.91	4.80	0.37	0.02	0.02	0.05	100
BBB	0.04	0.30	5.20	87.70	5.70	0.70	0.16	0.20	100
BB	0.03	0.11	0.61	6.80	81.65	7.10	2.60	1.10	100
B	0.01	0.09	0.55	0.88	7.90	75.67	8.70	6.20	100
CCC	0.00	0.01	0.31	0.84	2.30	8.10	62.54	25.90	100

Rating Migration (Transition) Table

The rating agencies periodically publish, in the form of a table, information about how issues that they have rated change over time. This table is called a *rating migration table* or *rating transition table*. The table is useful for investors to assess potential downgrades and upgrades. A rating migration table is available for different lengths of time. Exhibit 2.7 shows a hypothetical rating migration table for a 1-year period. The first column shows the ratings at the start of the year and the first row shows the ratings at the end of the year.

Let's interpret one of the numbers. Look at the cell where the rating at the beginning of the year is AA and the rating at the end of the year is AA. This cell represents the percentage of issues rated AA at the beginning of the year that did not change their rating over the year. That is, there were no downgrades or upgrades. As can be seen, 92.75% of the issues rated AA at the start of the year were rated AA at the end of the year. Now look at the cell where the rating at the beginning of the year is AA and at the end of the year is A. This shows the percentage of issues rated AA at the beginning of the year that were downgraded to A by the end of the year. In our hypothetical 1-year rating migration table, this percentage is 5.07%. One can view this figure as a probability. It is the probability that an issue rated AA will be downgraded to A by the end of the year.

A rating migration table also shows the potential for upgrades. Again, using Exhibit 2.7 look at the row that shows issues rated AA at the beginning of the year. Looking at the cell shown in the column AAA rating at the end of the year, there is the figure 1.60%. This figure represents the percentage of issues rated AA at the beginning of the year that were upgraded to AAA by the end of the year.

In general, the following hold for actual rating migration tables. First, the probability of a downgrade is much higher than for an upgrade for investment-grade bonds. Second, the longer the migration period, the lower the probability that an issuer will retain its original rating. That is, a 1-year rating migration table will have a lower probability of a downgrade for a particular rating than a 5-year rating migration table for that same rating.

Credit Watch

A rating agency may announce in advance that it is reviewing a particular credit rating, and may go further and state that the review is a precursor to a possible downgrade or upgrade. This announcement is referred to as putting the issue under *credit watch*. The outcome of a credit watch is in most cases likely to be a rating downgrade, however the review may reaffirm the current rating or possibly upgrade it.

During the credit watch phase the rating agency will advise investors to use the current rating with caution. When a rating agency announces that an issue is under credit watch, the price of the bonds will fall in the market as investors look to sell out of their holdings. This upward movement in yield will be more pronounced if an actual downgrade results. For example in October 1992 the government of Canada was placed under credit watch and subsequently lost its AAA credit rating. As a result there was an immediate and sharp sell-off in Canadian government eurobonds before the rating agencies had announced the actual results of their credit review.

Event Risk

Occasionally the ability of an issuer to make interest and principal payments changes seriously and unexpectedly because of an unforeseen event. This can include any number of idiosyncratic events that are specific to the corporation or to an industry, including a natural or industrial accident, a regulatory change, a takeover or corporate restructuring or even corporate fraud. This risk is referred to generically as *event risk* and will result in a downgrading of the issuer by the rating agencies. Because the price of the entity's securities will typically change dramatically or jump in price, this risk is sometimes referred to as *jump risk*.

Here are two actual examples of event risk. The first is the takeover in 1988 of RJR Nabisco for $25 billion through a leveraged buyout (LBO). The new company took on a substantial amount of debt to finance the acquisition of the firm. In the case of RJR Nabisco, the debt and equity after the LBO were $29.9 and $1.2 billion, respectively. Because of the need to service a larger amount of debt, the company's rating was downgraded.

RJR Nabisco's credit rating as assigned by Moody's dropped from A1 to B3. As a result, investors demanded a higher credit spread because of this new capital structure with a greater proportion of debt. The yield spread to a benchmark Treasury rate increased from about 100 bps to 350 bps.

A security example of event risk is the rapid decline of WorldCom corporate bonds in 2002. At the beginning of 2002, WorldCom enjoyed a triple A rating. Its 8.25% bonds due in 2031 were trading above par value at 106.68 in January of 2002. However, as rumors of WorldCom failing to meet its profit projections in 2002 began to swirl in February and March, WorldCom bonds began to drift downwards in value—trading at about 80 cents on the dollar by the beginning of April 2002. Then the bottom fell out. By mid-April, allegation of accounting "irregularities" were confirmed, and WorldCom bonds fell precipitously. Over a 2-week time period, World-Com bonds declined from a price of about 75 in mid-April to a price of about 42 by the end of April 2002. At the same time the rating agencies rapidly slashed WorldCom's credit rating to junk status. Still, the worst was yet to come. By June, the total amount of the accounting fraud was confirmed in the range of $10 billion, and WorldCom declared bankruptcy. Its bonds took another leg down in June of 2002 from a price of 45 down to 11. In the space of only six months, WorldCom went from a strong investment grade "Buy" to a distressed debt "Sell."

CHAPTER 3

Credit Default Swaps

By far, the most popular type of credit derivative is the credit default swap. Not only is this form of credit derivative the most commonly used standalone product employed by asset managers and traders, but it is also used extensively in structured credit products such as synthetic collateralized debt obligations and credit-linked notes.

A credit default swap is probably the simplest form of credit risk transference among all credit derivatives. Credit default swaps are used to shift credit exposure to a credit protection seller. They are similar to a credit default option discussed in Chapter 11 in that their primary purpose is to hedge the credit exposure to a reference obligation or issuer. In this sense, credit default swaps operate much like a standby letter of credit.

Our focus in this chapter is on the features, investment characteristics, and primary applications of credit default swaps. How they are used in structured credit products and how they are priced are covered in later chapters.

BASIC ELEMENTS OF CREDIT DEFAULT SWAPS

In a credit default swap, the documentation will identify the *reference entity* or the *reference obligation*. The reference entity is the issuer of the debt instrument. It could be a corporation, a sovereign government, or a bank loan.

When there is a reference entity, the party to the credit default swap has an option to deliver one of the issuer's obligation subject to prespecified constraints. So, if the reference entity is Ford Motor Credit Company, any one of acceptable senior bond issues of that issuer, for example, can be delivered. In contrast, a *reference obligation* is a specific obligation for which protection is being sought.

47

EXHIBIT 3.1   Credit Default Swap

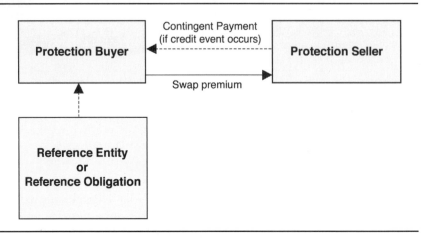

Credit default swaps can be classified as follows:

- Single-name credit default swaps
- Basket swaps

We'll discuss the difference between these types of swaps in this chapter.

In a credit default swap, the protection buyer pays a fee, the *swap premium*, to the protection seller in return for the right to receive a payment conditional upon the default of the reference obligation or the reference entity. Collectively, the payments made by the protection buyer are called the *premium leg*; the contingent payment that might have to be made by the protection seller is called the *protection leg*.

In the documentation of a trade, a default is defined in terms of a *credit event* and we shall use the terms "default" and "credit event" interchangeably throughout this book. Should a credit event occur, the protection seller must make a payment. This is shown in Exhibit 3.1.

Single-Name Credit Default Swaps

The interdealer market has evolved to where single-name credit default swaps for corporate and sovereign reference entities are standardized. While trades between dealers have been standardized, there are occasional trades in the interdealer market where there is a customized agreement. In the interdealer market, the tenor, or length of time of a credit default swap, is typically five years. The tenor of a swap is referred to as the "scheduled term" because a credit event will result in a payment by the protection seller, resulting in the credit default swap being terminated. Asset managers can have a dealer create a tenor equal to the maturity of the reference obligation or be constructed for a shorter time period to match the manager's investment horizon.

The *trade date* is the date the parties enter into the credit derivative transaction. The *effective date* is the date when contractual payments begin to accrue. The parties to the trade specify at the outset when the credit default swap will terminate. If no credit event has occurred by the maturity of the credit swap, then the swap terminates at the *scheduled termination date*—a date specified by the parties in the contract. However, the *termination date* under the contract is the earlier of the scheduled termination date or a date upon which a credit event occurs and notice is provided. Therefore, notice of a credit event terminates a credit default swap.

Calculation of the Swap Premium

The standard contract for a single-name credit default swap in the inter-dealer market calls for a quarterly payment of the swap premium. Typically, the swap premium is paid in arrears.

The quarterly payment is determined using one of the day count conventions in the bond market. A day count convention indicates the number of days in the month and the number of days in a year that will be used to determine how to prorate the swap premium to a quarter. The possible day count conventions are (1) actual/actual, (2) actual/360, and (3) 30/360. The day count convention used in the U.S. government bond market is actual/actual, while the convention used in the corporate bond market is 30/360. The day count convention used for credit default swaps is actual/360. This is the same convention used in the interest rate swap market. A day convention of actual/360 means that to determine the payment in a quarter, the actual number of days in the quarter are used and 360 days are assumed for the year. Consequently, the swap premium payment for a quarter is computed as follows:

$$\text{Quarterly swap premium payment}$$
$$= \text{Notional amount} \times \text{Annual rate (in decimal)}$$
$$\times \frac{\text{Actual no. of days in quarter}}{360}$$

Illustration of a Single-Name Credit Default Swap

As explained above, the underlying for a credit default swap can be a reference entity or a reference obligation. Prices are provided by credit derivative market makers for reference entities. Exhibit 3.2 shows the indica-

EXHIBIT 3.2   Credit Derivative Price Quotes for Auto Reference Entities
(June 16, 2003)

GRAB									Equity BBVM

10:54 **AUTOS**   PAGE 1 / 1

		3 Y − CDS Quotes				5 Y − CDS Quotes			
Autos		BID / ASK	CHG	TIME		BID / ASK	CHG	TIME	
AUTO AVERAGE	1)	120 / 151		8:12	14)	134 / 146		9:02	
BMW	2)	15 / 27		8:12	15)	31 / 38		9:02	
CONTINENTAL	3)	40 / 65		8:12	16)	65 / 80		8:12	
DCX	4)	90 / 120		8:12	17)	126 / 136	+1	9:02	
FIAT	5)	650 / 800		8:12	18)	550 / 590		8:12	
FORD	6)	285 / 310		8:12	19)	320 / 330		8:12	
GMAC	7)	210 / 260		8:12	20)	275 / 285		8:12	
PEUGEOT	8)	30 / 45		8:12	21)	45 / 55		8:12	
RENAULT	9)	55 / 70		8:12	22)	74 / 80		8:12	
SCANIA	10)	35 / 50		8:12	23)	48 / 56		8:12	
VALEO	11)	20 / 43		8:12	24)	35 / 55		8:12	
VOLKSWAGEN	12)	60 / 70		8:12	25)	70 / 76		8:12	
VOLVO	13)	40 / 50		8:12	26)	53 / 58		8:12	

Tel: +34 91 537 6087
INDICATIVE PRICES FOR CREDIT DEFAULT SWAPS ON STANDARD
ISDA 1999 DOCUMENTATION WITH 3 CREDIT EVENTS. MATURITIES
ARE ON QUARTERLY BASIS. PRICES VARY DEPENDING UPON THE
CREDIT QUALITY OF THE COUNTERPARTY.

BBVA

Australia 61 2 9777 8600   Brazil 5511 3048 4500   Europe 44 20 7330 7500   Germany 49 69 920410
Hong Kong 852 2977 6000 Japan 81 3 3201 8900 Singapore 65 6212 1000 U.S. 1 212 318 2000 Copyright 2003 Bloomberg L.P.
H021-57-1 16-Jun-03 10:54:48

Source: Bloomberg Financial Markets.

tive CDS price screen from BBVM, a European bank, on June 16, 2003. These quotes are for auto manufacturers covering both 3-year and 5-year swaps. The screen shows that BBVM is prepared to trade as protection buyer or protection seller on a reference entity. Notice three items at the bottom of the exhibit. First, the payments are quarterly. Second, the swap premium will depend on the counterparty who seeks to trade with BBVM. Finally, the definition of a credit event is specified in terms of the ISDA definitions. We will discuss these definitions later in this chapter.

Let's illustrate the mechanics of a single-name credit default swap where the reference entity is a corporation. Look at the quote for "Ford," which means Ford Motor Credit, Inc, and for the 5-year swap. The bid-ask spread is 320–330. This means that BBVM is willing to sell protection for 330 bps (the ask price) and buy protection for 320 bps (the bid price).While not shown here, the credit default swap would reference a basket of deliverable obligations issued by Ford, which would be viewed as BBB1 rated. The terms of a physically settled credit default swap (discussed below) in this case may state that the reference obligation meet certain terms with regard to maturity, and may state that certain securities such as asset-backed securities or convertibles are not deliverable. If an asset manager wished to see all the reference obligations of the reference entity, on Bloomberg he or she would type "Ford <CORP> TK <go>." This lists all bonds issued by Ford. In theory, all of these bonds are deliverable assets for a credit default contract that is written on Ford as an entity and which is physically settled. However, according to the requirements of one of both counterparties, the actual basket of deliverable assets may be limited, for instance according to maturity or bond class.

Suppose, for purposes of our illustration, that an asset manager wants to buy protection for $10 million notional on Ford and the swap premium (price) is 330 bps. The notional amount is not the par value of an acceptable bond issue of Ford. For example, suppose that a bond issue of Ford is trading at 80 (par value being 100). If an asset manager owns $12.5 million par value of the bond issue and wants to protect the current market value of $10 million (= 80% of $12.5 million), then the asset manager will want a $10 million notional amount. If a credit event occurs, the asset manager will deliver the $12.5 million par value of the bond and receive a cash payment of $10 million.

As noted earlier, the standard contract for a single-name credit default swap in the interdealer market calls for a quarterly payment of the swap premium. The day count convention used for credit default swaps is actual/360. Since the notional amount for our hypothetical swap is $10 million and assume there are 92 actual days in the first quarter, then if the annual rate is 330 bps (0.033), the quarterly swap premium payment made by the protection buyer would be:

$$\$10,000,000 \times 0.033 \times \frac{92}{360} = \$84,333.33$$

In the absence of a credit event occurring, the protection buyer will make a quarterly swap premium payment (in arrears) that varies based on the actual number of days in the quarter. If a credit event occurs, the protection seller pays the protection buyer the notional amount, $10 million in our illustration, and receives from the protection buyer an acceptable bond issue of Ford Motor Credit Company.

Basket Default Swaps

In a basket default swap, there is more than one reference entity. Typically, in a basket default swap, there are three to five reference entities. There are different types of basket default swap. They are classified as follows:

■ Nth to default swaps
■ Subordinate basket default swaps
■ Senior basket default swaps

In the following sections we describe each type.

Nth to Default Swaps

In an N*th-to-default swap*, the protection seller makes a payment to the protection buyer only after there has been a default for the Nth reference entity and no payment for default of the first (N-1) reference entities. Once there is a payout for the Nth reference entity, the credit default swap terminates. That is, if the other reference entities that have not defaulted subsequently do default, the protection seller does not make any payout.

For example, suppose that there are five reference entities. In a *first-to-default basket swap*, a payout is triggered after there is a default for only one of the reference entities. There are no other payouts made by the protection seller even if the other four reference entities subsequently have a credit event. If a payout is triggered only after there is a second default from among the reference entities, the swap is referred to as a *second-to-default basket swap*. So, if there is only one reference entity for which there is a default over the tenor of the swap, the protection seller does not make any payment. If there is a default for a second reference entity while the swap is in effect, there is a payout by the protection seller and the swap terminates. The protection seller does not make any payment for a default that may occur for the three remaining reference entities.

Subordinate and Senior Basket Credit Default Swaps

In a *subordinate basket default swap* there is (1) a maximum payout for each defaulted reference entity and (2) a maximum aggregate payout over the tenor of the swap for the basket of reference entities. For example, assume there are five reference entities and that (1) the maximum payout is $10 million for a reference entity and (2) the maximum aggregate payout is $10 million. Also assume that defaults result in the following losses over the tenor of the swap:

Loss resulting from default of first reference entity = $6 million
Loss result from default of second reference entity = $10 million
Loss result from default of third reference entity = $16 million
Loss result from default of fourth reference entity = $12 million
Loss result from default of fifth reference entity = $15 million

When there is a default for the first reference entity, there is a $6 million payout. The remaining amount that can be paid out on any subsequent defaults for the other four reference entities is $4 million. When there is a default for the second reference entity of $10 million, only $4 million will be paid out. At that point, the swap terminates.

In a *senior basket default swap* there is a maximum payout for each reference entity, but the payout is not triggered until after a specified threshold is reached. To illustrate, again assume there are five reference entities and the maximum payout for an individual reference entity is $10 million. Also assume that there is no payout until the first $40 million of default losses (the threshold). Using the hypothetical losses above, the payout by the protection seller would be as follows. The losses for the first three defaults is $32 million. However, because the maximum loss for a reference entity, only $10 million of the $16 million is applied to the $40 million threshold. Consequently, after the third default, $26 million ($6 million + $10 million + $10 million) is applied toward the threshold. When the fourth reference entity defaults, only $10 million is applied to the $40 million threshold. At this point, $36 million is applied to the $40 million threshold. When the fifth reference entity defaults in our illustration, only $10 million is relevant since the maximum payout for a reference entity is $10 million. The first $4 million of the $10 million is applied to cover the threshold. Thus, there is a $6 million payout by the protection seller.

Comparison of Riskiness of Different Default Swap

Let's compare the riskiness of each type of default swap from the perspective of the protection seller. This will also help reinforce an understanding of the different types of swaps.[1] We will assume that for the basket default swaps there are the same five reference entities. Six credit default swaps, ranked by highest to lowest risk for the reasons to be explained, are:

1. *$50 million swap portfolio of five different single-name credit default swaps*: For each single-name credit default swap the notional amount is $10 million. Consequently, the aggregate payout if each reference entity pays out its full notional amount is $50 million.
2. *Subordinate basket default swap*: The maximum for each reference entity is $10 million with a maximum aggregate payout of $10 million.

---

[1] The illustration and discussion in this section draws from "*Nth* to Default Swaps and Notes: All About Default Correlation," *CDO Insight* (May 30, 2003) UBS Warburg.

3. *First-to-default swap*: The maximum payout is $10 million for the first reference entity to default.
4. *$10 million swap portfolio five different single-name credit default swaps*: As with the $50 million portfolio, there are five single-name credit default swaps but the notional amount per swap is $2 million instead of $10 million. The aggregate payout, if all five reference entities pays out their notional amount, is $10 million.
5. *Fifth-to-default swap*: The maximum payout for the fifth reference entity to default is $10 million.
6. *Senior basket default swap*: There is a maximum payout for each reference entity of $10 million, but there is no payout until a threshold of $40 million is reached.

Consider first the $50 million swap portfolio comprising of five different single-name credit default swaps. If there are $10 million of losses for each of the references entities, the protection seller for the swap portfolio will have to pay out $50 million. In contrast, the other five default swaps have a maximum payout of $10 million, but their relative risks differ. So the $50 million portfolio swap is the riskiest.

All but the senior basket default swap requires the protection seller to make a pay out from the very first loss reference entity that defaults (subject to the maximum payout on the loss for the individual reference entities). Consequently, the senior basket default swap exposes the protection seller to the least risk.

Now let's look at the relative risk of the other four default swaps with a $10 million maximum payout: subordinate basket default swap, first-to-default swap, $10 million swap portfolio, and fifth-to-default swap. Consider first the subordinate basket swap versus first-to-default swap. Suppose that the loss for the first reference entity to default is $8 million. In the first-to-default swap the payout required by the protection seller is $8 million and then the swap terminates (i.e., there are no further payouts that must be made by the protection seller). For the subordinate basket swap, after the payout of $8 million of the first reference entity to default, the swap does not terminate. Instead, the protection seller is still exposed to $2 million for any default loss resulting from the other four reference entities. Consequently, the subordinate basket default swap has greater risk than the first-to-default swap.

Now compare the first-to-default swap to the $10 million swap portfolio. The first-to-default swap has greater risk but the reason is not as simple as in the other comparisons made above. To see why the answer requires some analysis assume that the loss of all reference entities defaulting is 50% of the notional amount. This means that for the first reference entity to default, the default loss is 50% of the $10 million for the first-to-default swap, $5 million, and therefore the protection seller for this swap makes a payment of $5 million. No further payments are made. For the $10 million swap portfolio, recall that each single-name credit default swap has a notional amount of $2 million. Consequently, the payout is only $1 million (the assumed 50% of notional amount) on the default and since there are five reference entities the total payout would be $5 million. For the protection seller of the $10 million swap portfolio, the only way that there will be a $5 million payout is if all five reference entities default.

The analysis of the relative risk therefore depends on (1) the specific pattern of defaults that is realized and (2) the percentage of the notional amount that results in a loss upon default. For example, suppose that for the first reference entity to default the default loss is 10% of the notional amount. For the first-to-default swap, the payout that must be made by the protection seller is $1 million (10% of $10 million) while only $0.2 million (10% of $2 million for a single-name credit default swap) is made by the protection seller for the $10 million swap portfolio. Should there be either (1) another reference entity that defaults with a default loss percentage that exceeds 40% of the notional amount ($0.8 million = 40% of $2 million) or (2) all four remaining reference entities default with an average default loss percentage that is greater than 10% of the notional amount ($0.2 million per single-name credit default swap and therefore $0.8 million for all four), then the protection seller of the $10 million swap portfolio would pay more than the first-to default protection seller. There are many scenarios that can be evaluated, but the likely situations are such that the protection seller in the first-to-default swap would incur a greater payout than the protection seller in the $10 million swap portfolio.[2]

Finally, the $10 million swap portfolio has less risk than the fifth-to-default swap. The reason is that there is only one way the protection seller of the fifth-to-default swap will make a greater payment than the protection seller of the swap portfolio is (1) if all reference entities default and (2) the average percentage default loss for each reference entity is less than the default loss percentage of the last reference entity to default in the fifth-to-default swap.[3]

MARKET TERMINOLOGY

Newcomers to the credit default swap market sometimes get confused regarding market terminology. The first potential source of confusion arises because market participants attempt to relate a position in the

[2] "Nth to Default Swaps and Notes: All About Default Correlation," p. 6.
[3] "Nth to Default Swaps and Notes: All About Default Correlation," p. 6

derivative market to a position in the cash market. The second potential source has to do with the use of the term "swap" to describe the transaction when the payment is contingent on the a credit event occurring.

Cash versus Credit Default Swap Market Terminology

Participants in derivatives markets find it helpful to compare their exposure (long or short) in the derivative market to that of an exposure in the cash market. Sometimes the relationship is straightforward. For example, a long position in a Treasury bond futures contract is equivalent to a long position in the Treasury bond market; a short position in a Treasury bond futures contract is equivalent to a short position in the Treasury bond market. In other cases, the relationship is not straightforward. For example, in a generic interest rate swap, the fixed-rate payer is said to be "short the bond market" and the fixed-rate receiver is said to be "long the bond market." This is because for the fixed-rate payer, the value of an interest rate swap increases when interest rates increase. A position in the cash market whereby the value of the position increases when interest rates increase is a short bond position. Similarly, for the fixed-rate receiver, the value of an interest swap increases when interest rates decrease and therefore is equivalent to being long a bond.

The terminology of the position of the parties in a credit default swap can be confusing. To "go long" an instrument generally is to purchase it. In the cash market, going long a bond means one is buying a bond and so receiving the coupon payments; the bond buyer has therefore taken on credit risk exposure to the issuer. In a credit default swap, going long is to buy the swap, but the buyer is purchasing protection and therefore paying the swap premium; the buyer has no credit exposure on the reference entity and has in effect "gone short" on the reference obligation (the equivalent of shorting a bond in the cash market and paying coupon). So buying a credit default swap (buying protection) is frequently referred to in the credit derivatives market as "shorting" the reference obligation.

Swap versus Option Nomenclature

A credit default swap may be properly classified as credit insurance, and the swap premium paid by the protection buyer may be classified as an insurance premium. The protection seller has literally "insured" the protection buyer against any credit losses on the reference obligation.

While the term "swap" is used to describe this credit derivative, it should be clear that it has an option-type payoff. That is, it does not have the characteristics of the typical swap found in the derivatives market. For example, in a plain vanilla or generic interest rate swap, two parties swaps payments periodically. One of the counterparties pays a fixed rate (called the "swap rate") and the other party pays a floating rate. The payments are made by both parties over the term of the swap agreement. Moreover, the payments are not contingent on some event and the occurrence of any event does not terminate the swap agreement. This is not a characteristic of the credit default swap.

The question is then: Why is the transaction referred to as a *swap*? The reason has to due with the way one characterizes an option. There are two attributes for characterizing a derivative as an option. The first attribute is that there is an asymmetric payoff. The second attribute involves the price performance feature. While a credit default swap does have an asymmetric payoff, its price performance is like that of a swap rather than an option. The price performance of an option depends on the price of the underlying. When a credit-risky bond is the underlying, it is the credit spread that affects the price of the bond. So the price performance mechanism for an option is as follows: changes in the credit spread affect the price of the underlying bond which, in turn, changes the price of the option. In the case of a credit default swap, the change in the credit spread directly affects the price of the transaction rather than through its effect on the reference obligation (i.e., underlying bond). This is a characteristic of a swap such as an interest rate swap where the price of a swap depends directly on interest rates. It is for this reason that a credit default swap is referred to as a swap.

LEGAL DOCUMENTATION

Credit derivatives are privately negotiated agreements traded over the counter. The lack of an exchange-traded product means that in the United States there is very little regulation from either the Securities and Exchange Commission or the Commodity Futures Trading Commission. Instead, credit derivatives are regulated through the content of the individually negotiated contracts. The International Swaps and Derivatives Association (ISDA) has recognized the need to provide a common format for credit derivative documentation.[4]

Although the first credit derivatives began to appear on the financial market scene in 1993, it was not until 1998 that the ISDA developed a

---

[4] ISDA is the recognized global trade association representing participants in the swaps and derivatives markets. These markets include interest rate derivatives, commodities, equity swaps, swaptions, and credit derivatives. ISDA was established in 1985 by a consortium of large broker-dealers and money center banks that were active in the interest rate swap market. For more information see the ISDA's web site: www.ISDA.org.

standard contract to capture these trades. Establishing an industry standard by which to document a derivatives transaction is an important step in the development of any derivative market. It indicates that a critical mass of trading had come together such that all participants in the market recognize the need for a common reference point.

In addition to the definitions of credit events, ISDA developed the *ISDA Master Agreement.* This is the authoritative contract used by industry participants because it established international standards governing privately negotiated derivative trades (all derivatives, not just credit derivatives). The Master Agreement reduces legal uncertainty by providing uniform contractual terms for all derivative participants. It also provides for a reduction in counterparty credit risk by allowing for the netting of contractual obligations. The original Master Agreement was introduced in 1987 and has been revised periodically. The latest version as of this writing is the *2002 ISDA Master Agreement.*

In 1998, ISDA released its contract form for credit derivatives. The documentation is primarily designed for either credit default swaps or total return swaps. However, the contract form is sufficiently flexible that it also can be used as a framework for documenting credit options, which are other credit derivatives discussed in Chapter 11. In our discussion of the credit default swaps in this chapter, key provisions of the ISDA credit swap contract and other relevant provisions from ISDA publications are covered.

The appendix is the ISDA's confirmation form for credit derivative transactions, "Exhibit A to 2003 ISDA Credit Derivatives Definitions." The confirmation sets forth the terms and conditions for the transaction. The definitions for a credit event are specified in a publication by the ISDA that we will discuss shortly. Those definitions are incorporated into the confirmation in "check box" format.

CREDIT EVENTS

The most important section of the documentation for a credit default swap is what the parties to the contract agree constitutes a credit event that will trigger a credit default payment. Definitions for credit events are provided by the ISDA. First published in 1999, there have been periodic supplements and revisions of these definitions

1999 ISDA Credit Derivative Definitions

The *1999 ISDA Credit Derivatives Definitions* (referred to as the "1999 Definitions") provides a list of eight possible credit events:

1. Bankruptcy
2. Credit event upon merger
3. Cross acceleration
4. Cross default
5. Downgrade
6. Failure to pay
7. Repudiation
8. Restructuring

These eight events attempt to capture every type of situation that could cause the credit quality of the reference entity to deteriorate, or cause the value of the reference obligation to decline.

The parties to a credit default swap may include all of these events, or select only those that they believe are most relevant. We describe each below. As explained later, there has been standardization of the credit events that are used in credit default swaps in the United States and Europe. Nevertheless, and this cannot be overemphasized, this does not preclude a credit protection buyer from including broader credit protection.

Bankruptcy

Bankruptcy means that a reference issuer either:

1. Is dissolved.
2. Becomes insolvent or unable to pay its debts as they become due.
3. Makes a general assignment, arrangement or composition for the benefit of creditors.
4. Institutes, or has instituted against it, a proceeding seeking a judgment of insolvency or bankruptcy, or any relief under any bankruptcy or insolvency law.
5. Has a petition presented for its winding-up or liquidation.
6. Has a resolution passed for its winding-up, official management, or liquidation.
7. Seeks or becomes subject to the appointment of an administrator, provisional liquidator, conservator, receiver, trustee, custodian or other similar official for all or substantially all of its assets.
8. Has a secured party take possession of all or substantially all of its assets, or has a distress, execution, attachment, sequestration or such other legal process levied, enforced or sued on against all or substantially all of its assets.
9. Causes or is subject to any event with respect to it which, under the applicable laws of any jurisdiction, has an analogous effect to any of the events specified in items 1–8.

10. Takes any action in furtherance of, or indicating its consent to, approval of, or acquiescence in, any of the foregoing acts.

In sum, bankruptcy includes any official (court directed) or private action which results in an issuer relinquishing control of its assets, operations, or management. The reference issuer may initiate these proceedings itself, or it may be forced to act by outside parties. Bankruptcy also occurs if the issuer cannot pay its outstanding debts as they become due. Consequently, poor operating performance and lack of short-term financing can force a bankruptcy.

Credit Event Upon Merger

Credit event upon merger means that the reference issuer has consolidated, amalgamated or merged with another entity, or has transferred all or substantially all of its assets to another entity, and the creditworthiness of the resulting, surviving or transferee entity is materially weaker than that of the reference issuer before the consolidation. For instance, if the combined entity has a lower credit rating after a merger than the reference entity before the merger, a credit event has occurred, subject to a determination of materiality.

Materiality is a term negotiated by the swap parties. Materiality can be defined as a single step downgrade in the issuer's credit rating, or a several step downgrade.

Cross Acceleration

Cross acceleration means the occurrence of a default, event of default, or some other similar condition (other than a failure to make any required payment) with respect to another outstanding obligation of the reference entity, which has resulted in the other obligation becoming due and payable before it would otherwise become due and payable. In other words, if the reference issuer defaults on any other bond, loan, lease, or obligation, for purposes of the credit default swap, this counts for a credit event as if the issuer had defaulted on the reference obligation.

Cross Default

Cross default is defined similarly to cross acceleration except that the other outstanding obligations are capable of being declared due and payable before such time as they would otherwise become due and payable. The distinction between cross acceleration and cross default is a fine one. For practical purposes a cross acceleration is an actual default event on another outstanding obligation, while a cross default is an event which provides the obligation holder with the ability to declare a default. In this respect, cross default provisions are preemptive—they kick in before the issuer defaults on an outstanding obligation.

Downgrade

Downgrade means a reduction in credit rating of the reference entity, or if the reference obligation is no longer rated by any rating agency. The parties to the agreement can specify below what level of credit rating a credit event will occur. Generally, the *specified rating* is set equal to the reference entity's current credit rating so that any downgrade results in a credit event. The parties can also specify the applicable rating agencies, although any nationally recognized statistical rating organization usually qualifies.

Failure to Pay

Failure to pay means that, after giving effect to any applicable grace period, the reference entity fails to make, when due, any payments equal to or exceeding any required payment of any outstanding obligation. Failure to pay is a more narrow case of cross acceleration and cross default. Under the latter two conditions, the failure to perform under any loan or bond covenant constitutes a credit event. However, under failure to pay, the lack of a cash payment constitutes a credit event.

Repudiation

Repudiation means that the reference entity refutes, disclaims, repudiates, rejects or challenges the validity of, in whole or part, any of its outstanding obligations. Basically, if the reference entity refuses to pay on any of its obligations, the protection buyer may declare a credit event on the reference obligation.

Restructuring

Restructuring means a waiver, deferral, restructuring, rescheduling, standstill, moratorium, exchange of obligations, or other adjustment with respect to any obligation of the reference entity such that the holders of those obligations are *materially* worse off from either an economic, credit, or risk perspective. The terms that can be changed would typically include, but are not limited to, one or more of the following: (1) a reduction in the interest rate; (2) a reduction in the principal; (3) a rescheduling of the principal repayment schedule (e.g., lengthening the maturity of the obligation) or postponement of an interest payment; or (4) a change in the level of seniority of the obligation in the reference entity's debt structure. In other words, if the reference entity works out a deal with its creditors on any outstanding obligation where the revised terms of that obligation are *materially* less favorable to the creditors, then the protection buyer may declare a credit event on the reference obligation.

Restructuring is the most controversial credit event that may be included in a credit default swap. The reason why it is so controversial is easy to understand. A protection buyer benefits from the inclusion of a restructuring as a credit event and feels that eliminating restructuring as a credit event will erode its credit protection. The protection seller, in contrast, would prefer not to include restructuring since even routine modifications of obligations that occur in lending arrangements would trigger a payout to the protection buyer.

Moreover, if the reference obligation is a loan and the protection buyer is the lender, there is a dual benefit for the protection buyer to restructure a loan. The first benefit is that the protection buyer receives a payment from the protection seller. Second, the accommodating restructuring fosters a relationship between the lender (who is the protection buyer) and its customer (the corporate entity that is the obligor of the reference obligation).

Because of this problem, the *Restructuring Supplement to the 1999 ISDA Credit Derivatives Definitions* (the "Supplement Definition") issued in April 2001 provided a modified definition for restructuring. There is a provision for the limitation on reference obligations in connection with restructuring of loans made by the protection buyer to the borrower that is the obligor of the reference obligation. This provision requires the following in order to qualify for a restructuring: (1) There must be four or more holders of the reference obligation; and (2) there must be a consent to the restructuring of the reference obligation by a supermajority (66⅔%). In addition, the supplement limits the maturity of reference obligations that are physically deliverable when restructuring results in a payout triggered by the protection buyer.

Consequently, in the credit default swap market, until 2003, the parties to a trade had the following three choices for restructuring: (1) no restructuring; (2) restructured based on the 1999 Definition for restructuring, referred to as "full restructuring" or "old restructuring;" or (3) restructuring as defined by the Restructuring Supplement Definition, referred to as "modified restructuring." Modified restructuring is typically used in the North American while full restructuring is used in Europe. When the reference entity is a sovereign, restructuring is often full restructuring.

Whether restructuring is included and, if it is included, whether it is old restructuring or modified restructuring affects the swap premium. Specifically, all other factors constant, it is more expensive if restructuring is included. Moreover, old restructuring results in a larger swap premium than modified restructuring.

2003 ISDA Credit Derivative Definitions

As the credit derivatives market developed, market participants learned a great deal about how to better define credit events, particularly with the record level of high-yield corporate bond default rates in 2002 and the sovereign defaults, particularly the experience with the 2001–2002 Argentina debt crisis. In January 2003, the ISDA published its revised credit events definitions in the *2003 ISDA Credit Derivative Definitions* (the "2003 Definitions"). It is these revised definitions that apply to the confirmation form shown in the appendix.

The revised definitions reflected amendments to several of the definitions for credit events set forth in the 1999 Definitions. Specifically, there were amendments for bankruptcy, repudiation, and restructuring. The major change was to restructuring whereby the ISDA allows parties to a given trade to select from among the following four definitions: (1) no restructuring; (2) full restructuring, with no modification to the deliverable reference obligations aspect; (3) modified restructuring (which is typically used in North America); or (4) "modified modified restructuring." The last choice is a new one and was included to address issues that arose in the European market.

TERMINATION VALUE AND SETTLEMENT

The *termination value* for a credit default swap is calculated at the time of the credit event, and the exact procedure that is followed to calculate the termination value will depend on the settlement terms specified in the contract. This will be either cash settlement or physical settlement.

Cash Settlement

A credit default swap contract may specify a predetermined payout value on occurrence of a credit event. This may be the nominal value of the swap contract. Such a swap is known in some markets as a *digital credit derivative*. Alternatively, the termination value can be calculated as the difference between the nominal value of the reference obligation and its market value at the time of the credit event. This arrangement is more common with cash-settled contracts.

Determining the market value of the reference obligation at the time of the credit event may be a little problematic: The issuer of the obligation may well be in default or administration (bankruptcy). The *calculation agent* usually makes the termination payment calculation. The calculation agent is usually the credit protection seller, although both parties to the trade can be joint calculation agents. When used as part of a structured credit product, the calculation agent is usually an independent third party.

Physical Settlement

With *physical settlement*, on occurrence of a credit event the buyer delivers the reference obligation to the seller, in return for which the seller pays the face value of the delivered asset to the buyer. The contract may specify a number of alternative issues of the reference entity that the buyer can deliver to the seller. These are known as *deliverable obligations*. This may apply when a credit default swap has been entered into on a reference entity rather than a specific obligation issued by that entity (i.e., when there is a reference entity rather than a reference obligation).

Where more than one deliverable obligation is specified, the protection buyer will invariably deliver the one that is the cheapest on the list of eligible deliverable obligations. This gives rise to the concept of the *cheapest-to-deliver*, as encountered with government bond futures and agency futures, and is in effect an embedded option afforded the protection buyer.

Many credit default swap contracts that are physically settled name a reference entity rather than a reference obligation. Upon default, the protection buyer often has a choice of deliverable bonds with which to effect settlement. The broader the definition of deliverable bonds is in the credit default swap documentation, the longer the list of the eligible delivery obligations: as long as the bond meets prespecified requirements for seniority and maturity, it may be delivered. Contrast this with the position of the bondholder in the cash market, who is aware of the exact issue that he is holding in the event of default. Default swap sellers may receive potentially any bond from the basket of deliverable instruments that rank *pari passu* with the cash bond issue— this is the delivery option afforded the protection buyer.

In practice, therefore, the protection buyer will deliver the cheapest-to-deliver bond from the deliverable basket, exactly as it would for an exchange-traded government futures contract. This delivery option has debatable value in theory, but significant value in practice. For instance the bonds of a reference entity that might be trading cheaper in the market include:

- The bond with the lowest coupon
- A convertible bond
- An illiquid bond
- A very-long-dated bond

Modified restructuring, described earlier in this chapter, specifically restricts the delivery of long-dated bonds where restructuring is the credit event that triggers a contract payout. When old restructuring is used a long-dated bond may be delivered and therefore the delivery option does carry value in the market. Similarly for an option contract, this value increases the closer the contract holder gets to the "strike price," which for a credit default swap is a credit event. We discuss this further in Chapter 4 when we discuss the "basis" for a credit default swap.

Relative Benefits of Cash versus Physical Settlement

In theory, the value of protection is identical irrespective of which settlement option is selected. However under physical settlement the protection seller can gain if there is a recovery value that can be extracted from the defaulted asset; or its value may rise as the fortunes of the issuer improve.

Swap market-making banks often prefer cash settlement as there is less administration associated with it. It is also more suitable when a credit default swap is used as part of a structured credit product, because such vehicles may not be set up to take delivery of physical assets.

Another advantage of cash settlement is that it does not expose the protection buyer to any risks should there not be any deliverable obligations in the market, for instance due to shortage of liquidity in the market—were this to happen, the buyer may find the value of its settlement payment reduced. A final advantage of cash settlement is greater certainty of settlement than the cheapest-to-deliver bond.

Nevertheless physical settlement is widely used because counterparties wish to avoid the difficulties associated with determining the market value of the reference obligation under cash settlement. Physical settlement also permits the protection seller to take part in the creditor negotiations with the reference entity's administrators, which may result in improved terms for them as holders of the obligation.

CONDITIONS TO PAYMENT

In order for a payment to be collected by the protection buyer upon the occurrence of a credit event, three conditions must be satisfied:

1. The affected party must deliver a credit event notice.
2. The affected party must deliver a notice of publicly available information.
3. The calculation agent must determine that materiality exists.

Credit Event Notice

A *credit event notice* is an irrevocable notice given by one party to the credit default swap to its counterparty that a credit event has occurred. ISDA allows for the notice to be given in writing or orally, including by telephone, but the parties may negotiate their preferred type of notice.

Notice of Publicly Available Information

A *notice of publicly available information* is a notice that confirms the occurrence of a credit event. This notice must reference a source of "publicly available information," which can include any internationally recognized published or electronically displayed news source such as the *Wall Street Journal*, Reuters electronic terminals, or Bloomberg terminals. Additionally, the parties to the credit default swap can specify a minimum number of publicly available information sources that must confirm the occurrence of a credit event (see the appendix to this chapter).

Calculation Agent and the Determination of Materiality

The *calculation agent* is the party designated to determine the required payments under the credit derivative transaction. For a payment to occur, the calculation agent must determine that materiality exists.

Materiality is a term that is negotiated by the parties. For instance, if the reference obligation is a high-yield corporate bond, materiality can be defined in terms of a price decline. The parties to the trade can state what dollar or percentage decline in value of the reference obligation is sufficient to qualify as a material credit event. Usually, materiality is stated as a 1% to 5% price decline from the initial price (referred to as the "price decline requirement"). The initial price may equal the reference (strike) price, or the reference price may be set at a different value.

Conversely, instead of a price decline, materiality can be defined in terms of increasing credit spreads. Recall that an increase in credit spreads for a reference issuer means a decline in value for a reference obligation of that issuer. Therefore, materiality can be defined in terms of a minimum credit spread increase (the "spread widening requirement") that must occur before a credit event is recognized.

Materiality, however, is determined by the calculation agent. The calculation agent is usually a point of negotiation in ISDA agreements. Almost always, the dealer who is selling the credit derivative wishes to remain the calculation agent. However, this raises a potential conflict of interest because the dealer/calculation agent might not want to recognize a credit event to prevent its payment obligation to the protection buyer.

Fortunately, ISDA provides for a dispute resolution provision in the contract. In the event that a party to the credit default swap does not agree with a determination made by the calculation agent, the disputing party has the right to require that the determination be made by a disinterested third party that is a dealer of credit derivative instruments. The calculation agent gets to pick the disinterested third party, but only after consultation with the disputing party.

The determination made by the third party is binding on the credit derivative participants unless there is manifest error. The costs, if any, from using the third party are borne by the disputing party if the third party substantially agrees with the calculation agent, and are borne by the nondisputing party if the third party does not substantially agree with the calculation agent. Bottom line: if the disputing party believes that the dealer/calculation agent has not properly recognized a credit event, it can challenge the dealer, but it must be prepared to pay any costs associated with the challenge should its dispute prove unjustified.

The parties can agree to be joint calculation agents. This can alleviate conflicts of interest. However, if the joint calculation agents cannot agree, the same dispute resolution techniques apply.

It is rare for the parties to a credit derivative trade to use an outside calculation agent. The norm is that the broker/dealer is usually the calculation agent, and if there is a dispute, then the parties to the trade turn to an outside calculation agent to resolve the disagreement. This is because it is expensive and time consuming to use an outside calculation agent. Also, the parties to the swap have the best knowledge of the terms of the trade. In contrast, an independent third-party calculation agent is almost always named whenever credit derivative contracts are used as part of structured finance vehicles such as synthetic collateralized debt obligations discussed in Chapter 7. Rating agencies such as Moody's specify that a third-party be named to carry out this role. For some structures, a third-party is required only to confirm that a credit event has occurred. Subsequent market valuations are then carried out by the swap dealer. In this case, the third-party is known as a *verification agent* and not a calculation agent.

Upon the occurrence of a credit event, the calculation agent must determine the current market value of the reference obligation to determine if there has been a material decline in value. This is accomplished by obtaining third-party quotes from other dealers and taking the average of the bids, offers, or midmarket quotes. This is just one more check and balance to ensure that the calculation agent performs its determinations in an objective fashion.

APPLICATIONS OF CREDIT DEFAULT SWAPS

As mentioned at the outset of this chapter, credit default swaps can be used by an asset manager or trader as a standalone vehicle or can be used in structured credit products. Below we discuss the main applications of credit default swaps by asset managers and traders.

Reducing Credit Exposure

Consider an asset manager that holds a large portfolio of bonds issued in a particular sector (say, utilities) and believes that spreads in this sector will widen in the short term. Prior to credit derivatives, in order to reduce this credit exposure the asset manager would have to sell bonds; however, this may crystallize a mark-to-market loss and may conflict with the asset manager's long-term investment strategy. An alternative approach would be to enter into a credit default swap, purchasing protection for the short term; if spreads do widen, these swaps will increase in value and may be sold at a profit in the secondary market. Alternatively, the asset manager may enter into total return swaps on the desired credits.

Consider now the case of an asset manager wishing to mitigate credit risk from a growing portfolio (say, one that has just been launched). Exhibit 3.3 shows an example of an unhedged credit exposure to a hypothetical portfolio containing credit-risky assets. It illustrates the manager's expectation of credit risk building up to $250 million as the portfolio is

EXHIBIT 3.3   Reducing Credit Exposure

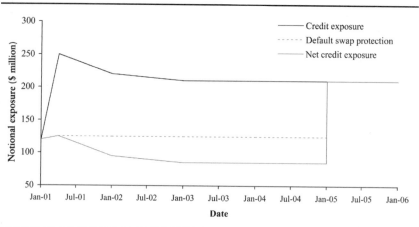

ramped up, and then reducing to a more stable level as the credits become more established. A 3-year credit default swap entered into shortly after provides protection on half of the notional exposure, shown as the broken line shown in the exhibit. The net exposure to credit events has been reduced by a significant margin.

Credit Switches and Zero-Cost Credit Exposure

Protection buyers utilizing credit default swaps must pay a the swap premium in return for laying off their credit risk exposure. An alternative approach for an asset manager involves the use of "credit switches" for specific sectors of the portfolio. In a credit switch the portfolio manager purchases credit protection on one reference obligation or pool of assets, and simultaneously sells protection on another reference obligation or pool of assets. (A pool of assets would be concentrated on one sector, such as utility company bonds.)

So, for example, the asset manager would purchase protection for a particular fund and sell protection on another fund. Typically the entire transaction would be undertaken with one investment bank, which would price the structure so that the net cash flows would be zero. This has the effect of synthetically diversifying the credit exposure of the asset manager, enabling it to gain and/or reduce exposure to sectors desired.

Enhancing Portfolio Returns

Asset managers can derive premium income by trading credit exposures in the form of credit default swaps issued with structured credit notes. The multitranching aspect of structured credit products enables specific credit exposures (credit spreads and outright default), and their expectations, to be sold to specific areas of demand. By using structured notes such as credit-linked notes, tied to the assets in the reference pool of the asset manager, the trading of credit exposures is crystallized as added yield on the asset manager's fixed income portfolio. In this way the asset manager has enabled other market participants to gain an exposure to the credit risk of a pool of assets but not to any other aspects of the portfolio, and without the need to hold the assets themselves.

APPENDIX: CONFIRMATION FOR CREDIT DERIVATIVES TRANSACTION

EXHIBIT A to 2003 ISDA Credit Derivatives Definitions

[Headed paper of Party A]

Date:

To: [Name and Address or Facsimile Number of Party B]

From: [Party A]

Re: Credit Derivative Transaction

Dear _____:

The purpose of this [letter] (this "Confirmation") is to confirm the terms and conditions of the Credit Derivative Transaction entered into between us on the Trade Date specified below (the "Transaction"). This Confirmation constitutes a "Confirmation" as referred to in the ISDA Master Agreement specified below.

The definitions and provisions contained in the 2003 ISDA Credit Derivatives Definitions (the "Credit Derivatives Definitions"), as published by the International Swaps and Derivatives Association, Inc., are incorporated into this Confirmation. In the event of any inconsistency between the Credit Derivatives Definitions and this Confirmation, this Confirmation will govern.

[This Confirmation supplements, forms a part of, and is subject to, the ISDA Master Agreement dated as of [date], as amended and supplemented from time to time (the "Agreement"), between you and us. All provisions contained in the Agreement govern this Confirmation except as expressly modified below.][1]

The terms of the Transaction to which this Confirmation relates are as follows:

THE FOOTNOTES TO THIS CONFIRMATION ARE PROVIDED FOR CLARIFICATION ONLY AND DO NOT CONSTITUTE ADVICE AS TO THE STRUCTURING OR DOCUMENTATION OF A CREDIT DERIVATIVE TRANSACTION.

ISDA has not undertaken to review all applicable laws and regulations of any jurisdiction in which the Credit Derivatives Definitions may be used. Therefore, parties are advised to consider the application of any relevant jurisdiction's regulatory, tax, accounting, exchange or other requirements that may exist in connection with the entering into and documenting of a privately negotiated credit derivative transaction.

1   Include if applicable. If the parties have not yet executed, but intend to execute, an ISDA Master Agreement include, instead of this paragraph, the following: "This Confirmation evidences a complete and binding agreement between you and us as to the terms of the Transaction to which this Confirmation relates. In addition, you and we agree to use all reasonable efforts promptly to negotiate, execute and deliver an agreement in the form of an ISDA Master Agreement, with such modifications as you and we will in good faith agree. Upon the execution by you and us of such an agreement, this Confirmation will supplement, form part of, and be subject to that agreement. All provisions contained in or incorporated by reference in that agreement upon its execution will govern this Confirmation except as expressly modified below. Until we execute and deliver that agreement, this Confirmation, together with all other documents referring to an ISDA Master Agreement (each a "Confirmation") confirming transactions (each a "Transaction") entered into between us (notwithstanding anything to the contrary in a Confirmation), shall supplement, form a part of, and be subject to, an agreement in the form of the 1992 ISDA Master Agreement (Multicurrency – Cross Border) if any Confirmation dated prior to the date of this Confirmation refers to that ISDA Master Agreement and otherwise the 2002 ISDA Master Agreement as if we had executed an agreement in such form (but without any Schedule except for the election of [English Law][the laws of the State of New York] as the governing law and [specify currency] as the Termination Currency) on the Trade Date of the first such Transaction between us. In the event of any inconsistency between the provisions of that agreement and this Confirmation, this Confirmation will prevail for the purpose of this Transaction."

1.   General Terms:

        Trade Date: [   ]

        Effective Date: [   ]

        Scheduled Termination Date: [   ]

        Floating Rate Payer: [Party A][Party B] (the "Seller").

        Fixed Rate Payer: [Party A][Party B] (the "Buyer").

        Calculation Agent:[2]   [   ]

        Calculation Agent City:[3]   [   ]

        Business Day:[4]   [   ]

        Business Day Convention: [Following][Modified Following][Preceding] (which, subject to Sections 1.4 and 1.6 of the Credit Derivatives Definitions, shall apply to any date referred to in this Confirmation that falls on a day that is not a Business Day[5]).

        Reference Entity: [   ]

        [Reference Obligation(s):][6]   [   ]

                            [The obligation[s] identified as follows:
                            Primary Obligor: [   ]
                            Guarantor: [   ]
                            Maturity: [   ]
                            Coupon: [   ]
                            CUSIP/ISIN: [   ]

---

2   If the Calculation Agent is a third party, the parties may wish to consider any documentation necessary to confirm its undertaking to act in that capacity. If a person is not specified, the Credit Derivatives Definitions provide that the Calculation Agent will be the Seller.
3   If a city is not specified, the Credit Derivatives Definitions provide that the Calculation Agent City will be the city in which the office through which the Calculation Agent is acting for purposes of the Credit Derivative Transaction is located.
4   The Credit Derivatives Definitions provide a fallback to days on which commercial banks and foreign exchange markets are generally open to settle payments in the jurisdiction of the currency of the Floating Rate Payer Calculation Amount.
5   The Credit Derivatives Definitions provide a fallback to the Following Business Day Convention.
6   Specify if required. A Reference Obligation must be specified for Credit Derivative Transactions to which Cash Settlement applies. If a Reference Obligation is specified for Credit Derivative Transactions to which Physical Settlement applies then, subject to the second paragraph of Section 2.20(b)(i) and Sections 2.32(a) and 2.33(a), such Reference Obligation is a Deliverable Obligation even though at the time of delivery it does not fall into the Obligation Category or lacks any or all Deliverable Obligation Characteristics.

All Guarantees:	[Applicable][Not Applicable]
Reference Price:	[%][7]

2.   Fixed Payments:

[Fixed Rate Payer Calculation Amount:[8]	[ ]]
[Fixed Rate Payer Period End Date:[9]	[ ]]
Fixed Rate Payer Payment Date[s]:	[ ], [ ], [ ] and [ ]
[Fixed Rate:	[ ]][10]
[Fixed Rate Day Count Fraction:[11]	[ ]]
[Fixed Amount:	[ ]]

3.   Floating Payment:

Floating Rate Payer Calculation Amount:[12]	[ ]
Conditions to Settlement:	Credit Event Notice

                   Notifying Party: Buyer [or Seller]

                   [Notice of Physical Settlement][13]

                   [Notice of Publicly Available Information Applicable][14]

                   [Public Source(s):[   ]][15]

---

7   If a percentage is not so specified, the Credit Derivatives Definitions provide that the Reference Price will be one hundred per cent.

8   If an amount is not specified, the Credit Derivatives Definitions provide that the Fixed Rate Payer Calculation Amount will be the Floating Rate Payer Calculation Amount.

9   If a date is not specified, the Credit Derivatives Definitions provide that the Fixed Rate Payer Period End Date will be each date specified in the related Confirmation as a Fixed Rate Payer Payment Dat e.

10   The Credit Derivatives Definitions provide that the Fixed Rate means a rate, expressed as a decimal, equal to the per annum rate specified here.

11   If a Fixed Rate Day Count Fraction is not specified, the Credit Derivatives Definitions provide a fallback to Actual/360 as the Fixed Rate Day Count Fraction.

12   Specify an amount or, for amortizing Transactions, refer to amounts listed in an amortization schedule.

13   Notice of Physical Settlement is a required Condition to Settlement in respect of Credit Derivative Transactions to which Physical Settlement is applicable. It is not applicable in relation to Credit Derivative Transactions to which Cash Settlement is applicable.

14   If Notice of Publicly Available Information is intended to be a Condition to Settlement, the parties should include a reference to it here.

15   If Notice of Publicly Available Information has been selected by the parties and a Public Source is not specified, the Credit Derivatives Definitions provide that the Public Sources will be Bloomberg Service, Dow Jones Telerate Service, Reuter Monitor Money Rates Services, Dow Jones News Wire, Wall Street Journal, New York Times, Nihon Keizai Shinbun, Asahi Shinbun, Yomiuri Shinbun, Financial Times, La Tribune, Les Echos and The Australian Financial Review (and successor publications), the main source(s) of business news in the

[Specified Number:[   ]][16]

Credit Events: The following Credit Event[s] shall apply to this Transaction:

[Bankruptcy]

[[Failure to Pay]

    [Grace Period Extension Applicable][17]

    [Grace Period:][18]

    Payment Requirement: [   ]][19]

[Obligation Default]

[Obligation Acceleration]

[Repudiation/Moratorium]

[Restructuring]

    [[Restructuring Maturity Limitation and Fully
        Transferable Obligation: [Applicable][20]]

    [[Modified Restructuring Maturity Limitation and
        Conditionally Transferable Obligation:
                [Applicable][21]]

---

jurisdiction in which the Reference Entity is organized and any other internationally recognized published or electronically displayed news sources.

16   If Notice of Publicly Available Information has been selected by the parties and a number of Public Sources is not specified, the Credit Derivatives Definitions provide that the Specified Number will be two.

17   Specify whether the parties intend Grace Period Extension to apply. If Grace Period Extension is not specified here as being applicable, Grace Period Extension will not apply to the Credit Derivative Transaction.

18   If Grace Period Extension is applicable, the parties may also wish to specify the number of days in the Grace Period. Parties should specify whether the Grace Period is to be measured in calendar days. If a number of days is not so specified, Grace Period will be the lesser of the applicable grace period with respect to the relevant Obligation and thirty calendar days. If at the later of the Trade Date and the date as of which an Obligation is issued or incurred, no grace period with respect to payments or a grace period with respect to payments of less than three Grace Period Business Days is applicable under the terms of that Obligation, a Grace Period of three Grace Period Business Days shall be deemed to apply to that Obligation. Unless Grace Period Extension is specified as applicable to a Credit Derivative Transaction, this deemed Grace Period will expire no later than the Scheduled Termination Date.

19   Payment Requirement is relevant to the Failure to Pay Credit Event. If a Payment Requirement is not specified, the Credit Derivatives Definitions provide that the Payment Requirement will be USD 1,000,000 or its equivalent in the relevant Obligation Currency as of the occurrence of the relevant Failure to Pay.

20   Specify whether the parties intend Restructuring Maturity Limitation and Fully Transferable Obligation, as set forth in Section 2.32 of the Credit Derivatives Definitions, to apply. If Restructuring Maturity Limitation and Fully Transferable Obligation are specified as applicable, the Restructuring Maturity Limitation Date is the date that is the earlier of 30 months following the Restructuring Date and the latest final maturity date of any Restructured Bond or Loan (but in no event a date earlier than the Scheduled Termination Date or a date later than 30 months following the Scheduled Termination Date) and only Fully Transferable Obligations may constitute Deliverable Obligations. The parties cannot specify that Restructuring Maturity Limitation and Fully Transferable Obligation *and* Modified Restructuring Maturity Limitation and Conditionally Transferable Obligation both apply. If Restructuring Maturity Limitation is not specified as being applicable, Restructuring Maturity Limitation will not apply to the Credit Derivative Transaction.

21   Specify whether the parties intend Modified Restructuring Maturity Limitation and Conditionally Transferable Obligation, as set forth in Section 2.33 of the Credit Derivatives Definitions, to apply. If Modified Restructuring Maturity Limitation and Conditionally Transferable Obligation are specified as applicable, the Modified Restructuring Maturity Limitation Date is the later of (x) 60 months for a Restructured Bond or Loan (and 30 months for other Deliverable Obligations) following the Restructuring Date and (y) the Scheduled Termination Date, and only Conditionally Transferable Obligations may constitute Deliverable Obligations. The parties cannot specify that Restructuring Maturity

[[Multiple Holder Obligation:] [22]

[Applicable]]

[Default Requirement: [   ]][23]

Obligation(s):

Obligation Category (Select only one):	Obligation Characteristics (Select all that apply):

[ ]   Payment
[ ]   Borrowed
      Money
[ ]   Reference
      Obligations
      Only[24]
[ ]   Bond
[ ]   Loan
[ ]   Bond or Loan
	[ ] Not Subordinated
	[ ] Specified Currency:
	      [ ][25]
	[ ] Not Sovereign Lender
	[ ] Not Domestic Currency
	      [Domestic Currency
	      means: [ ]][26]
	[ ] Not Domestic Law
	[ ] Listed
	[ ] Not Domestic Issuance

[and:]

[Specify any other obligations of a Reference Entity.]

[Excluded Obligations:][27]   [   ]

4.   Settlement Terms:

     Settlement Method: [Cash Settlement] [Physical Settlement]

     [[Terms Relating to Cash Settlement:] [28]

Limitation and Fully Transferable Obligation *and* Modified Restructuring Maturity Limitation and Conditionally Transferable Obligation both apply. If Modified Restructuring Maturity Limitation is not specified as being applicable, Modified Restructuring Maturity Limitation will not apply to the Credit Derivative Transaction.

22   Unless Not Applicable is specified, the Credit Derivatives Definitions provide that Restructuring gs are limited to Multiple Holder Obligations.

23   Default Requirement is relevant to the Obligation Acceleration, Obligation Default, Repudiation/Moratorium and Restructuring Credit Events. If a Default Requirement is not specified, the Credit Derivatives Definitions provide that the Default Requirement will be USD 10,000,000 or its equivalent in the relevant Obligation Currency as of the occurrence of the relevant Credit Event.

24   If Reference Obligations Only is specified as the Obligation Category, no Obligation Characteristics should be specified.

25   Specify Currency. The Credit Derivatives Definitions provide that, if no currency is so specified, Specified Currency means the lawful currencies of any of Canada, Japan, Switzerland, the United Kingdom and the United States of America and the euro (and any successor currency to any such currency). The Credit Derivatives Definitions provide that these currencies may be referred to collectively in a Confirmation as the "Standard Specified Currencies".

26   If no currency is specified, the Credit Derivatives Definitions provide that Domestic Currency will be the lawful currency and any successor currency of (a) the relevant Reference Entity, if the Reference Entity is a Sovereign, or (b) the jurisdiction in which the relevant Reference Entity is organized, if the Reference Entity is not a Sovereign. In no event shall Domestic Currency include any successor currency if such successor currency is the lawful currency of any of Canada, Japan, Switzerland, the United Kingdom or the United States of America or the euro (or any successor currency to any such currency).

27   Unless specified here as an Excluded Obligation, the Reference Obligation will be an Obligation.

28   Include if Cash Settlement applies.

[Valuation Date:][29]

[Single Valuation Date:
[   ] Business Days][30]

[Multiple Valuation Dates:
[   ] Business Days[31]; and
each [   ] Business Days thereafter[32]
Number of Valuation Dates: [   ]][33]

[Valuation Time:][34]

[Quotation Method: [Bid][Offer][Mid-market]][35]

[Quotation Amount: [   ][Representative Amount][36]

[Minimum Quotation Amount:][37]

[Dealer(s):   ][38]

[Settlement Currency:][39]

[Cash Settlement Date: [   ] Business Days][40]

[Cash Settlement Amount:][41]

[Quotations: [Include Accrued Interest][Exclude Accrued Interest]][42]

---

29   Include if the Cash Settlement Amount is not a fixed amount. The Credit Derivatives Definitions provide that if neither Single Valuation Date nor Multiple Valuation Dates is specified here, Single Valuation Date will apply.
30   If the number of Business Days is not specified, the Credit Derivatives Definitions provide that this will be five Business Days.
31   If the number of Business Days is not specified, the Credit Derivatives Definitions provide that this will be five Business Days.
32   If the number of Business Days is not specified, the Credit Derivatives Definitions provide that this will be five Business Days.
33   If the number of Valuation Dates is not specified, the Credit Derivatives Definitions provide that there will be five Valuation Dates.
34   If no time is specified, the Credit Derivatives Definitions provide that the Valuation Time will be 11:00 a.m. in the principal trading market for the Reference Obligation.
35   If no Quotation Method is specified, the Credit Derivatives Definitions provide that Bid shall apply.
36   Specify either an amount in a currency or Representative Amount. If no Quotation Amount is specified, the Credit Derivatives Definitions provide that the Quotation Amount will be the Floating Rate Payer Calculation Amount.
37   If no amount is specified, the Credit Derivatives Definitions provide that the Minimum Quotation Amount will be the lower of (i) USD 1,000,000 (or its equivalent in the relevant Obligation Currency) and (ii) the Quotation Amount.
38   Specify the Dealers. If no Dealers are specified here, the Calculation Agent will select the Dealers in consultation with the parties.
39   If no currency is specified, the Credit Derivatives Definitions provide that the Settlement Currency will be the currency of denomination of the Floating Rate Payer Calculation Amount.
40   If a number of Business Days is not specified, the Credit Derivatives Definitions specify three Business Days.
41   If no amount is so specified, the Credit Derivatives Definitions provide that the Cash Settlement Amount will be the greater of (a) (i) Floating Rate Payer Calculation Amount multiplied by (ii) the Reference Price minus the Final Price and (b) zero.
42   If neither Include Accrued Interest nor Exclude Accrued Interest is specified with respect to Quotations, the Credit Derivatives Definitions provide that the Calculation Agent will determine, after consultation with the parties, based on then current market practice in the market of the Reference Obligation, whether such Quotations shall include or exclude accrued but unpaid interest.

[Valuation Method:[43]   [Market] [Highest][44]
                                             [Average Market] [Highest] [Average Highest][45]
                                             [Blended Market] [Blended Highest][46]
                                             [Average Blended Market] [Average Blended Highest]][47]]

[Terms Relating to Physical Settlement:] [48]

[Physical Settlement Period: [   ] Business Days][49]

[Deliverable Obligations: [Include Accrued Interest] [Exclude Accrued Interest][50]

---

43   Include if the Cash Settlement Amount is not a fixed amount.

44   One of these Valuation Methods may be specified for a Credit Derivative Transaction with only one Reference Obligation and only one Valuation Date. If no Valuation Method is specified in such circumstances, the Credit Derivatives Definitions provide that the Valuation Method shall be Highest.

45   One of these three Valuation Methods may be specified for a Credit Derivative Transaction with only one Reference Obligation and more than one Valuation Date. If no Valuation Method is specified in such circumstances, the Credit Derivatives Definitions provide that Average Highest shall apply.

46   One of these Valuation Methods may be specified for a Credit Derivative Transaction with more than one Reference Obligation and only one Valuation Date. If no Valuation Method is specified in such circumstances, the Credit Derivatives Definitions provide that Blended Highest shall apply.

47   One of these Valuation Methods may be specified for a Credit Derivative Transaction with more than one Reference Obligation and more than one Valuation Date. If no Valuation Method is specified in such circumstances, the Credit Derivatives Definitions provide that Average Blended Highest shall apply.

48   Include if Physical Settlement applies. Subject to contrary agreement between the parties, the Partial Cash Settlement Terms contained in the Credit Derivatives Definitions apply automatically in the context of events rendering it impossible or illegal for Buyer to Deliver or for Seller to accept Delivery of the Deliverable Obligations on or prior to the Latest Permissible Physical Settlement Date. This should be distinguished from the Partial Cash Settlement of Consent Required Loans, Partial Cash Settlement of Assignable Loans and Partial Cash Settlement of Participations provisions, which are elective. If applicable for any reason, the Partial Cash Settlement Terms will apply in the form prescribed in the Credit Derivatives Definitions unless contrary provision is made by the parties in the Confirmation.

49   If a number of Business Days is not specified, the Credit Derivatives Definitions provide that the Physical Settlement Period will be, with respect to a Deliverable Obligation, the maximum number of Business Days for settlement in accordance with then current market practice of such Deliverable Obligation, as determined by the Calculation Agent after consultation with the parties.

50   Specify whether, in respect of Deliverable Obligations with an outstanding principal balance, the Deliverable Obligation is to include or exclude accrued but unpaid interest. If neither "Include Accrued Interest" nor "Exclude Accrued Interest" is specified here, the Credit Derivatives Definitions provide that the Deliverable Obligations shall exclude accrued but unpaid interest.

Deliverable Obligations:

Deliverable Obligation Category (Select only one):	Deliverable Obligation Characteristics (Select all that apply):
[ ] Payment [ ] Borrowed Money [ ] Reference Obligations Only[51] [ ] Bond [ ] Loan [ ] Bond or Loan	[ ] Not Subordinated [ ] Specified Currency: [ ][52] [ ] Not Sovereign Lender [ ] Not Domestic Currency [ ] [Domestic Currency means: [ ][53] [ ] Not Domestic Law [ ] Listed [ ] Not Contingent [ ] Not Domestic Issuance [ ] Assignable Loan [ ] Consent Required Loan [ ] Direct Loan Participation Qualifying Participation Seller: [ ][54] [ ] Transferable [ ] Maximum Maturity [ ][55] [ ] Accelerated or Matured [ ] Not Bearer

[and:]

[Specify any other obligations of a Reference Entity.]

[Excluded Deliverable
Obligations:][56]   [   ]

---

51   If Reference Obligations Only is specified as the Deliverable Obligation Category, no Deliverable Obligation Characteristics should be specified.

52   Specify Currency. The Credit Derivatives Definitions provide that, if no currency is so specified, Specified Currency means the lawful currencies of any of Canada, Japan, Switzerland, the United Kingdom and the United States of America and the euro (and any successor currency to any such currency). The Credit Derivatives Definitions provide that these currencies may be referred to collectively in a Confirmation as the "Standard Specified Currencies".

53   If no currency is specified, the Credit Derivatives Definitions provide that Domestic Currency will be the lawful currency and any successor currency of (a) the relevant Reference Entity, if the Reference Entity is a Sovereign, or (b) the jurisdiction in which the relevant Reference Entity is organized, if the Reference Entity is not a Sovereign. In no event shall Domestic Currency include any successor currency if such successor currency is the lawful currency of any of Canada, Japan, Switzerland, the United Kingdom or the United States of America or the euro (or any successor currency to any such currency).

54   If Direct Loan Participation is specified as a Deliverable Obligation Characteristic, specify any requirements for the Qualifying Participation Seller here. If requirements are not so specified, the Credit Derivatives Definitions provide that there shall be no Qualifying Participation Seller, with the result that only a participation pursuant to a participation agreement between the Buyer and Seller will constitute a Direct Loan Participation.

55   Specify maximum period to maturity from the Physical Settlement Date.

56   Unless specified as an Excluded Deliverable Obligation, the Reference Obligation will, subject to the second paragraph of Section 2.20(b)(i) and Sections 2.32(a) and 2.33(a), be a Deliverable Obligation even though at the time of delivery it does not fall into the Obligation Category or lacks any or all Deliverable Obligation Characteristics.

[Partial Cash Settlement of Consent Required Loans Applicable][57]

[Partial Cash Settlement of Assignable Loans Applicable][58]

[Partial Cash Settlement of Participations Applicable][59]

Escrow: [Applicable][Not Applicable]

5.   Notice and Account Details:

Telephone and/or
Facsimile Numbers and
Contact Details for Notices:
                    Buyer: [   ]
                    Seller: [   ]

Account Details

    Account Details of
    Buyer: [   ]

    Account Details of Seller: [   ]

[6.   Offices[60]

Seller: [   ]

Buyer: [   ]]

---

57   Include if the parties intend that the Partial Cash Settlement Terms are to be applicable in relation to Consent Required Loans.
58   Include if the parties intend that the Partial Cash Settlement Terms are to be applicable in relation to Assignable Loans.
59   Include if the parties intend that the Partial Cash Settlement Terms are to be applicable in relation to Direct Loan Participations.
60   If necessary, specify the Offices through which the parties are acting for the purposes of the Credit Derivative Transaction.

Closing

Please confirm your agreement to be bound by the terms of the foregoing by executing a copy of this Confirmation and returning it to us [by facsimile].

Yours sincerely,

[PARTY A]

By: _____
     Name:
     Title:

Confirmed as of the date
first above written:

[PARTY B]

By: _____
     Name:
     Title:

Source: International Swaps and Derivatives Association, Inc. Reproduced with permission.

CHAPTER 4

Asset Swaps and the Credit Default Swap Basis

An investor who seeks to earn a credit spread on a fixed rate credit-risky bond and minimize interest rate risk can do so by using an *asset swap*. In an asset swap, the investor enters into the following two transactions simultaneously: buys the fixed rate credit-risky bond and enters into an interest rate swap.

While an asset swap is not a true credit derivative, it is closely associated with the credit derivatives market because it explicitly sets out the price of credit as a spread over an investor's funding cost, typically the London interbank offered rate (LIBOR). Although it allows the acquiring of credit risk while minimizing interest rate risk, it does not allow an investor to protect against or transfer credit risk. It is because of this shortcoming of an asset swap that other types of derivative instruments and structured products, particularly credit default swaps, were created.

An early method for pricing the single-name credit default swaps described in Chapter 10 was by recourse to the asset swap spread of the reference entity, as the default swap spread should (in theory) be equal to the asset swap spread of the reference asset. At the end of this chapter, we consider the use of this technique, before looking at the issues that cause the pricing of a credit default swap to differ from that of an asset swap on the same reference entity.

In order to understand an asset swap, it is necessary to understand an interest rate swap. Consequently, we begin this chapter with a description of the basic features of an interest rate swap.

INTEREST RATE SWAP

To understand an asset swap, it is necessary to understand an interest rate swap. In an *interest rate swap*, two parties agree to exchange periodic interest payments. The amount of the interest payments exchanged is based on a specified notional amount. In the most common type of interest rate swap, one party agrees to pay the other party fixed interest payments at designated dates for the life of the contract. This party is referred to as the *fixed-rate payer*. The fixed rate that the fixed-rate payer must make is called the *swap fixed rate* or simply *swap rate*. The other party, who agrees to make payments that float with some reference rate, is referred to as the *fixed-rate receiver*. The fixed-rate payer is also referred to as the *floating-rate receiver* and the fixed-rate receiver is also called the *floating-rate payer*. The type of swap that we have just described is called a *plain vanilla swap*.

The reference rates that have been used for the floating rate in an interest rate swap are those on various money market instruments: Treasury bills, the LIBOR, commercial paper, bankers acceptances, certificates of deposit, the federal funds rate, and the prime rate. The most common is LIBOR.

The payments between the counterparties are usually netted. For example, if the fixed-rate payer must pay $1.50 million and the fixed-rate receiver must pay $1.25 million, than rather than writing checks for the respective amounts, the fixed-rate party makes a payment of $0.25 million (= $1.50 million − $1.25 million) to the fixed-rate receiver. We shall refer to this netted payment between the two parties as the "cash flow for the swap" for the period. We note that throughout the literature the terms "swap payments" and "cash flows" are used interchangeably. However, we will use the term swap payments to mean the payment made by a counterparty before any netting and cash flow to mean the netted amount.

The *swap rate* is some "spread" above the Treasury yield curve with the same term to maturity as the swap. This spread is called the *swap spread*. The convention that has evolved for quoting an interest rate swap rate is that a dealer sets the floating rate equal to the reference rate and then quotes the swap spread.

Interest rate swaps are over-the-counter (OTC) instruments. Consequently, a risk that the two parties face when they enter into an interest rate swap is that the other party will fail to fulfill its obligations as set forth in the swap agreement. That is, swap agreements create another form of credit exposure: counterparty credit risk, where each party faces credit risk and, therefore, there is bilateral counterparty risk.

When interest rates change, the value of an interest rate swap changes. For example, consider the position of the fixed-rate payer. Suppose that an investor enters into a 5-year interest rate swap in which the swap rate is 6.15%. Suppose six months later that interest rates in the market increase such that, for an interest rate swap with a 4.5-year tenor, the swap rate is greater than 6.15%. This is an advantage to the investor. This is because the investor need only pay 6.15% to receive the reference rate but the market is demanding that any fixed-rate payer make a payment in excess of 6.15% to receive the reference rate. Thus, a rise in interest rates will increase the value of an interest rate swap for the fixed-rate payer. For the fixed-rate receiver, there is a corresponding decline in the value of the swap.

If, instead of an increase in interest rates leading to an increase in the swap rate, there is decrease in interest rates such that the fixed swap rate six-months after the inception of the interest rate swap declines below 6.15%, the investor is disadvantaged. This is because the market is requiring a fixed-rate payer to exchange less than 6.15% to get the reference rate. As a result, a rise in the fixed swap rate decreases the value of an interest rate swap for the fixed-rate payer and increases it by the same amount for the fixed-rate receiver.

The relationship between the changes in interest rates that leads to a change in the swap rate and the corresponding change in value for the swap counterparties is summarized below:

	Change in value for the:	
	Fixed-rate payer	Fixed-rate receiver
Increase in rates	Increases	Decreases
Decrease in rates	Decreases	Increases

Interest Rate Swaptions

There are options on interest rate swaps. These derivative instruments are called *swaptions* and they should be understood because they are used in variations of asset swaps as explained later. A swaption grants the option buyer the right to enter into an interest rate swap at a future date. The time until expiration of the swap, the term of the swap, and the swap rate are specified. The swap rate is the strike rate for the option.

There are two types of swaptions. A *pay fixed swaption* (also called a *payer's swaption*) entitles the option buyer to enter into an interest rate swap in which the buyer of the option pays a fixed rate and receives a floating rate. If the option buyer has the right to enter into the swap at the expiration date of the option, the option is referred to as a *European style swaption*. In contrast, if the option buyer has the right to enter into the swap at any time until the expiration date, the option is referred to as an *American style swaption*. For example, suppose that a European pay fixed swaption has a strike rate equal to 6.5%, a term of three years, and expires in two years. This means that at the end of two years the buyer of this pay fixed swaption has the right to enter into a 3-year interest rate swap in which the buyer pays 6% (the swap rate which is equal to the strike rate) and receives the reference rate.

In a *receive fixed swaption* (also called a *receiver's swaption*) the buyer of the swaption has the right to enter into an interest rate swap that requires paying a floating rate and receiving a fixed rate. For example, for a European receive fixed swaption with a strike rate of 6.25%, a swap term of four years, and an expiration date of year, the buyer of this has the right at the end of the next year to enter into an 4-year interest rate swap in which the buyer receives a swap rate of 7% (i.e., the strike rate) and pays the reference rate.

INVESTOR STRUCTURED ASSET SWAP

Now that we understand an interest rate swap, we can explain what an asset swap is. As explained earlier, in an asset swap an investor buys a fixed-rate, credit-risky bond for which it is willing to accept credit exposure and at the same time enters into an interest rate swap. An investor creates this structure by entering into the following terms in an interest rate swap:

- The investor will agree to be the fixed-rate payer.
- The term of the swap selected by the investor will match the maturity of the credit-risky bond purchased.
- The timing of the swap payments will match the timing of the cash flow of the credit-risky bond purchased.

If the issuer defaults on the issue, the investor must continue to make payments to the dealer and is therefore still exposed to the credit risk of the issuer.

Let's now illustrate a basic asset swap. Suppose that an investor purchases $20 million par value of a 6.85%, 5-year bond for a rated single-A telecom company at par value. The coupon payments are semiannual. At the same time, the investor enters into a 5-year interest rate swap with a dealer where the investor is the fixed-rate payer and the payments are made semiannually. Suppose that the swap rate is 6.00% and the investor receives 6-month LIBOR plus 45 bps.

Let's look at the cash flow for the investor every six months for the next five years:

	Receive from telecom bonds:	6.85%
−	Payment to dealer on swap:	6.00%
+	Payment from dealer on swap:	6-month LIBOR
	Net received by investor:	0.85% + 6-month LIBOR

Thus, regardless of how interest rates change, if the telecom issuer does not default on the issue, the investor earns a 85 bps over 6-month LIBOR. Effectively, the investor has converted a fixed-rate, single-A 5-year bond into a 5-year floating-rate bond with a spread over 6-month LIBOR. Thus, the investor has created a synthetic floating-rate bond. While our illustration has demonstrated how an asset swap can convert a fixed-rate bond into a synthetic floating-rate bond, an asset swap can also be used to convert a floating-rate bond into a synthetic fixed-rate bond.

ASSET SWAP STRUCTURE (PACKAGE) CREATED BY A DEALER

In our description of an asset swap, the investor bought the credit-risky bond and entered into an interest rate swap with a dealer. Typically, an asset swap combines the sale of a credit-risky asset owned by an investor to a counterparty, at par and with no interest accrued, with an interest rate swap. This type of asset swap structure or package is referred to as a *par asset swap*. If there is a default by the issuer of the credit-risky bond, the asset swap transaction is terminated and the defaulted bonds are returned to the investor plus or minus any mark-to-market on the asset swap transaction. Hence, the investor is still exposed to the bond issuer's credit risk.

The coupon on the bond in the par asset swap is paid in return for LIBOR, plus a spread if necessary. This spread is the *asset-swap spread* and is the price of the asset swap. In effect the asset swap allows investors that are LIBOR-based funded to receive the asset-swap spread. This spread is a function of the credit risk of the underlying credit-risky bond. The asset-swap spread may be viewed as equivalent to the price payable on a credit default swap written on that asset.

To illustrate this asset swap structure, suppose that in our previous illustration the swap rate prevailing the market is 6.30% rather than 6.00%. The investor owns the telecom bonds and sells them to a dealer at par with no accrued interest. The asset swap agreement between the dealer and the investor is as follows:

- The term is five years.
- The investor agrees to pay the dealer 6.30% semiannually.

■ The dealer agrees to pay the investor every six months 6-month LIBOR plus an asset-swap spread of 30 bps.

Let's look at the cash flow for the investor every six months for the next five years for this asset swap structure

	Received from telecom bonds:	6.85%
−	Payment to dealer on swap:	6.30%
+	Payment from dealer on swap:	6-month LIBOR + 30 bps
	Net received by investor:	0.85% + 6-month LIBOR

In our first illustration of an asset swap given earlier, the investor is creating a synthetic floater without a dealer. The investor owns the bonds. The only involvement of the dealer is as a counterparty to the interest rate swap. In the second structure, the dealer is the counterparty to the asset swap structure and the dealer owns the underlying credit-risky bonds. If there is a default, the dealer returns the bonds to the investor.

Illustration Using Bloomberg

We can illustrate the asset swap spread for a credit-risky corporate bond using Bloomberg screens. In Exhibit 4.1 we show the 7% 2007 bond

EXHIBIT 4.1   Bloomberg YA Screen for British Telecom 7% 2007 Bond, June 11, 2003

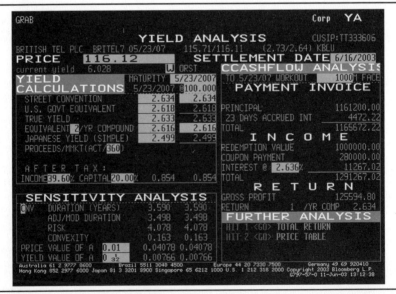

Source: Bloomberg Financial Markets. ©Bloomberg L.P. Used with permission.

EXHIBIT 4.2 Bloomberg ASW Screen for British Telecom 7% 2007 Bond, June 11, 2003

```
GRAB                                               Corp   ASW
Curve Source: CMPN
              ASSET  SWAP  CALCULATOR             Page  1 of 3
BRITISH TEL PLC  BRITEL7 05/23/07   115.72/116.12   (2.73/2.63) KBLU
    Currency                Bond              Underlying Curves
From USD  To USD  Buy/Sell S Par Amt    1000 M   Price Date  US        US
   [US]    [US]   Workout   5/23/07 @ 100.0000     6/11/03   23<SWDF#>  23
                             Swap                 Crv Settle  R<B/A/M>R
Spot F/X   1.000      Coupon  Day Count Freq       6/16/03   BGN       BGN
                 Fixed    2.01452% 30E/360   1           Z-Spread
Trade Settlement Floating 1.16470% ACT/360   4            65.7 bp
   6/16/03       Swap Par Amt(FLT)   1000 M
           Gross  Spread  Valuation
                                       Money        Spread(bp)
       Implied Value 118.8394          27.2M   =      70.4
              Swapped  Spread  Details
   Calculate 3                          Money        Spread(bp)
   1:Bond Price   116.12  /  2.63354%
     Swap Price   100      Cash Out  16.1200    -161.2M  =  -417.3 bp
   2:Swap Rate    2.01452% Bond Cpn   7.0000     188.4M  =   487.7
     Redemption Premium / Discount    0.0000%     0.0    =    0.0
     Funding Spread    0.0 bp                     0.0M   =    0.0
   3:Swapped Spread                                          70.4 bp
1 <Go> for X-currency spread summary, 2 <Go> to save, 3 <Go> to update swap crv
Australia 61 2 9777 8600        Brazil 5511 3048 4500    Europe 44 20 7330 7500    Germany 49 69 920410
Hong Kong 852 2977 6000 Japan 81 3 3201 8900 Singapore 65 6212 1000 U.S. 1 212 318 2000 Copyright 2003 Bloomberg L.P.
                                                                G797-57-1 11-Jun-03 13:13:26
```

Source: Bloomberg Financial Markets. ©Bloomberg L.P. Used with permission.

issued by British Telecom plc, a United Kingdom telecomm company. The bond is denominated in U.S. dollars. The screen is Bloomberg's YA page for yield analysis, and shows the bond as at June 11, 2003, at an offered price of 116.12. Combining this with an interest rate swap to create our asset swap will convert the bond's fixed coupon to a floating-rate coupon for the bondholder.

To see what the spread for this bond would be in an asset swap, we call up screen ASW. This is shown at Exhibit 4.2 and we see that the swap spread for this bond, which is rated Baa1 by Moody's and A– by S&P, is 70.4 bps. The bond price on the screen is user-input at 116.12. Another screen can be used to see the bond spread over other references and benchmarks, and is shown at Exhibit 4.3. We see that the interpolated spread over Treasuries is 93 bps (two-thirds down in the lower left-hand corner). This compares to a spread of just over 60 bps over Treasuries on issue. In other words, the bond has cheapened in the market since issue in May 1997, when it was priced off the U.S. 10-year active. This is not surprising as the issuer has been downgraded since that time.

EXHIBIT 4.3 Determination of British Telecom Yield Spreads for 7% 2007 Bond, Using YAS Screen, June 11, 2003

GRAB					Corp	YAS
YIELD & SPREAD ANALYSIS				CUSIPTT333606	PCS KBLU	
BRITISH TEL PLC BRITEL7 05/23/07		115.71/116.11	(2.73/2.64) KBLU			
SETTLE 6/16/03	FACE AMT	1000 M	or PROCEEDS		1,165,672.22	

1) YA	YIELDS	2) YASD	RISK &	BRITEL7 05/23/07		
PRICE	116.120000		HEDGE	workout		HEDGE BOND
YIELD	2.616 Ist		RATIOS	5/23/07 OAS		OAS
SPRD	129.90 bp yld-decimals3/3		Mod Dur	3.54	3.57	2.84
versus			Risk	4.129	4.158	2.900
3yr T 2 05/15/06		BENCHMARK	Convexity	0.15	0.15	0.10
PRICE 101-30+	Save Delete		Workout HEDGE Amount:1,428 M			
YIELD 1.317 %	sd: 6/12/03		OAS HEDGE Amount:1,434 M			

Yields are: Semi-Annual					
3) OAS	SPREADS	4) ASW	5) FPA	FINANCING	
OAS:	95.9 CRV# CMT VOL Opt		Repo% 0.990	(360/365)360	Days 1
OAS:	65.3 CRV# I52		Int Income	194.44	Carry P&L
ASSET SWAP:	(A/A) 69.4 TED: -60.3		Fin Cost	-32.06	162.39
ISPRD	60.2 CRV# I52 US $ SWAP 30/360		Amortiz	-110.27<->	52.12
Yield Curve:I25	US TREASURY ACTIVES		Forwrd Prc	116.103761	
+ 93	v 3.9yr (1.686 %) INTERPOLATED		Prc Drop	0.016239	
+ 130	v 3yr (1.32) T 2 05/15/06		Drop (bp)	0.13	
+ 56	v 5yr (2.05) T 2 ⅝ 05/15/08		Accrued Interest /100	0.447222	
- 54	v 10yr (3.16) T 3 ⅝ 05/15/13		Number Of Days Accrued	23	
- 162	v 30yr (4.24) T 5 ⅜ 02/15/31				

Australia 61 2 9777 8600   Brazil 5511 3048 4500   Europe 44 20 7330 7500   Germany 49 69 920410
Hong Kong 852 2977 6000 Japon 81 3 3201 8900 Singapore 65 6212 1000 U.S. 1 212 318 2000 Copyright 2003 Bloomberg L.P.
G797-57-0 11-Jun-03 13:11:37

Source: Bloomberg Financial Markets. ©Bloomberg L.P. Used with permission.

Selecting the credit-risky industrials yield curve for USD (numbered I52 on Bloomberg), we see that the asset swap spread is actually 69.4 for this bond. This is because the screen has calculated the asset swap spread over a more specific yield curve, rather than the generic inter-bank LIBOR curve used by screen ASW.

USING SWAPTIONS TO REMOVE UNWANTED STRUCTURAL FEATURES

There are variations of the basic asset swap structure to remove unwanted noncredit structural features of the underlying credit-risky bond. The simplest example of an asset swap variation to remove an unwanted noncredit structural feature is when the bond is callable. If the bond is callable, then the future cash flows of the bond are uncertain because the issue can be called. Moreover, the issue is likely to be called if interest rates decline below the bond's coupon rate.

This problem can be handled in the case where the investor buys the bond and enters into an interest rate swap. The tenor of the interest rate swap would still be for the term of the bond. However, the investor would also enter into a swaption in which the investor has the right to effectively terminate the swap from the time of the first call date for the bond to the maturity date of the bond. In the swaption, since the investor is paying fixed and receiving floating, the swaption must be one in which the investor receives fixed and pays floating. Specifically, the investor will enter into a receive fixed swaption.

In the asset swap that is structured with a dealer, this is simpler to do. The transaction can be structured such that the asset swap is terminated if the bonds are called.

THE ASSET SWAP—CREDIT DEFAULT SWAP BASIS

In this section, we consider the difference in spread premium between asset swaps and credit default swaps written on the same reference asset.[1] We begin with a look at asset swap pricing.

Asset-Swap Pricing

There are two approaches to pricing default swaps—*static replication* and *modeling*. The former approach is based on the assumption that if one can replicate the cash flows of the structure which one is trying to price using a portfolio of tradable instruments, then the price of the structure should equal the value of the replicating portfolio. As explained below, an asset swap is the static replication approach to pricing default swaps. In situations where either the nature of the instrument we are trying to price cannot be replicated or that we do not have access to prices for the instruments we would use in the replicating portfolio, it may become necessary to use a modeling approach. This approach is explained in Chapter 10.

Consequently, the asset swap market is a reasonably reliable indicator of the returns required for individual credit exposures, and provides a mark-to-market framework for reference assets as well as a hedging mechanism. As explained above, a par asset swap typically combines the sale of an asset such as a fixed-rate corporate bond to a counterparty, at par and with no interest accrued, with an interest-rate swap. The coupon on the bond is paid in return for LIBOR, plus a spread if necessary. This spread is the asset-swap spread and is the price of the asset swap. In effect the asset swap allows market participants that pay LIBOR-based funding to receive

---

[1] This section draws from Moorad Choudhry, "Some Issues in the Asset-Swap Pricing of Credit Default Swaps," in Frank J. Fabozzi (ed.), *Professional Perspectives on Fixed Income Portfolio Management: Volume 4* (Hoboken, NJ: John Wiley & Sons, 2003).

the asset-swap spread. This spread is a function of the credit risk of the underlying bond asset, which is why it may be viewed as equivalent (in theory) to the price payable on a credit default swap written on that asset.

The generic pricing is given by

$$Y_a = Y_b - ir$$

where

Y_a = is the asset swap spread
Y_b = is the asset spread over the benchmark
ir = is the interest-rate swap spread

The asset spread over the benchmark is simply the bond (asset) redemption yield over that of the government benchmark. The interest-rate swap spread reflects the cost involved in converting fixed-coupon benchmark bonds into a floating-rate coupon during the life of the asset (or default swap), and is based on the swap rate for that maturity.

The theoretical basis for deriving a default swap price from the asset swap rate can be illustrated by looking at a basis-type trade involving a cash market reference asset (bond) and a credit default swap written on this bond. This is similar in approach to the risk-neutral or *no-arbitrage* concept used in derivatives pricing. The theoretical trade involves:

- A long position in the cash market floating rate note (FRN) priced at par, and which pays a coupon of LIBOR + X bps.
- A long position (bought protection) in a default swap written on the same FRN, of identical term-to-maturity and at a cost of Y bps.

The buyer of the bond is able to fund the position at LIBOR. In other words, the bondholder has the following net cash flow:

$$(100 - 100) + [(LIBOR + X) - (LIBOR + Y)]$$

or X – Y bps.

In the event of default, the bond is delivered to the protection seller in return for payment of par, enabling the bondholder to close out the funding position. During the term of the trade, the bondholder has earned X – Y bps while assuming no credit risk. For the trade to meet the no-arbitrage condition, we must have X = Y. If X ≠ Y, the investor would be able to establish the position and generate a risk-free profit.

This is a logically tenable argument as well as a reasonable assumption. The default risk of the cash bondholder is identical in theory to that of the default seller. In the next section we illustrate an asset swap pricing

EXHIBIT 4.4   Credit Default Swap and Asset Swap Hedge

example, before looking at why in practice there exist differences in pricing between credit default swaps and cash market reference assets.

Asset Swap Pricing Example

XYZ plc is a Baa2-rated corporate. The 7-year asset swap for this entity is currently trading at 93 bps; the underlying 7-year bond is hedged by an interest rate swap with an Aa2-rated bank. The risk-free rate for floating rate bonds is LIBID minus 12.5 bps (assume the bid-offer spread is 6 bps). This suggests that the credit spread for XYZ plc is 111.5 bps. The credit spread is the return required by an investor for holding the credit of XYZ plc. The protection seller is conceptually long the asset, and so would short the asset to hedge its position. This is illustrated in Exhibit 4.4. The price charged for the default swap is the price of shorting the asset, which works out as 111.5 bps each year.

Therefore we can price a credit default swap written on XYZ plc as the present value of 111.5 bps for seven years, discounted at the interest-rate swap rate of 5.875%. This computes to a credit default swap price of 6.25%. We list the terms below:

Reference:	XYZ plc
Term:	7 years
Interest rate swap rate:	5.875%
Asset swap:	LIBOR plus 93 bps

Default swap pricing:

Benchmark rate:	LIBID minus 12.5 bps
Margin:	6 bps
Credit default swap:	111.5 bps
Default swap price:	6.252%

The Credit Default Swap Basis

A number of factors observed in the market serve to make the price of credit risk that has been established synthetically using credit default swaps to differ from its price as traded in the cash market using asset swaps. In fact, identifying (or predicting) such differences gives rise to arbitrage opportunities that may be exploited by basis trading in the cash and derivative markets.[2] The difference between the synthetic credit risk premium and the cash market premium is known as the *basis*. It is shown as

$$\text{CDS premium} - \text{ASW spread} = \text{basis}$$

The basis is usually positive, occasionally negative, and arises from a combination of several factors. These factors include the following:

- Bond identity: The bondholder is aware of the exact issue that they are holding in the event of default; however, default swap sellers may receive potentially any bond from a basket of deliverable instruments that rank *pari passu* with the cash asset, where physical settlement is required. This is the delivery option afforded the long swap holder.
- The borrowing rate for a cash bond in the repo market may differ from LIBOR if the bond is to any extent *special*. This does not impact the default swap price which is fixed at inception.
- Certain bonds rated AAA (such as U.S. agency securities) sometimes trade below LIBOR in the asset swap market; however, a bank writing protection on such a bond will expect a premium (positive spread over LIBOR) for selling protection on the bond.
- Depending on the precise reference credit, the default swap may be more liquid than the cash bond, resulting in a lower default swap price, or less liquid than the bond, resulting in a higher price.
- Default swaps may be required to pay out on credit events that are technical defaults, and not the full default that impacts a cash bondholder; protection sellers may demand a premium for this additional risk.
- The default swap buyer is exposed to counterparty risk during the term of the trade, unlike the cash bondholder.

For these and other reasons the default swap price often differs from the cash market price for the same asset. This renders continued reliance on the asset-swap pricing technique a trifle problematic. Therefore banks are increasingly turning to credit pricing models, based on the same models used to price interest rate derivatives, when pricing credit derivatives.

---

[2] This is known as trading the *credit default basis* and involves either buying the cash bond and buying a default swap written on this bond, or selling the cash bond and selling a credit default swap written on the bond.

EXHIBIT 4.5   Bloomberg DES Page for Air Products & Chemicals Bond

```
APD 6.5 07 Corp DES                                    N172 Corp   DES
SECURITY DESCRIPTION                        Page 1/ 1
AIR PROD & CHEM  APD6 ½ 07/12/07   104.7376/104.7376  (5.46/5.46) BFV  @20:28
┌──────────────────────────────┬─────────────────────────┬──────────────────────┐
│ ISSUER INFORMATION           │ IDENTIFIERS             │ 1) Additional Sec Info│
│ Name AIR PRODUCTS & CHEMICALS│ Common   011391176      │ 2) Identifiers        │
│ Type Chemicals-Specialty  ·  │ ISIN    XS0113911761    │ 3) Ratings            │
│ Market of Issue EURO NON-DOLLAR│ BB number  EC2705415  │ 4) Fees/Restrictions  │
├──────────────────────────────┤─────────────────────────┤ 5) Sec. Specific News │
│ SECURITY INFORMATION         │ RATINGS                 │ 6) Involved Parties   │
│ Country US      Currency EUR │ Moody's      A3      *+ │ 7) Custom Notes       │
│ Collateral Type SR UNSUB     │ S&P          A          │ 8) Issuer Information  │
│ Calc Typ(  1)STREET CONVENTION│ Composite   A3         │ 9) ALLQ               │
├──────────────────────────────┤─────────────────────────┤ 10) Pricing Sources   │
│ Maturity   7/12/2007 Series  │ ISSUE SIZE              │ 11) Related Securities │
│ NORMAL                       │ Amt Issued              │ 12) Issuer Web Page   │
├──────────────────────────────┤ EUR 300,000.00    (M)   │                       │
│ Coupon  6 ½        FIXED     │ Amt Outstanding         │                       │
│ ANNUAL        ACT/ACT        │ EUR 300,000.00    (M)   │                       │
├──────────────────────────────┤ Min Piece/Increment     │                       │
│ Announcement Dt  6/30/00     │ 100,000.00/  1,000.00   │                       │
│ Int. Accrual Dt  7/12/00     │ Par Amount    1,000.00  │                       │
│ 1st Settle Date  7/12/00     │─────────────────────────│                       │
│ 1st Coupon Date  7/12/01     │ BOOK RUNNER/EXCHANGE    │                       │
│ Iss Pr  99.7800 Reoffer  99.78│ ABN,DB                 │ 65) Old DES           │
│ SPR @ FPR  130.0 vs DBR 6 07/07│ LUXEMBOURG            │ 66) Send as Attachment│
│ NO PROSPECTUS                │                         │                       │
│ UNSEC'D.                     │                         │                       │
└──────────────────────────────┴─────────────────────────┴──────────────────────┘
 Australia 61 2 9777 8600      Brazil 5511 3048 4500   Europe 44 20 7330 7500   Germany 49 69 920410
 Hong Kong 852 2977 6000 Japan 81 3 3201 8900 Singapore 65 212 1000 U.S. 1 212 318 2000  Copyright 2002 Bloomberg L.P.
                                                                        G432-212-0 18-Jan-02 20:28:32
 Bloomberg
 PROFESSIONAL
```

Source: Bloomberg Financial Markets. Used with permission.

Illustration Using Bloomberg

Observations from the market illustrate the difference in price between asset swaps on a bond and a credit default swap written on that bond, reflecting the factors stated in the previous section. We show this now using a euro-denominated corporate bond.

The bond is the Air Products & Chemicals 6.5% bond due July 2007. This bond is rated A3/A as shown in Exhibit 4.5, the description page from Bloomberg. The asset swap price for that specific bond to its term to maturity as at January 18, 2002 was 41.6 bps. This is shown in Exhibit 4.6. The relevant swap curve used as the pricing reference is indicated on the screen as curve 45, which is the Bloomberg reference number for the euro swap curve and is shown in Exhibit 4.7.

We now consider the credit default swap page on Bloomberg for the same bond, which is shown in Exhibit 4.8. For the similar maturity range the credit default swap price would be approximately 115 bps. This differs significantly from the asset swap price, and gives a basis value of 73.4.

EXHIBIT 4.6   Asset Swap Calculator Page ASW on Bloomberg, January 18, 2002

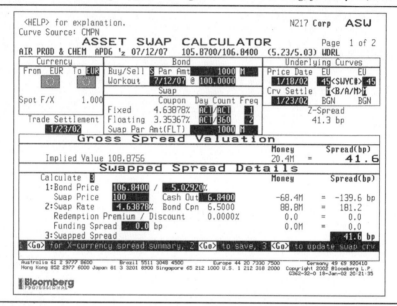

Source: Bloomberg Financial Markets. ©Bloomberg L.P. Used with permission.

EXHIBIT 4.7   Euro Swap Curve on Bloomberg, January 18, 2002

```
<HELP> for explanation, <MENU> for similar functions.    N217 Corp   SWDF
Screen Printed
New  Euro  Currency        SWAP CURVE
                  Cash Rates       Type O <page> to view more cash rates.
Term   1 wk    1 mo    2 mo    3 mo    4 mo    5 mo    6 mo    9 mo    1yr
Bid    3.3420  3.3490  3.3460  3.3450  3.3470  3.3490  3.3510  3.3890  3.5060
Ask    3.3420  3.3490  3.3460  3.3450  3.3470  3.3490  3.3510  3.3890  3.5360
Updt   10:02   10:02   10:02   10:02   10:02   10:02   10:02   10:02   18:00
                        Swap Rates
Term   18 mo   2 yr    30 mo   3 yr    4 yr    5 yr    6 yr    7 yr    8 yr
Bid    3.6910  3.8970          4.1800  4.3780  4.5500  4.7000  4.8300  4.9280
Ask    3.7060  3.9270          4.2100  4.3980  4.5700  4.7300  4.8500  4.9480
Updt   17:31   18:00           18:00   17:59   17:59   18:00   18:02   18:02
Src    CMPN    CMPN            CMPN    CMPN    CMPN    CMPN    CMPN    CMPN
                     Long Term Swap Rates
Term   9 yr    10 yr   11 yr   12 yr   15 yr   20 yr   25 yr   30 yr
Bid    5.0050  5.0650          5.1700  5.2780  5.3550  5.3600  5.3530
Ask    5.0250  5.0850          5.1900  5.2980  5.3750  5.3900  5.3730
Updt   18:02   18:02           18:02   18:02   18:02   18:00   18:02
Src    CMPN    CMPN            CMPN    CMPN    CMPN    CMPN    CMPN

Daytype / Frequency Conventions        IRSB <Go> for Sprd vrs Benchmark
Cash Rates   ACT/360
Swap Rates   30/360 , 1               Enter <Menu> to select another crv
                                      For old SWYC, enter SWYC OLD <GO>.
```

Source: Bloomberg Financial Markets. ©Bloomberg L.P. Used with permission.

EXHIBIT 4.8   Default Swap Page CDSW for Air Products & Chemicals Bond, January 18, 2002

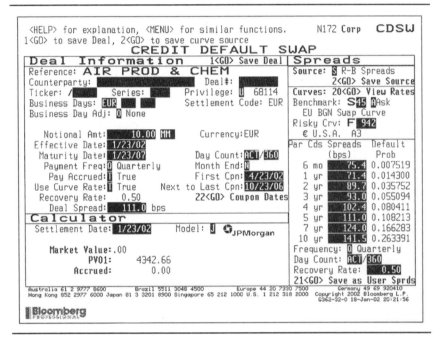

Source: Bloomberg Financial Markets. ©Bloomberg L.P. Used with permission.

From the screen we can see that the benchmark curve is the same as that used in the calculation shown in Exhibit 4.7. However, the corporate curve used as the pricing reference is indicated as the euro-denominated, U.S. issuer A3 curve, and this is shown in Exhibit 4.9. This is page CURV on Bloomberg, and is the fair value corporate credit curve constructed from a basket of A3 credits. The user can view the list of bonds that are used to construct the curve on following pages of the same screen. For comparison we also show the Bank A3 rated corporate credit yield curve, in Exhibit 4.10.

Prices observed in the market will invariably show this pattern of difference between the asset swap price and the credit default swap price. The page CDSW on Bloomberg uses the generic risky curve to calculate the default swap price, and adds the credit spread to the interest rate swap curve (shown in Exhibit 4.10). However, the ASW page is the specific asset swap rate for that particular bond, to the bond's term to maturity. This is another reason why the prices of the two instruments will differ significantly.

EXHIBIT 4.9   Fair Market Curve, Euro A3 Sector

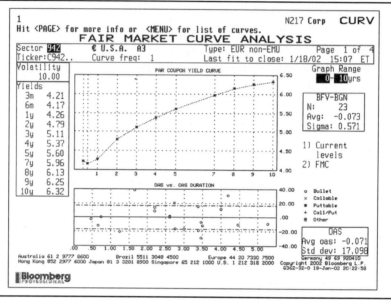

Source: Bloomberg Financial Markets. ©Bloomberg L.P. Used with permission.

EXHIBIT 4.10   Fair Market Curve, Euro Banks A3 Sector

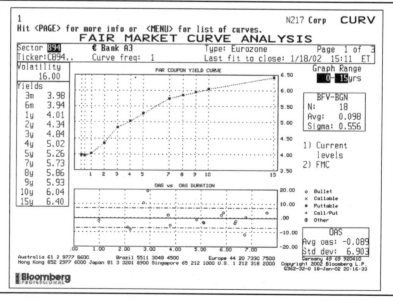

Source: Bloomberg Financial Markets. ©Bloomberg L.P. Used with permission.

EXHIBIT 4.11   CDSW Page with Discounted Spreads Model Selected

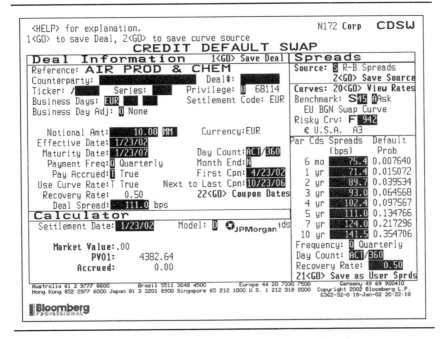

Source: Bloomberg Financial Markets. ©Bloomberg L.P. Used with permission.

On Bloomberg the user can select either the JPMorgan Chase credit default swap pricing model or a generic discounted credit spreads model. These are indicated by "J" or "D" in the box marked "Model" on the CDSW page. Exhibit 4.11 shows this page with the generic model selected. Although there is no difference in the swap prices, as expected the default probabilities have changed under this setting.

Our example illustrates the difference in swap prices that we discussed earlier, and can be observed for any number of corporate credits across sectors. This suggests that middle-office staff and risk managers who use the asset swap technique to independently value credit default swap books are at risk of obtaining values that differ from those in the market. This is an important issue for credit derivative market-making banks.

CHAPTER 5

Total Return Swaps

A *total return swap* is a swap in which one party makes periodic floating rate payments to a counterparty in exchange for the total return realized on a reference asset (or underlying asset). The reference asset could be one of the following:

- Credit-risky bond
- A loan
- A reference portfolio consisting of bonds or loans
- An index representing a sector of the bond market
- An equity index

Our focus in this chapter is on total return swaps, where the reference asset is one of the first four types listed above. We first explain how a total return swap can be used when the reference asset is a credit-risky bond and a loan. While these types of total return swaps are more aptly referred to as total return *credit* swaps, we will simply refer to them as total return swaps. When the bond index consists of a credit risk sector of the bond market, the total return swap is referred to as a *total return bond index swap* or in this chapter as simply a *total return index swap*. We will explain how a total return index swap offers asset managers and hedge fund managers greater flexibility in managing a bond portfolio. In the appendix to this chapter we explain the pricing of total return swaps.

ECONOMICS OF A TOTAL RETURN SWAP

A total return of a reference asset includes all cash flows that flow from it as well as the capital appreciation or depreciation of the reference

EXHIBIT 5.1   Total Return Swaps

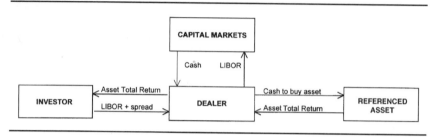

asset. The floating rate is a reference interest rate (typically LIBOR) plus or minus a spread. The party that agrees to make the floating rate payments and receive the total return is referred to as the *total return receiver* or the *swap buyer*; the party that agrees to receive the floating rate payments and pay the total return is referred to as the *total return payer* or *swap buyer*. Total return swaps are viewed as unfunded credit derivatives, because there is no up-front payment required.

If the total return payer owns the underlying asset, it has transferred its economic exposure to the total return receiver. Effectively then, the total return payer has a neutral position that typically will earn LIBOR plus a spread. However, the total return payer has only transferred the economic exposure to the total return receiver; it has not transferred the actual asset. The total return payer must continue to fund the underlying asset at its marginal cost of borrowing or at the opportunity cost of investing elsewhere the capital tied up by the reference assets.

The total return payer may not initially own the reference asset before the swap is transacted. Instead, after the swap is negotiated, the total return payer will purchase the reference asset to hedge its obligations to pay the total return to the total return receiver. In order to purchase the reference asset, the total return payer must borrow capital. This borrowing cost is factored into the floating rate that the total return receiver must pay to the swap seller. Exhibit 5.1 diagrams how a total return credit swap works.

In the exhibit the dealer raises cash from the capital markets at a funding cost of straight LIBOR. The cash that flows into the dealer from the capital markets flows right out again to purchase the reference asset. The asset provides both interest income and capital gain or loss depending on its price fluctuation. This total return is passed through in its entirety to the investor according to the terms of the total return swap. The investor, in turn, pays the dealer LIBOR plus a spread to fulfill its obligations under the swap.

From the dealer's perspective, all of the cash flows in Exhibit 5.1 net out to the spread over LIBOR that the dealer receives from the investor. Therefore, the dealer's profit is the spread times the notional amount of the total return swap. Furthermore, the dealer is perfectly hedged. It has no risk position except for the counterparty risk of the investor. Effectively, the dealer receives a spread on a riskless position.

In fact, if the dealer already owns the reference asset on its balance sheet, the total return swap may be viewed as a form of credit protection that offers more risk reduction than a credit default swap. A credit default swap has only one purpose: To protect the investor against default risk. If the issuer of the reference asset defaults, the credit default swap provides a payment. However, if the underlying asset declines in value but no default occurs, the credit protection buyer receives no payment. In contrast, under a total return swap, the reference asset owned by the dealer is protected from declines in value. In effect, the investor acts as a "first loss" position for the dealer because any decline in value of the reference asset must be reimbursed by the investor.

The investor, on the other hand, receives the total return on a desired asset in a convenient format. There are several other benefits in using a total return swap as opposed to purchasing a reference asset itself. First, the total return receiver does not have to finance the purchase of the reference asset itself. Instead, the total return receiver pays a fee to the total return payer in return for receiving the total return on the reference asset. Second, the investor can take advantage of the dealer's "best execution" in acquiring the reference asset. Third, the total return receiver can achieve the same economic exposure to a diversified basket of assets in one swap transaction that would otherwise take several cash market transactions to achieve. In this way a total return swap is much more efficient means for transacting than via the cash market. Finally, an investor who wants to short a credit-risky asset such as a corporate bond will find it difficult to do so in the market. An investor can do so efficiently by using a total return swap. In this case the investor will use a total return swap in which it is a total return payer.

There is a drawback of a total return swap if an asset manager employs it to obtain credit protection. In a total return swap, the total return receiver is exposed to both credit risk and interest rate risk. For example, the credit spread can decline (resulting in a favorable price movement for the reference asset), but this gain can be offset by a rise in the level of interest rates. This is the same unfavorable feature of a credit derivative instrument shared by an option on a credit-risky bond described in Chapter 11.

Total Return Swap Compared to an Interest Rate Swap

It is worthwhile comparing market conventions for a total return swap to that of an interest rate swap. A plain vanilla or generic interest rate swap involves the exchange of a fixed-rate payment for a floating-rate payment. A *basis swap* is a special type of interest rate swap in which both parties exchange floating-rate payments based on a different reference interest rate. For example, one party's payments may be based on 3-month LIBOR, while the other parties payment is based on the 6-month Treasury rate. In a total return swap, both parties pay a floating rate.

The quotation convention for a generic interest rate swap and a total return swap differ. In a generic interest rate swap, the fixed-rate payer pays a spread to a Treasury security with the same tenor as the swap and the fixed-rate receiver pays the reference rate flat (i.e., no spread or margin). The payment by the fixed-rate receiver (i.e., floating-rate payer) is referred to as the *funding leg*. For example, suppose an interest rate swap quote for a 5-year, 3-month LIBOR-based swap is 50. This means that the fixed-rate payer agrees to pay the 5-year Treasury rate that exists at the inception of the swap and the fixed-rate receiver agrees to pay 3-month LIBOR. In contrast, the quote convention for a total return swap is that the total return receiver receives the total return flat and pays the total return payer a interest rate based on a reference rate (typically LIBOR) plus or minus a spread. That is, the funding leg (i.e., what the total return receiver pays includes a spread).

Illustration

Let's illustrate a total return swap where the reference asset is a corporate bond. Consider an asset manager who believes that the fortunes of XYZ Corporation will improve over the next year so that the company's credit spread relative to U.S. Treasury securities will decline. The company has issued a 10-year bond at par with a coupon rate of 9% and therefore the yield is 9%. Suppose at the time of issuance, the 10-year Treasury yield is 6.2%. This means that the credit spread is 280 bps and the asset manager believes it will decrease over the year to less than 280 bps.

The asset manager can express this view by entering into a total return swap that matures in one year as a total return receiver with the reference asset being the 10-year, 9% XYZ Corporation's bond issue. For simplicity, assume that the total return swap calls for an exchange of payments semiannually. Suppose the terms of the swap are that the total return receiver pays the 6-month Treasury rate plus 160 bps in order to receive the total return on the reference asset. The notional amount for the contract is $10 million.

Suppose that at the end of one year the following occurs:

■ The 6-month Treasury rate is 4.8% initially.
■ The 6-month Treasury rate for computing the second semiannual payment is 5.4%.
■ At the end of one year the 9-year Treasury rate is 7.6%.
■ At the end of one year the credit spread for the reference asset is 180 bps.

First let's look at the payments that must be made by the asset manager. The first swap payment made by the asset manager is 3.2% (4.8% plus 160 bps divided by two) multiplied by the $10 million notional amount. The second swap payment made is 3.5% (5.4% plus 160 bps divided by two) multiplied by the $10 million notional amount. Thus,

First swap payment paid: $10 million × 3.2% = $320,000
Second swap payment paid: $10 million × 3.5% = $350,000
Total payments: $670,000

The payments that will be received by the asset manager are the two coupon payments plus the change in the value of the reference asset. There will be two coupon payments. Since the coupon rate is 9% the amount received for the coupon payments is $900,000.

Finally, the change in the value of the reference asset must be determined. At the end of one year, the reference asset has a maturity of nine years. Since the 9-year Treasury rate is assumed to be 7.6% and the credit spread is assumed to decline from 280 bps to 180 bps, the reference asset will sell to yield 9.4%. The price of a 9%, 9-year bond selling to yield 9.4% is 97.61. Since the par value is $10 million, the price is $9,761,000. The capital loss is therefore $239,000. The payment to the total return receiver is then:

Coupon payment = $900,000
Capital loss   = $239,000
Swap payment   = $661,000

Netting the swap payment made and the swap payment received, the asset manager must make a payment of $9,000 ($661,000 – $670,000).

Notice that even though the asset manager's expectations were realized (i.e., a decline in the credit spread), the asset manager had to make a net outlay. This illustration highlights one of the disadvantages of a total return swap noted earlier: The return to the investor is dependent on both credit risk (declining or increasing credit spreads) and market risk (declining or increasing market rates). Two types of market interest rate risk can affect the price of a fixed-income asset. *Credit independent market risk* is the risk that the general level of interest rates will change over the term of the swap. This type of risk has nothing to do with the credit deterioration of the reference asset. *Credit dependent market interest rate risk* is the risk that the discount rate applied to the value of an asset will change based on either perceived or actual default risk.

In the illustration, the reference asset was adversely affected by market interest rate risk, but positively rewarded for accepting credit dependent market interest rate risk. To remedy this problem, a total return receiver can customize the total return swap transaction. For example, the asset manager could negotiate to receive the coupon income on the reference asset plus any change in value due to changes in the credit spread. Now the asset manager has expressed a view exclusively on credit risk; credit independent market risk does not affect the swap value. In this case, in addition to the coupon income, the asset manager would receive the difference between the present value of the reference asset at a current spread of 280 bps and the present value of the reference asset at a credit spread of 180 bps.

APPLICATIONS OF A TOTAL RETURN SWAP

As explained in Chapter 3, an asset manager typically uses a credit default swap to hedge a credit exposure. However, a total return swap is typically used to increase credit exposure. A total return swap transfers all of the economic exposure of a reference asset to the total return receiver. In exchange for accepting this exposure, the total return receiver pays a floating interest rate to the total return payer.

Total return swap applications fall into three categories:

1. Asset managers using a total return swap for leveraging purposes.
2. Asset managers using a total return swap as a more transnationally efficient means for implementing a portfolio management strategy.
3. Bank managers using a total return swap as an efficient vehicle for transferring credit risk and as a means for reducing capital charges.

Below we provide two applications of total return swaps and further when total return index swaps are discussed.

Creating a Synthetic Repo

There are a number of reasons why asset managers may wish to enter into total swap arrangements. As noted above, one of these is to reduce or remove credit risk. Using total return swaps as a credit derivative instrument, a party can remove exposure to an asset without having to sell it. In a vanilla total return swap the total return payer retains rights to the reference asset, although in some cases servicing and voting rights may be transferred. This assumes that the reference asset is on the payer's balance sheet.

The total return receiver gains an exposure to the reference asset without having to pay out the cash proceeds that would be required to purchase it. As the maturity of the swap rarely matches that of the reference asset, in a positive yield curve environment the swap receiver may gain from the positive funding or carry that derives from being able to roll over short-term funding of a longer-term asset. The total return payer on the other hand benefits from protection against interest rate and credit risk for a specified period of time, without having to liquidate the asset itself. At the maturity of the swap the total return payer may reinvest the asset if it continues to own it, or it may sell the asset in the open market. In this respect a total return swap is in essence a *synthetic repo*.

A total return swap agreement entered into as a credit derivative is a means by which banks can take on unfunded off-balance sheet credit exposure. Higher-rated banks that have access to London interbank bid rate (LIBID) funding can benefit by funding on-balance sheet assets that are credit protected through a credit derivative such as a total return swap, assuming the net spread of asset income over credit protection premium is positive.

A total return swap conducted as a synthetic repo is usually undertaken to effect the temporary removal of assets from the balance sheet. This may be desired for a number of reasons, for example if the institution is due to be analyzed by credit rating agencies, or if the annual external audit is due shortly. Another reason a bank may wish to temporarily remove lower credit-quality assets from its balance sheet is if it is in danger of breaching capital limits in between the quarterly return periods. In this case, as the return period approaches, lower quality assets may be removed from the balance sheet by means of a total return swap, which is set to mature after the return period has passed.

However, this is a semantic point associated with the motivation of the total return payer. If effected for regulatory capital reasons a total return swap is akin to a synthetic repo; if effected for credit speculation reasons it becomes a credit derivative. In Chapter 7 we discuss a special type of funded total return swap as used in synthetic structured credit products.

Use in the Bank Loan Market

Let's use an actual case to see how a total return swap can be employed in the bank loan market.[1] Consider the details of a 3-year swap on a term

---

[1] This illustration is an expanded discussion of a bank loan swap presented by Keith Barnish, Steve Miller, and Michael Rushmore in "The New Leveraged Loan Syndication Market," *The Journal of Applied Corporate Finance* (Spring 1997), pp. 79–88.

bank loan. A large AA insurance company purchased a 3-year total return swap on a $10 million piece of Riverwood International's Term Loan B. Term Loan B was actually a tranche of $250 million, but the insurance company only wanted credit exposure to a portion of the term loan.

This demonstrates one of the advantages of a credit derivative in general: customization. An investor may like the credit risk of a particular bank loan tranche, but may not have sufficient appetite for the whole loan. A total return credit swap allows the investor to choose a big or small piece of credit exposure depending on the investor's appetite for the credit risk. Furthermore, the term loan had a maturity of 10 years while the holding period horizon of the insurance company was three years. Therefore, the total return swap can accommodate the insurance company's investment horizon while the term loan does not.

The seller of the swap (i.e., the total return payer) was a large institutional bank. In order for the insurance company to purchase the total return swap, the bank effectively loaned the insurance company the $10 million notional amount of the swap. The bank in fact did not disburse $10 million to the insurance company, but instead charged the insurance company interest on $10 million dollars as if the bank had loaned the full amount. In this transaction, the bank charged the insurance company LIBOR + 75 bps. Since the insurance company's normal borrowing rate was 12.5 bps over LIBOR, the bank effectively charged the insurance company a swap processing fee of 62.5 bps, equivalent to $62,500 on an annual basis. In addition to the annual fee, the insurance company was required to put up $1 million of collateral as security for the effective loan. This $1 million was invested in U.S. Treasury securities.

In return for paying this fee, the insurance company received the total return on the Riverwood International term loan. The total return included the floating interest on the term loan of LIBOR + 300 bps plus any gain or loss in market value of the loan. In sum, the bank passed through the swap to the insurance company all of the interest payments and price risk as if the insurance company had the term loan on the asset side of its balance sheet.

The benefit to the insurance company was the net interest income earned on the swap. The insurance company agreed to pay LIBOR + 75 bps to the bank in return for LIBOR + 300 bps received from the Riverwood International term loan. The annual net interest income from the swap paid to the insurance company was:

$$\$10,000,000 \times [(\text{LIBOR} + 300 \text{ bps}) - (\text{LIBOR} + 75 \text{ bps})]$$
$$= \$10,000,000 \times 2.25\% = \$225,000$$

Provided that Riverwood International did not default on any portion of the term loan, the insurance company also received the interest income on the Treasury securities.

Why would the bank want to enter into this transaction? Perhaps, the bank bit off more than it wanted to chew when it purchased the full tranche from Riverwood International. The total return swap with the insurance company allowed the bank to reduce its credit exposure and collect a fee. In effect, the bank got paid to reduce its credit risk.

And what about the insurance company? Was this a good deal for it? The answer is yes if we consider the alternative to the total return swap. Assume, that instead of the total return swap, the insurance company could have purchased a $10 million portion of the Riverwood International term loan at its normal financing cost of LIBOR + 12.5 bps, held the term loan on its balance sheet for three years, and then sold it at the end of its holding period. The question we need to answer is which alternative provided a greater return: the total return swap, or the outright purchase of the term loan?

Exhibit 5.2 details the holding period returns to the two alternatives. In the first case, the insurance company borrows $1 million at its normal financing rate to purchase the Treasury security collateral and receives three annual net payments of $225,000 from the bank as well as interest income on the Treasury securities. Additionally, in year 3, the insurance company receives back the $1 million of collateral. These cash flows are discounted at the insurance company's cost of capital of 3-year LIBOR + 12.5 bps.

In the second case, the insurance company receives the full payment of LIBOR + 300 bps on the term loan, but must finance the full $10 million for three years. It receives an annual cash flow of $950,000, and sells its investment at the end of three years for $10 million.

To keep the analysis simple, assume that the insurance company bought a 3-year U.S. Treasury note as collateral with a maturity equal to the tenor of the swap and with an annual coupon of 6.00%, that 1-year LIBOR remains constant at 5.78125%, and that there is no change in value of the Riverwood International term loan. The discount rate for present value purposes is 5.90625% (LIBOR + 12.5 bps).

Under the swap, the insurance company will receive each year a cash flow of $225,000 from the bank and $60,000 from the Treasury note. In addition, in year 3, the insurance company will receive back its $1 million collateral contribution. Under the outright purchase of the term loan, the insurance company will receive each year a cash flow of $950,000. At the end of three years the insurance company sells the term loan in the market for its original investment of $10 million.

EXHIBIT 5.2   Investment Returns for a Total Return Bank Loan Credit Swap

Assumptions

Asset	$10,000,000 bank term loan
Maturity	Three years
1-year LIBOR	5.78125% (constant)
3-year Treasury	6.00%
Discount rate	5.90625%
Term loan value remains constant	

	Investment Alternatives	
	Credit Swap	Purchase Term Loan
Initial investment	($1,000,000)	($10,000,000)
Annual cash flows (loan value remains constant)		
Year 1	$285,000	$950,000
Year 2	285,000	950,000
Year 3	1,285,000	10,950,000
Present value of annual cash flows	$1,604,983	$10,961,833
Net present value	$604,983	$961,833
IRR	29%	9%
Initial investment	($1,000,000)	($10,000,000)
Annual cash flows (loan value declines by $1,000,000)		
Year 1	$285,000	$950,000
Year 2	285,000	950,000
Year 3	285,000	9,950,000
Present value of annual cash flows	$763,132	$10,120,431
Net present value	($236,868)	$120,431
IRR	-7%	6%

Exhibit 5.2 details these assumptions as well as a comparison of the cash flows for each alternative.

As can be seen from the exhibit, the outright purchase of the term loan results in a higher net present value than the total return swap. The net present value for the term loan is $961,833 and for the total return swap it is $604,983, a difference of $356,850. However, the total return swap requires a much smaller capital requirement than the outright purchase of the term loan. Even though the total return swap results in lower total cash flows, it provides an internal rate of return (IRR) which is three times greater than that of the term loan purchase.

This example demonstrates the use of leverage in a total return swap. The smaller capital commitment of the total return swap allows the insurance company to earn a higher rate of return on its investment than the outright purchase of the term loan. In fact, the leverage implicit in this total return swap is 10:1. Economically, the total return swap is more efficient because it allows the insurance company to access the returns of the bank loan market with a smaller required investment.

However, what if the value of the term loan had declined at the end of three years? Assume that over the 3-year holding period, the value of the Riverwood International bank loan declined in value to $9 million. With the total return swap arrangement, the $1 million loss in value would wipe out the posted collateral value. At the end of year three, the insurance company would receive only the cash flow from the interest income, $225,000 from the swap, and $60,000 in interest from the posted collateral.

Under the purchase scenario, the insurance company would receive back $9 million of its committed capital. Additionally, in each year the insurance company would receive the $950,000 interest income from the term loan. Exhibit 5.2 also compares the two investment choices under the assumption of a $1 million decline in loan value.

Under the total return swap, the net present value of the investment is now a negative $236,868. Conversely, a decline in loan value of $1 million still leaves the purchase scenario with a positive net present value of $120,431. Comparing the IRR on the two investments, we now see that the total return swap yields a negative IRR of –7%, while the purchase of the term loan yields a positive IRR of 6%—slightly more than the insurance company's cost of borrowed funds. Exhibit 5.2 demonstrates that the embedded leverage in the total return swap can be a double-edged sword. It can lead to large returns on capital, but can also result in rapid losses.

TOTAL RETURN INDEX SWAPS

Thus far our focus has been on a single reference asset. Total return index swaps are swaps where the reference asset is the return on a market index. The market index can be an equity index or a bond index. Our focus will be on bond indexes.

Broad-based bond market indexes such as the Lehman, Salomon Smith Barney, and Merrill Lynch indexes have subindexes that represent major sectors of the bond market. For example, there is the Treasury and agency sector, the credit sector (i.e., investment grade corporate bonds, at one time referred to as the corporate sector), the mortgage sector (consisting of agency residential mortgage-backed securities), the commercial mortgage-backed securities (CMBS) sector, and the asset-backed securities (ABS) sector. The non-Treasury sectors offer a spread to Treasuries and are hence referred to as "spread sectors." The spread in the mortgage sector is primarily compensation for the prepayment risk associated with investing in this sector. Spread to compensate for credit risk is offered in the credit spread sector, of course, and the CMBS and ABS sectors. There are also indexes available for other credit spread sectors of the bond market: high-yield corporate bond sector and emerging market bond sector. Thus, a total return index swap in which the underlying index is a credit spread sector allows an asset manager to gain or reduce exposure to that sector.

We conclude this chapter with a discussion of the flexibility offered asset managers and hedge fund managers by using total return swaps in which the index is a credit spread sector of the bond market.

Indexing a Credit Spread Sector by an Active Asset Manager

Bond portfolio strategies range from indexing to aggressive active strategies. The degree of active management can be quantified in terms of how much an asset manager deviates from the primary risk factors of the target index. A bond indexing strategy for a sector involves creating a portfolio so as to replicate the issues comprising the target sector's index. This means that the indexed portfolio is a mirror image of the target sector index or, put another way, that the *ex ante* tracking error is close to zero.

Why would an asset manager pursuing an active portfolio management strategy want to engage in an indexing strategy for a credit sector of the target index? Suppose that the asset manager's target index is the Lehman Brothers U.S. Aggregate Bond Index. Suppose further that the asset manager skills are such that she believes she can add value in the mortgage, CMBS, and ABS sectors but has no comparative advantage in the credit (corporate sector). The asset manager in this case can underweight the credit sector. However, the risk is that the credit sector will perform better than the other sectors in the target index and, as a result, the asset manager will underperform the target index. An alternative is to be neutral with respect to the credit sector and make active bets within the sectors of the target index that the asset manager believes value can be added. This approach requires that the asset manager follow an indexing strategy for the credit sector of the target index. However, in pursuing this strategy of creating a portfolio to replicate the credit sector, the asset manager will encounter several logistical problems.

First, the prices for each issue in the credit sector used by the organization that publishes the sector index may not be execution prices available to the asset manager. In fact, they may be materially different from the prices offered by some dealers. In addition, the prices used by organizations reporting the value of sector indexes are based on bid prices. Dealer ask prices, however, are the ones that the manager would have to transact at when constructing or rebalancing the indexed portfolio. Thus there will be a bias between the performance of the sector index and a portfolio that attempts to replicate the sector index that is equal to the bid-ask spread.

Furthermore, there are logistical problems unique to certain sectors in the bond market. For the credit sector, which consists of investment-grade corporate bonds, there are typically more than 4,000 issues. Because of the illiquidity for many of the issues, not only may the prices used by the organization that publishes the index be unreliable, but also many of the issues may not even be available.

Third, as bonds mature, their shrinking duration will force them out of this index. This will create natural turnover and higher transaction costs. Last, bonds pay consistent coupons that must be reinvested in the index.

In the absence of a total return swap, there are two methodologies that have been used to construct a portfolio to replicate the index representing the credit sector: stratified sampling methodology and the variance minimization methodology. With the stratified sampling approach (or also called the cellular approach) to indexing, the sector index is divided into cells representing the primary risk factors. The objective is then to select from all of the issues in the index one or more issues in each cell that can be used to represent that entire cell. The total dollar amount purchased of the issues from each cell will be based on the percentage of the index's total market value that the cell represents. For example, if X% of the market value of all the issues in the credit sector index is made up of single-A rated corporate bonds, then X% of the market value of the replicating portfolio should be composed of single-A rated corporate bond issues. The number of cells that the asset manager uses will depend on the dollar amount of the portfolio to be indexed. In indexing a portfolio of less than $50 million, for example, using a large number of cells would require purchasing odd lots of issues. This increases the cost of buying the issues to represent a cell, and thus would increase the *ex ante* tracking error. Reducing the number of cells to overcome this problem increases *ex ante* tracking error because the major risk factors of the indexed portfolio may differ materially from those of the index. For corporate bonds, for example, there is the concern of downgrade risk of individual corporate issues that would adversely affect tracking error. Exhibit 5.3 shows the findings of

EXHIBIT 5.3   Risk due to Downgrades as a Function of Portfolio Size—by Credit Quality

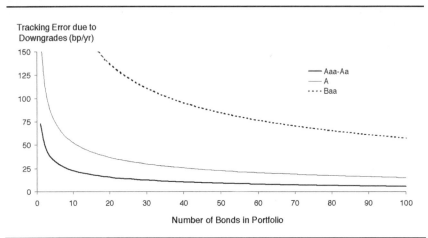

Source: Exhibit 14 in Lev Dynkin, Jay Hyman, and Vadim Konstantinovsky, "Sufficient Diversification in Credit Portfolios," *Journal of Portfolio Management* (Fall 2002), p. 100.

a Lehman Brothers study that demonstrates how many issues must be purchased to minimize tracking error due to downgrade risk.[2] As can be seen, if only a few issues are selected tracking error is high.

The variance minimization methodology is a more complicated approach than stratified sampling. This approach requires using historical data to estimate the variance of the tracking error for each issue in the index. The objective then is to minimize the variance of the tracking error in constructing the replicating portfolio.

The more efficient solution may be simply to use an total return index swap where the credit sector to be indexed is the underlying index for the swap.

Active Strategies

Active bond portfolio strategies involve constructing a portfolio that deviates from the target index. There are various strategies that can be employed. For example, one strategy is to construct a portfolio that is intentionally different from the duration of the target index based on the view of the asset manager regarding future interest rates. Another is to overweight a sector of the index based on the asset manager's view of

---

[2] Lev Dynkin, Jay Hyman, and Vadim Konstantinovsky, "Sufficient Diversification in Credit Portfolios," *Journal of Portfolio Management* (Fall 2002), pp. 89–114.

the relative performance of the sectors comprising the index. For example, if the credit sector is expected to outperform the other sectors, an asset manager may wish to overweight that sector. The asset manager can monetize this view by entering into a total return swap as the total return receiver. Again, as noted earlier, this is an efficient way to replicate the performance of the index.

Hedge funds manager can use total return swaps to create leverage in the same way described earlier when we showed how a synthetic repo can be created for a credit-risky bond. Moreover, suppose instead that a hedge fund manager believes that the credit sector will have a negative return. The manager can monetize this view by selling a total return swap. The advantage of the total return swap is that the credit sector can be shorted, a task that is extremely difficult and costly to do for individual bond issues in the credit sector.

Risk Control

Total return swaps can be sued as effective risk control instruments. Interest rate swaps can be used to control the duration of the portfolio. Total return swaps can be used to control the spread duration of a portfolio and, more specifically, the credit spread duration of a portfolio, that is the sensitivity of a portfolio to changes in credit spreads. Hedging a position with respect to credit spread risk means creating a cash and total return swap position whereby the credit spread duration is zero. An asset manager would want to hedge a portfolio that has exposure to credit spread risk if the credit spread duration of the portfolio differs from that of the target index. Total return swaps can be used to bring the portfolio's credit spread risk duration in line with the credit spread risk of the target index.

APPENDIX: THE VALUATION OF TOTAL RETURN SWAPS

In this appendix we explain the valuation of total return swaps. We begin with an intuitive approach.

An Intuitive Approach

A typical total return swap is to swap the return on a reference asset for a risk-free return, usually LIBOR. The cash flows for the swap buyer (i.e., the total return receiver) are shown in Exhibit 5.4. In the exhibit L_t LIBOR at time t, s is the spread to LIBOR, and R_t is the total return at time t. The cash flow outlay at time t per $1 of notional amount that

EXHIBIT 5.4   Cash Flows for the Total Return Receiver

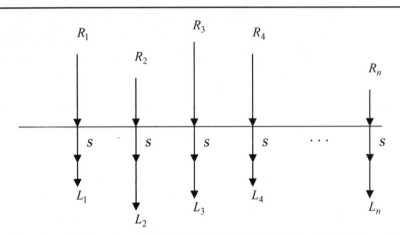

must be made by the swap buyer is $L_t + s$; the cash flow inflow at time t per \$1 of notional amount is R_t.

As a result, the pricing of total return swap is to decide the right spread, s, to pay on the fund (i.e., LIBOR) leg. Formally,

$$\hat{E}_0\left\{\sum_{j=1}^{n}\exp\left(-\int_0^{T_j}r(t)dt\right)[R_j-(L_j+s)]\right\}=0$$

where r is the risk-free discount rate.

In words, the spread should be set so that the expected payoffs of the total return swap the next cash flow is equal to zero.[3] To make the matter simple (we shall discuss more rigorous cases later), we view r, R, and L as three separate random variables. We then rearrange the above equation as

$$\hat{E}_0\left\{\sum_{j=1}^{n}\exp\left(-\int_0^{T_j}r(t)dt\right)(R_j-L_j)\right\}=\hat{E}_0\left\{\sum_{j=1}^{n}\exp\left(-\int_0^{T_j}r(t)dt\right)s\right\}$$

Exchange expectation and summation of the right-hand side gives

---

[3] We employ the standard risk-neutral pricing and discounting at the risk-free rate.

$$\hat{E}_0\left\{\sum_{j=1}^{n}\exp\left(-\int_0^{T_j}r(t)dt\right)\right\} = \sum_{j=1}^{n}\hat{E}_0\left[\exp\left(-\int_0^{T_j}r(t)dt\right)\right]$$

$$= \sum_{j=1}^{n}P(0, T_j)$$

as the sum of risk-free pure discount bond prices. This implies

$$\sum_{j=1}^{n}\hat{E}_0\left[\exp\left(-\int_0^{T_j}r(t)dt\right)R_j - L_j\right] = \sum_{j=1}^{n}P(0, T_j)s$$

The next step is to use the forward measure to simplify the left-hand side of the above equation:

$$\sum_{j=1}^{n}P(0, T_j)E_0^{F(j)}[R_j - L_j] = \sum_{j=1}^{n}P(0, T_j)s$$

Later we show that the forward measure expectation of an asset gives the forward price of the asset. Hence, the left-hand side of the above equation gives two forward curves, one on the asset return, R and the other on the LIBOR, L:

$$\sum_{j=1}^{n}P(0, T_j)[f_j^R - f_j^L] = \sum_{j=1}^{n}P(0, T_j)s$$

where f_j^i is the forward rate of i ($i = R$ or L) for j periods ahead. Therefore, the spread can be solved easily as

$$s = \frac{\sum_{j=1}^{n}P(0, T_j)[f_j^R - f_j^L]}{\sum_{j=1}^{n}P(0, T_j)}$$

The result intuitive: the spread is a weighted average of the expected difference between two floating-rate indexes. The weight is

$$\frac{P(0, T_j)}{\sum_{j=1}^{n} P(0, T_j)}$$

Note that all the weights should sum to one.

Using the Duffie-Singleton Model

The difference in two floating-rates is mainly due to their credit risk, otherwise they should both offer identical rates and give identical forward curves. As a consequence, to be rigorous about getting the correct result, we need to incorporate the credit risk in one of the indices.

Among various choices, the reduced form Duffie-Singleton model suits the best for this situation.[4] The Duffie-Singleton model that will be discussed in Chapters 9 and 10 defines the present value of any risky cash flow as

$$c_t = \left[\frac{S_{t+1} - S_t}{S_t} - L_{t+1} \right] N$$

where N is the notional, L is the LIBOR rate, S is the index level. As noted earlier, since both cash flows are random, it is a floating-floating swap. Also since the index is always higher than LIBOR because of credit risk, this swap requires a premium. As a result, the premium is computed as the sum of all future values, discounted and expected:

$$V = \sum_{j=1}^{n} E\left[\exp\left(\int_t^{T_j} [r(u) + q(u)] du \right) c_{T_j} \right]$$

where q is the "spread" in the Duffie-Singleton model that incorporates the recovery rate and default probability.

The Forward Measure

In this section, we show how the forward measure works and why a forward-adjusted expectation gives the forward value. We first state the

---

[4] Darrell Duffie and Kenneth Singleton, "Modeling the Term Structure of Defaultable Bonds," working paper, Stanford University (1997).

separation principle that leads to the forward measure. Based on the no-arbitrage principle, the current value of any asset is the risk-neutral expected value of the discounted future payoff:

$$C(t) = \hat{E}_t\left[\exp\left(-\int_t^T r(u)du\right)C(T)\right]$$

Separation principle states that if we adopt the forward measure, then the above equation can be written as

$$C(t) = \hat{E}_t\left[\exp\left(-\int_t^T r(u)du\right)C(T)\right]E_t^{F(T)}[C(T)]$$

where $E_t^{F(T)}[\cdot]$ is the forward measure. The derivation of this result can be found in a number of places.[5] Note that the first term is nothing but the zero coupon bond price:

$$P(t, T) = \hat{E}_t\left[\exp\left(-\int_t^T r(u)du\right)\right]$$

and hence

$$C(t) = P(t, T)E_t^{F(T)}[C(t)]$$

While we do not prove this result, we should note an intuition behind it. Let C be a zero coupon bond expiring at time u. Then the above result can be applied directly and gives

$$P(t, s) = P(t, T)E_t^{F(T)}[P(T, u)]$$

or equivalently

$$E_t^{F(T)}[P(T, s)] = \frac{P(t, s)}{P(t, T)}$$

---

[5] See: Farshid Jamshidian, "Pricing of Contingent Claims in the One Factor Term Structure Model," Merrill Lynch Capital Market, 1987; and Ren-Raw Chen, *Understanding and Managing Interest Rate Risks* (Singapore: World Scientific Publishing Company, 1996).

This is an indirect proof that the forward-adjusted expectation gives a forward value. The instantaneous forward rate can be shown to be the forward-adjusted expectation of the future instantaneous spot rate:

$$f(t, T) = -\frac{d \ln P(t, T)}{dT}$$

$$= -\frac{1}{P(t, T)} \hat{E}_t \left[\frac{d}{dT} \exp\left(-\int_t^T r(u) \, du \right) \right]$$

$$= \frac{1}{P(t, T)} \hat{E}_t \left[\exp\left(-\int_t^T r(u) \, du \right) r(T) \right]$$

$$= E_t^{F(T)} [r(T)]$$

The discrete forward rates, $f_D(t,w,T)$ for all w and T can be shown also as the forward-adjusted expectations of future discrete spot rates:

$$f_D(t, w, T) \equiv \frac{1}{\Psi(t, w, T)} - 1$$

$$= \frac{P(t, w)}{P(t, T)} - 1$$

$$= \frac{1}{P(t, T)} \hat{E}_t \left[\exp\left(-\int_t^T r(u) \, du \right) \frac{1}{P(w, T)} \right] - 1$$

$$= E_t^{F(T)} \left[\frac{1}{P(w, T)} - 1 \right]$$

where $t < w < T$.

CHAPTER 6

Credit-Linked Notes

Credit derivatives are grouped into *funded* and *unfunded* variants. In an unfunded credit derivative, typified by a credit default swap, the protection seller does not make an upfront payment to the protection buyer. In a funded credit derivative, typified by a credit-linked note (CLN), the investor in the note is the credit-protection seller and is making an upfront payment to the protection buyer when buying the note. Thus, the protection buyer is the issuer of the note. If no credit event occurs during the life of the note, the redemption value of the note is paid to the investor on maturity. If a credit event does occur, then on maturity a value less than par will be paid out to the investor. This value will be reduced by the nominal value of the reference asset that the CLN is linked to. In this chapter we discuss CLNs.

DESCRIPTION OF CLNS

Credit-linked notes exist in a number of forms, but all of them contain a link between the return they pay and the credit-related performance of the underlying asset. A standard CLN is a security, usually issued by an investment-graded entity, that has an interest payment and fixed maturity structure similar to a vanilla bond. The performance of the CLN, however, including the maturity value, is linked to the performance of a specified underlying asset or assets as well as that of the issuing entity. CLNs are usually issued at par. They are often used as a financing vehicle by borrowers in order to hedge against credit risk; CLNs are purchased by investors to enhance the yield received on their holdings. Hence, the issuer of the CLN is the protection buyer and the buyer of the note is the protection seller.

EXHIBIT 6.1   Bloomberg Screen SND: Definition of Credit-Linked Note

```
GRAB                                                       Mtge   SND
                                                        Page 11/ 12
Credit Linked Notes (CLN): A hybrid debt security that offers investors a
synthetic credit exposure to a specified Reference Entity or basket of
Reference Entities. This credit exposure can be gained through a variety of
methods including (but not limited to): a credit default swap, a credit
spread swap, a total return swap, or as a repackaged note where the issuer
passes through the risk of an underlying credit to the noteholder in exchange
for an enhanced return. For example, a note might provide for its principal
repayment to be reduced below par in the event that a reference obligation
defaults.
20) Example: EC771465 <CORP> DES. A note that is linked to the credit of
             Sodexho Alliance SA. Following a credit event on the underlying
             reference obligation, this note will be redeemed early at
             less than par.
Repackaged Notes: A debt instrument secured by an underlying asset where the
cashflows of that asset are reprofiled through a derivative contract while
the credit risk is passed through to the investor of the Repackaged Note.
21) Example: EC785183 <CORP> DES. A note that is secured by Roche Holdings
             convertible notes and a swap agreement. Following an event of
             default on all or part of the underlying, this note will be
             redeemed early at an amount based on the underlying.
             Page <FWD> for FFIEC 034 Structured Note Call Reporting Revision
Australia 61 2 9777 8600      Brazil 5511 3048 4500     Europe 44 20 7330 7500      Germany 49 69 920410
Hong Kong 852 2977 6000 Japan 81 3 3201 8900 Singapore 65 6212 1000 U.S. 1 212 318 2000 Copyright 2003 Bloomberg L.P.
                                                                    H021-57-0 30-May-03 11:38:24
```

Source: © Bloomberg L.P. Used with permission.

Essentially CLNs are hybrid instruments that combine a pure credit risk exposure with a vanilla bond. The CLN pays regular coupons; however the credit derivative element is usually set to allow the issuer to decrease the principal amount, and/or the coupon interest, if a specified credit event occurs.

Exhibit 6.1 shows a Bloomberg screen SND and its definition of the CLN.

To illustrate a CLN, consider a bank issuer of credit cards that wants to fund its credit card loan portfolio via an issue of debt. The bank is rated AA–. In order to reduce the credit risk of the loans, it issues a two-year CLN. The principal amount of the bond is 100 (par) as usual, and it pays a coupon of 7.50%, which is 200 bps above the two-year benchmark. The equivalent spread for a vanilla bond issued by a bank of this rating would be of the order of 120 bps. With the CLN though, if the incidence of bad debt amongst credit card holders exceeds 10% then the terms state that note holders will only receive back 85 per 100 par. The credit card issuer has in effect purchased a credit option that lowers its liability in the event that it suffers from a specified credit event, which in this case is an above-expected incidence of bad debts.

The cost of this credit option to the credit protection buyer is paid in the form of a higher coupon payment on the CLN. The credit card bank has issued the CLN to reduce its credit exposure, in the form of this particular type of credit insurance. If the incidence of bad debts is low, the CLN is redeemed at par. However if there a high incidence of such debt, the bank will only have to repay a part of its loan liability.

Investors may wish purchase the CLN because the coupon paid on it will be above what the credit card bank would pay on a vanilla bond it issued, and higher than other comparable investments in the market. In addition such notes are usually priced below par on issue. Assuming the notes are eventually redeemed at par, investors will also have realized a substantial capital gain.

As with credit default swaps, CLNs may be specified under cash settlement or physical settlement. Specifically:

- Under cash settlement, if a credit event has occurred, on maturity the protection seller receives the difference between the value of the initial purchase proceeds and the value of the reference asset at the time of the credit event.
- Under physical settlement, on occurrence of a credit event, the note is terminated. At maturity the protection buyer delivers the reference asset or an asset among a list of deliverable assets, and the protection seller receives the value of the original purchase proceeds minus the value of the asset that has been delivered.

Exhibit 6.2 illustrates a cash-settled CLN.

CLNs may be issued directly by a financial or corporate entity or via a Special Purpose Vehicle (SPV). They have been issued with the form of credit-linking taking on one or more of a number of different guises. For instance, a CLN may have its return performance linked to the issuer's, or a specified reference entity's, credit rating, risk exposure, financial performance or circumstance of default. Exhibit 6.3 shows Bloomberg screen CLN and a list of the various types of CLN issue that have been made. Exhibit 6.4 shows a page accessed from Bloomberg screen "CLN," which is a list of CLNs that have had their coupon affected by a change in the reference entity's credit rating.

Many CLNs are issued directly by banks and corporate borrowers, in the same way as conventional bonds. An example of such a bond is shown at Exhibit 6.5. This shows Bloomberg screen DES for a CLN issued by British Telecom plc, the 8.125% note due in December 2010. The terms of this note state that the coupon will increase by 25 bps for each one-notch rating downgrade below A–/A3 suffered by the issuer during the life of the note. The coupon will decrease by 25 bps for each

EXHIBIT 6.2   Credit-Linked Note

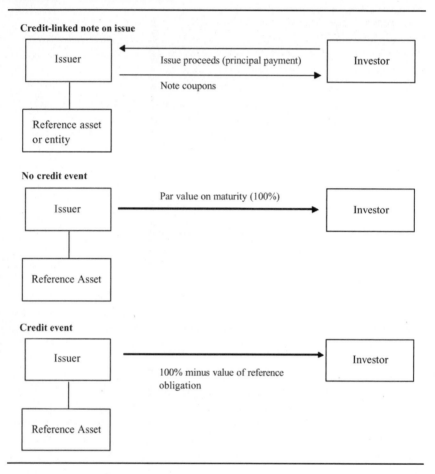

ratings upgrade, with a minimum coupon set at 8.125%. In other words, this note allows investors to take on a credit play on the fortunes of the issuer.

Exhibit 6.6 shows Bloomberg screen YA for this note, as at May 29, 2003. We see that a rating downgrade meant that the coupon on the note was now 8.375%.

Exhibit 6.7 is the Bloomberg DES page for a U.S. dollar denominated CLN issued directly by Household Finance Corporation (HFC).[1] Like the British Telecom bond, this is a CLN whose return is linked to the credit risk of the issuer, but in a different way. The coupon of the

---
[1] HFC was subsequently acquired by HSBC.

EXHIBIT 6.3 Bloomberg Screen CLN

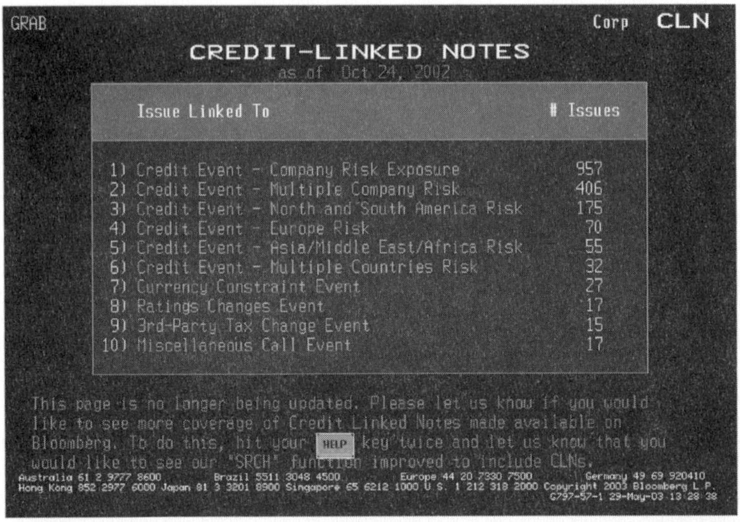

GRAB Corp CLN

CREDIT-LINKED NOTES

as of Oct 24, 2002

Issue Linked To	# Issues
1) Credit Event - Company Risk Exposure	957
2) Credit Event - Multiple Company Risk	406
3) Credit Event - North and South America Risk	175
4) Credit Event - Europe Risk	70
5) Credit Event - Asia/Middle East/Africa Risk	55
6) Credit Event - Multiple Countries Risk	32
7) Currency Constraint Event	27
8) Ratings Changes Event	17
9) 3rd-Party Tax Change Event	15
10) Miscellaneous Call Event	17

This page is no longer being updated. Please let us know if you would like to see more coverage of Credit Linked Notes made available on Bloomberg. To do this, hit your HELP key twice and let us know that you would like to see our "SRCH" function improved to include CLNs.

Australia 61 2 9777 8600 Brazil 5511 3048 4500 Europe 44 20 7330 7500 Germany 49 69 920410
Hong Kong 852 2977 6000 Japan 81 3 3201 8900 Singapore 65 6212 1000 U.S. 1 212 318 2000 Copyright 2003 Bloomberg L.P.
G797-57-1 29-May-03 13:28:38

Source: © Bloomberg L.P. Used with permission.

EXHIBIT 6.4 Bloomberg Screen Showing a Sample of CLNs Impacted by Change in Reference Entity Credit Rating, October 2002

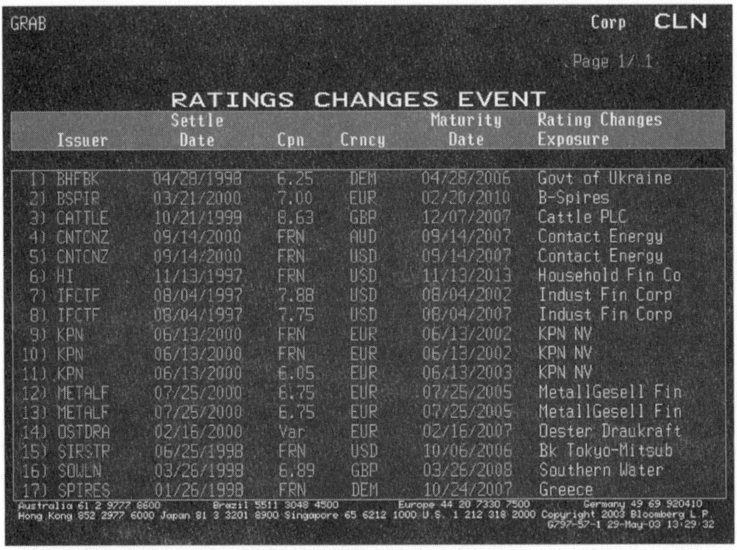

GRAB Corp CLN

Page 1/1

RATINGS CHANGES EVENT

Issuer	Settle Date	Cpn	Crncy	Maturity Date	Rating Changes Exposure
1) BHFBK	04/28/1998	6.25	DEM	04/28/2006	Govt of Ukraine
2) BSPIR	03/21/2000	7.00	EUR	02/20/2010	B-Spires
3) CATTLE	10/21/1999	6.63	GBP	12/07/2007	Cattle PLC
4) CNTCNZ	09/14/2000	FRN	AUD	09/14/2007	Contact Energy
5) CNTCNZ	09/14/2000	FRN	USD	09/14/2007	Contact Energy
6) HI	11/13/1997	FRN	USD	11/13/2013	Household Fin Co
7) IFCTF	08/04/1997	7.88	USD	08/04/2002	Indust Fin Corp
8) IFCTF	08/04/1997	7.75	USD	08/04/2007	Indust Fin Corp
9) KPN	06/13/2000	FRN	EUR	06/13/2002	KPN NV
10) KPN	06/13/2000	FRN	EUR	06/13/2002	KPN NV
11) KPN	06/13/2000	6.05	EUR	06/13/2003	KPN NV
12) METALF	07/25/2000	6.75	EUR	07/25/2005	MetallGesell Fin
13) METALF	07/25/2000	6.75	EUR	07/25/2005	MetallGesell Fin
14) OSTDRA	02/16/2000	Var	EUR	02/16/2007	Oester Draukraft
15) SIRSTR	06/25/1998	FRN	USD	10/06/2006	Bk Tokyo-Mitsub
16) SOWLN	03/26/1998	6.89	GBP	03/26/2008	Southern Water
17) SPIRES	01/26/1998	FRN	DEM	10/24/2007	Greece

Australia 61 2 9777 8600 Brazil 5511 3048 4500 Europe 44 20 7330 7500 Germany 49 69 920410
Hong Kong 852 2977 6000 Japan 81 3 3201 8900 Singapore 65 6212 1000 U.S. 1 212 318 2000 Copyright 2003 Bloomberg L.P.
G797-57-1 29-May-03 13:29:32

Source: © Bloomberg L.P. Used with permission.

EXHIBIT 6.5 Bloomberg Screen DES for British Telecom plc 8.125% 2010 Credit-Linked Note Issued on December 5, 2000

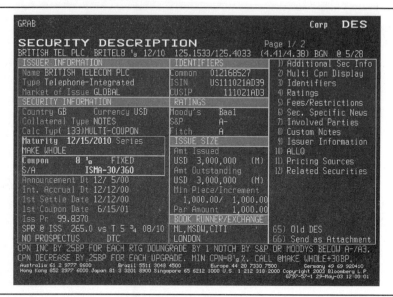

Source: © Bloomberg L.P. Used with permission.

EXHIBIT 6.6 Bloomberg Screen YA for British Telecom CLN, May 29, 2003

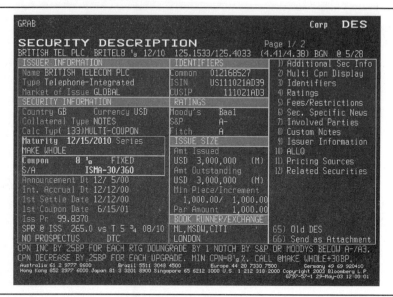

Source: © Bloomberg L.P. Used with permission.

EXHIBIT 6.7   Bloomberg DES Screen for Household Finance Corporation CLN

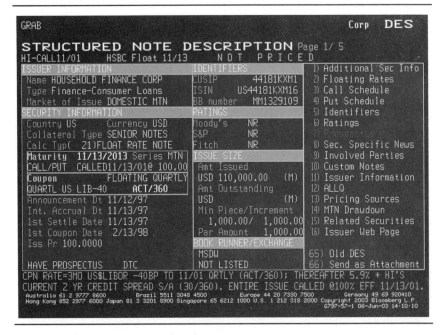

Source: © Bloomberg L.P. Used with permission.

HFC bond was issued as floating USD-LIBOR, but in the event of the bond not being called by November 2001, the coupon would be the issuer's two-year "credit spread" over a fixed rate of 5.9%. In fact, the issuer called the bond with effect from the coupon change date. Exhibit 6.8 shows the Bloomberg screen YA for the bond and how its coupon remained as at first issue until the call date.

Another type of credit-linking is evidenced from Exhibit 6.9, the Ford CLN Bloomberg DES page. This is a Japanese yen-denominated bond issued by Alpha-Spires, which is a medium-term note program vehicle (a SPV) set up by Merrill Lynch. The note itself is linked to the credit quality of Ford Motor Credit. In the event of a default of the reference name, the note will be called immediately. Exhibit 6.10 shows the rate fixing for this note as at the last coupon date. The screen snapshot was taken on June 6, 2003.

Structured products such as synthetic collateralized debt obligations (CDOs) described in Chapter 7 may combine both CLNs and credit default swaps, to meet issuer and investor requirements. For instance, Exhibit 6.11 shows a credit structure designed to provide a higher return for an investor on comparable risk to the cash market. An issuing

EXHIBIT 6.8 Bloomberg YA Screen for Household Finance Corporation CLN, June 6, 2003

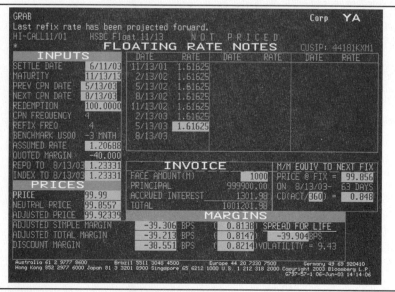

Source: © Bloomberg L.P. Used with permission.

EXHIBIT 6.9 Bloomberg DES Screen for Ford CLN

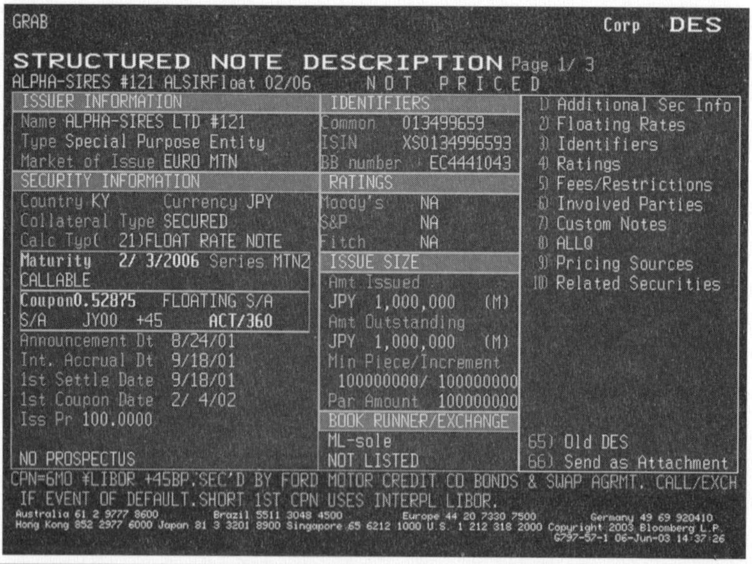

Source: © Bloomberg L.P. Used with permission.

EXHIBIT 6.10   Bloomberg YA Screen for Ford CLN, June 6, 2003

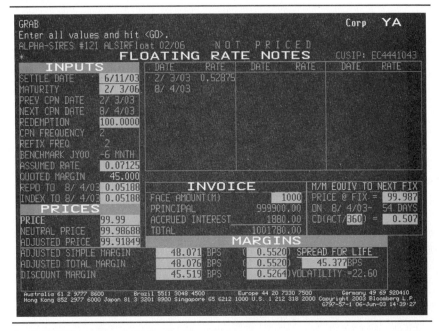

Source: © Bloomberg L.P. Used with permission.

EXHIBIT 6.11   CLN and Credit Default Swap Structure on Single Reference Name

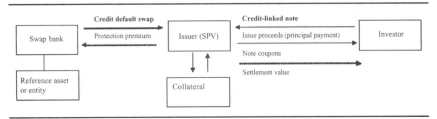

entity is set up in the form of a special purpose vehicle (SPV) which issues CLNs to the market. The structure is engineered so that the SPV has a neutral position on a reference asset. It has bought protection on a single reference name by issuing a funded credit derivative, the CLN, and simultaneously sold protection on this name by selling a credit default swap on this name. The proceeds of the CLN are invested in risk-free collateral such as Treasury bills or a Treasury bank account. The coupon on the CLN will be a spread over LIBOR. It is backed by the collateral account and the fee generated by the SPV in selling protection with the credit default swap. Investors in the CLN will have exposure to the reference asset or entity, and the repayment of the CLN is linked to the performance of the reference entity. If a credit event occurs, the maturity date of the CLN is brought forward and the note is settled as par minus the value of the reference asset or entity.

THE FIRST-TO-DEFAULT CREDIT-LINKED NOTE

A standard CLN is issued in reference to one specific bond or loan. An investor purchasing such a note is writing credit protection on a specific reference credit. A CLN that is linked to more than one reference credit is known as a *basket credit-linked note*. A development of the CLN as a structured product is the First-to-Default CLN (FtD), which is a CLN that is linked to a basket of reference assets. The investor in the CLN is selling protection on the first credit to default.[2] Exhibit 6.12 shows this progression in the development of CLNs as structured products, with the *fully-funded synthetic CDO*, described in Chapter 7, being the vehicle that uses CLNs tied to a large basket of reference assets.

An FtD CLN is a funded credit derivative in which the investor sells protection on one reference in a basket of assets, whichever is the first to default. The return on the CLN is a multiple of the average spread of the basket. The CLN will mature early on occurrence of a credit event relating to any of the reference assets. Settlement on the CLN can be either of the following:

- Physical settlement, with the defaulted asset(s) being delivered to the noteholder.
- Cash settlement, in which the CLN issuer pays redemption proceeds to the noteholder calculated as

$$\text{Principal amount} \times \text{Reference asset recovery value}$$

EXHIBIT 6.12   Progression of CLN Development

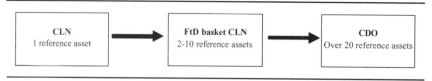

---

[2] "Default" here meaning a credit event as defined in the ISDA definitions.

EXHIBIT 6.13 First-to-Default CLN Structure

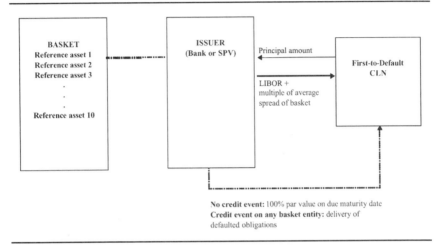

No credit event: 100% par value on due maturity date
Credit event on any basket entity: delivery of
defaulted obligations

In practice, it is not the "recovery value" that is used but the market value of the reference asset at the time the credit event is verified. Recovery of a defaulted asset follows a legal process of administration and/or liquidation that can take some years, and so the final recovery value may not be known with certainty for some time. Because the computation of recovery value is so difficult, holders of a CLN may prefer physical settlement where they take delivery of the defaulted asset.

Exhibit 6.13 shows a generic FtD credit-linked note.

To illustrate, consider an FtD CLN issued at par with a term-to-maturity of five years and linked to a basket of five reference assets with a face value (issued nominal amount) of $10 million. An investor purchasing this note will pay $10 million to the issuer. If no credit event occurs during the life of the note, the investor will receive the face value of the note on maturity. If a credit event occurs on any of the assets in the basket, the note will redeem early and the issuer will deliver a deliverable obligation of the reference entity, or a portfolio of such obligations, for a $10 million nominal amount. An FtD CLN carries a similar amount of risk exposure on default to a standard CLN, namely the recovery rate of the defaulted credit. However its risk exposure prior to default is theoretically lower than a standard CLN, as it can reduce default probability through diversification. The investor can obtain exposure to a basket of reference entities that differ by industrial sector and by credit rating.

The matrix shown in Exhibit 6.14 illustrate how an investor can select a credit mix in the basket that diversifies risk exposure across a wide range—we show a hypothetical mix of reference assets to which an

EXHIBIT 6.14   Diversified Credit Exposure to Basket of Reference Assets: Hypothetical Reference Asset Mix

	Automobiles	Banks	Electronics	Insurance	Media	Telecoms	Utilities
AAA							
Aa1							
Aa2				SunAlliance			
Aa3		RBoS					
A1							
A2							Powergen
A3	Ford					British Telecom	
Baa1			Philips		News Intl		
Baa2							
Baa3							

issued FtD could be linked. The precise selection of names will reflect investors' own risk/return profile requirements.

The FtD CLN creates a synthetic credit entity that features a note return with enhanced spread. Investors receive a spread over LIBOR that is the average return of all the reference assets in the basket. This structure serves to diversify credit risk exposure while benefiting from a higher average return. If the pool of reference assets is sufficiently large, the structure becomes similar to a single-tranche CDO. This is discussed in Chapter 7.

CHAPTER 7

Synthetic Collateralized Debt Obligation Structures

The collateralized debt obligation (CDO), first introduced in 1988, was a natural advancement of securitization technology. A CDO is essentially a structured finance product in which a distinct legal entity known as a *special purpose vehicle* (SPV)[1] issues bonds or notes against an investment in cash flows of an underlying pool of assets. These assets can be bonds, commercial bank loans or a mixture of both bonds and loans. Originally CDOs were developed as repackaging structures for high-yield bonds and illiquid instruments such as certain convertible bonds, but they have developed into sophisticated investment management vehicles in their own right. Through the 1990s, CDOs were the fastest growing asset class in the asset-backed securities market, due to a number of features that made them attractive to issuers and investors alike. A subsequent development was the *synthetic* CDO, a structure that uses credit derivatives in its construction and is therefore called a *structured credit product*. The synthetic CDO structure is the subject of this chapter. We begin with a review of CDOs.

REVIEW OF COLLATERALIZED DEBT OBLIGATIONS

A *cash flow* CDO structure is represented by an issue of the notes whose interest and principal payments are linked to the performance of the underlying assets of the structure. These underlying assets are the *collat-*

---

[1] A special purpose vehicle is also referred to as a *special purpose entity* (SPE) or *special purpose company* (SPC).

eral for the issued notes, hence the name. There are many similarities between CDOs and other asset-backed securities (ABS), which predated them. The key difference between CDOs and other ABS and multiasset repackaged securities is that the collateral pool in a CDO is generally (though not always) actively managed by a collateral portfolio manager.

Generally, CDOs feature a multitranche overlying note structure, with most or all of the notes being rated by one or more rating agency. The priority of payment of the issued securities reflects the credit rating for each note, with the most senior note being the highest rated. The term *waterfall* is used to refer to the order of cash flow payments. Sufficient underlying cash flows must be generated by the issuing vehicle in order to meet the fees of third-party agency servicers and all the note issue liabilities. The issued securities may pay a fixed or floating coupon, usually on a semi-annual, quarterly, or monthly basis, with senior note issues rated from AAA to A and junior and mezzanine notes rated BBB to B. There may be unrated subordinated and *equity* pieces issued. The equity note is actually a bond, and represents the shareholding interest in the vehicle; it's return is variable and linked to the performance of the collateral pool. Investors in the subordinated notes receive their coupon after payment of servicing fees and the coupon on senior notes.

The equity and subordinated note are the first loss pieces and, as they carry the highest risk, have a higher expected return compared to that of the underlying collateral. The most junior note is called the *first loss* piece because any losses suffered by the vehicle, which reduces the vehicle's ability to fully service its liabilities, will impact the junior note first. This follows traditional securitization technology and is a natural result of the tranching of the notes into an order of seniority. The first loss piece will be the lowest rated note, or (as is common with CDO structures), an unrated note. The principal value of the first loss note is reduced to cover losses on the structure, up to its par value, after which further losses will then be taken out of the next junior note. Equity note tranches in CDOs have a more volatile risk-reward profile then the other note tranches, because they are the first loss piece and also because they receive any surplus cash generated by the vehicle.

There are two types of CDOs, *collateralized bond obligations* (CBOs) and *collateralized loan obligations* (CLOs). As the names suggest, the primary difference between each type is the nature of the underlying assets; a CBO will be collateralized by a portfolio of bonds while a CLO will represent an underlying pool of bank loans. Following this distinction, CDOs can be broken into two main types, *balance sheet* CDOs and *arbitrage* CDOs. Balance sheet CDOs are most akin to a traditional securitization; they are created to remove assets from the balance sheet of the originator, usually a bank, in order to reduce regulatory capital requirements, increase return on capital or free up lending lines. An arbitrage CDO is created when the originator, who may be a bank or fund manager, wishes to exploit a yield differential existing between the underlying assets and the overlying notes. This may be achieved by active management of the underlying portfolio, which might consist of high-yielding or emerging market bonds. Arbitrage CDOs are categorized further into *cash flow* and *market value* CDOs. Almost invariably balance sheet CDOs are cash flow transactions. Put simply, a cash flow CDO is one in which the underlying collateral generates sufficient cash flow to pay the principal and interest on the issued notes, as well as the servicing fees of third-party agents. In a market value CDO, the collateral manager actively runs the portfolio and, by means of this trading activity, generates sufficient returns to pay the CDO obligations. The underlying securities are marked-to-market on a daily basis in the same manner as a trading book.

Banks and financial institutions use CDOs to diversify their sources of funding, to manage portfolio risk, and to obtain regulatory capital relief. Investors are attracted to the senior notes in a transaction because these allow them to earn relatively high yields compared to other asset-backed bonds of a similar credit rating. Other advantages for investors include:

- Exposure to a diversified range of credits.
- Access to the fund management and credit analysis skills of the portfolio manager.
- Generally, a lower level of uncertainty and risk exposure compared to a single bond of similar rating.

Cash Flow CDO Structures

Generally cash flow CDOs will be categorized as either balance sheet or arbitrage deals. Arbitrage CDOs are further categorized as cash flow or market value deals. A later development, the *synthetic* CDO, now accounts for a growing number of transactions. We show a "family tree" of CDOs in Exhibit 7.1.

Cash Flow CDO

Cash flow CDOs are similar to other asset-backed securitizations involving an SPV. Bonds or loans are pooled together and the cash flows from these assets used to back the liabilities of the notes issued by the SPV into the market. As the underlying assets are sold to the SPV, they are removed from the originator's balance sheet; hence the credit risk associated with these assets is transferred to the holders of the issued notes. The originator also obtains funding by issuing the notes. The generic structure is illustrated at Exhibit 7.2.

EXHIBIT 7.1　The CDO Family

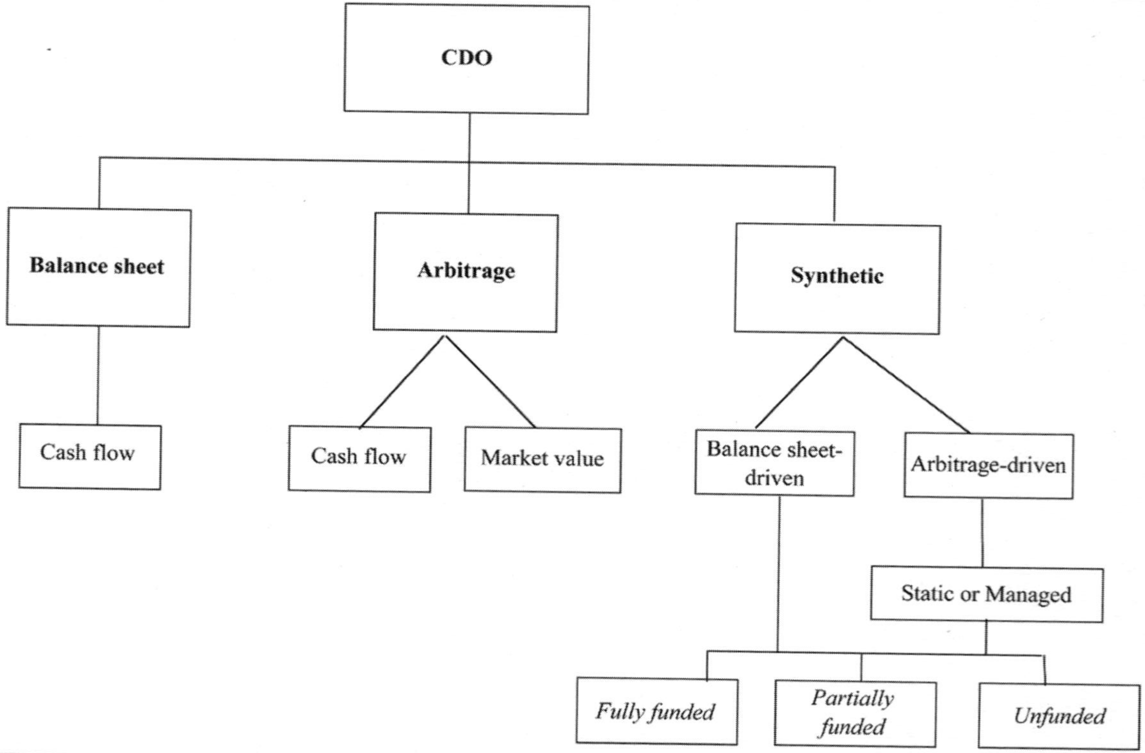

EXHIBIT 7.2 Generic Cash Flow CDO

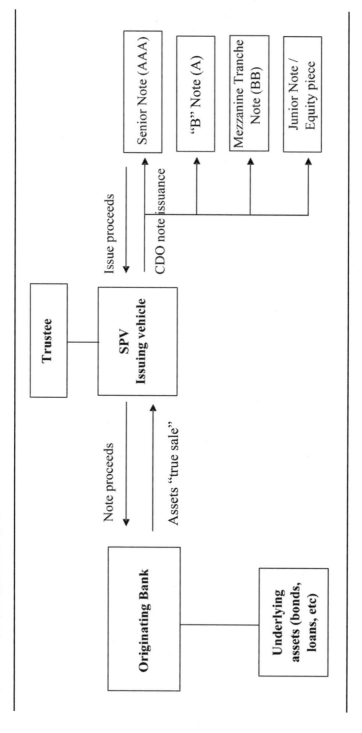

Banks and other financial institutions are the primary originators of *balance sheet CDOs*. These are deals securitizing banking assets such as commercial loans of investment grade or subinvestment grade rating. The main motivations for entering into this arrangement are to:

- Obtain regulatory relief.
- Increase return on capital via the removal of lower yielding assets from the balance sheet.
- Secure alternative and/or cheaper sources of funding.
- Free up lending capacity with respect to an industry or group of borrowers.

Investors are often attracted to balance sheet CDOs because they are perceived as offering a higher return than say, credit card ABS, at a similar level of risk exposure. They also represent a diversification away from traditional structured finance investments. The asset pool in a balance sheet CDO is static, that is it is not traded or actively managed by a portfolio manager; for this reason the structure is similar to more traditional ABS or repackaging vehicles. The typical note tranching is:

- Senior note, AAA-rated, and 90%–95% of the issue
- Mezzanine note, BBB-rated, 1%–3%
- Subordinated note, A-rated, 3%–5%
- Equity note, non-rated, 1%–2%

The cash flows of the underlying assets are used to fund the liabilities of the overlying notes. As the notes carry different ratings, there is a *priority of payment* that must be followed, which is the cash flow waterfall. The most senior payment must be paid in full before the next payment can be met, all the way until the most junior liability is discharged. If sufficient funds are not available, the most senior notes must be paid off before the junior liabilities can be addressed.

The waterfall process for interest payments is shown at Exhibit 7.3. Before paying the next priority of the waterfall, the vehicle must pass a number of compliance tests on the level of its underlying cash flows. These include interest coverage and principal (par) coverage tests.

During the life of the CDO transaction, a portfolio administrator will produce a periodic report detailing the quality of the collateral pool. This report is known as an investor or *Trustee* report and also shows the results of the compliance tests that are required to affirm that the notes of the CDO have maintained their credit rating.

Arbitrage CDOs are classified into either cash flow CDOs or market value CDOs. An arbitrage CDO will be designated as one of these two

EXHIBIT 7.3 Interest Cash Flow Waterfall for Cash Flow CDO

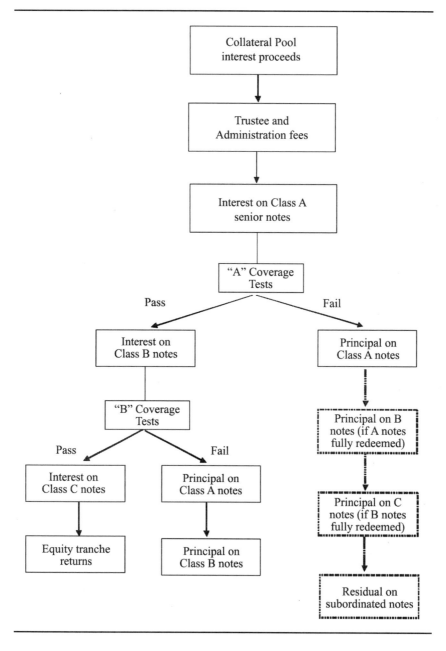

types depending on the way the underlying asset pool is structured to provide value (cash proceeds) in the vehicle. The distinction is that:

- A cash flow CDO will have a collateral pool that is usually static, and which generates sufficient interest to cover fees, expenses and overlying liabilities, and sufficient principal to repay notes on maturity.
- In a market value CDO the collateral pool is usually actively traded, and marked-to-market on a daily basis. The daily mark for all the assets indicates the total value of the collateral pool and this value must always be sufficient to cover the principal and interest liabilities.

Because market value deals are such a small part of the CDO market, we will not review them in this book.

A cash flow arbitrage CDO has certain similarities with a balance sheet CDO, and if it is a static pool CDO it is also conceptually similar to an ABS deal.[2] The priority of payments is similar, starting from expenses, Trustee and servicing fees, senior noteholders, and so on down to the most junior noteholder. Underlying assets on cash flow arbitrage deals are commonly lower-rated bonds, commercial bank loans, high-yield debt and emerging market sovereign bonds. The basic structure is designed to split the aggregate credit risk of the collateral pool into various tranches, which are the overlying notes, each of which has a different credit exposure from the other. As a result each note exhibits a different risk/reward profile, and so will attract itself to different classes of investor.

The different risk profiles of the issued notes results because they are subordinated, that is, the notes are structured in descending order of seniority. In addition, the structure makes use of *credit enhancements* to varying degrees, which may include:

- *Overcollateralization*: The overlying notes are lower in value compared to the underlying pool; for example, $250 million nominal of assets are used as backing for $170 million nominal of issued bonds.
- *Cash reserve accounts*: A reserve is maintained in a cash account and used to cover initial losses; the funds may be sourced from part of the proceeds.
- *Excess spread*: Cash inflows from assets that exceed the interest service requirements of liabilities.
- *Insurance wraps*: Insurance cover against losses suffered by the asset pool, for which an insurance premium is paid for as long as the cover is needed.

---

[2] Except that in a typical ABS deal such as a consumer or trade receivables deal, or a residential MBS deal, there are a large number of individual underlying assets, whereas with a CBO or CLO there may be as few as 20 underlying loans or bonds.

The quality of the collateral pool is monitored regularly and reported on by the portfolio administrator, who produces the investor report. This report details the results of various *compliance tests*, which are undertaken at individual asset level as well as aggregate level. Compliance tests include:

- *Weighted average spread and weighted average rating*: The average interest spread and average credit rating of the assets, which must remain at a specified minimum.
- *Concentration*: There will be a set maximum share of the assets that may be sourced from particular emerging markets, industrial sectors, and so on.
- *Diversity score*: This is a statistical value that is calculated via a formula set by the rating agency analyzing the transaction. It measures the level of diversity of the assets, in other words how different they are— and hence how uncorrelated in their probability of default—from each other.

These tests are calculated on a regular basis and also each time the composition of the assets changes, for example because certain assets have been sold, new assets purchased or because bonds have paid off ahead of their legal maturity date. If the test results fall below the required minimum, trading activity is restricted to only those trades that will improve the test results.

Certain other compliance tests are viewed as more important, since if any of them are "failed," the cash flows will be diverted from the normal waterfall and will be used to begin paying off the senior notes until the test results improve. These include:

- *Overcollateralization*: The overcollateralisation level (OC test) vis-à-vis the issued notes must remain above a specified minimum, for instance it must be at 120% of the par value of the senior note.
- *Interest coverage*: The level of interest receivables (IC test) on assets must be sufficient to cover interest liabilities, but also to bear default and other losses.

Compliance tests are specified as part of the process leading up to the issue of notes, in discussion between the originator and the rating agency or rating agencies. The ratings analysis is comprehensive and focuses on the quality of the collateral, individual asset default probabilities, the structure of the deal, and the track record and reputation of the originator.

If a CDO vehicle fails an important compliance test such as the OC or IC test, the portfolio administrator will inform the deal originator (or fund manager). On this occurrence, an immediate restriction is placed on any further trading by the vehicle and the originator has 30 days to rectify the position. After this date, the only trading that is permitted is that required on a credit risk basis (to mitigate credit risk and possible further loss due to say, defaults in the portfolio). At the next coupon date, known as the determination date, if the compliance test is still being failed, then principal on the notes will begin to be paid off, in order of priority. Typically the most senior note will pay off first, although some deals have certain provisions in their deal documentation that state that another note may be paid off first.[3] During this phase, the CDO is also likely to be put on "credit watch" by the credit rating agency, with a view to possible downgrade, because the underlying portfolio will be viewed as having deteriorated in quality from the time of its original rating analysis.

SYNTHETIC CDOs

The ongoing development of securitization technology has resulted in more complex structures, as illustrated by the synthetic CDO. This structured credit product was introduced to meet differing needs of originators, where credit risk transfer is of more importance than funding considerations. Compared with cash flow CDO deals, which feature an actual transfer of ownership or *true sale* of the underlying assets to a separately incorporated legal entity, a synthetic securitization structure is engineered so that the credit risk of the assets is transferred by the sponsor or originator of the transaction, from itself, to the investors by means of credit derivative instruments. The originator is therefore the credit protection buyer and investors are the credit protection sellers. This credit risk transfer may be undertaken either directly or via an SPV. Using this approach, underlying or *reference* assets are not necessarily moved off the originator's balance sheet, so it is adopted whenever the primary objective is to achieve risk transfer rather than balance sheet funding. The synthetic structure enables removal of credit exposure without asset transfer, so may be preferred for risk management and regulatory capital relief purposes. For banking institutions, it also enables loan risk to be transferred without selling the loans themselves, thereby allowing customer relationships to remain unaffected.

---

[3] For example, with the EuroCredit I CDO, originated by Intermediate Capital Group and arranged by Morgan Stanley in 1999, and which closed in 2000, the deal documentation states that the Class 3 note pays off prior to the Class 1 and Class 2 notes.

EXHIBIT 7.4   CDO Market Volume Growth in Europe

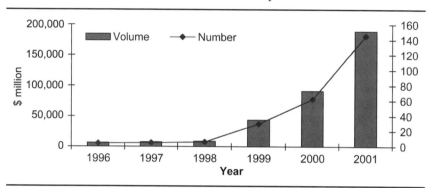

Note: Volume includes rated debt and credit default swap tranches and unrated super-senior tranches for synthetic CDOs, and excludes equity tranches.
Source: Moody's; Bank of America, Bloomberg. Used with permission.

Synthetic CDOs make use of credit derivatives, both *unfunded* credit derivatives such as credit default swaps and *funded* credit derivatives such as credit-linked notes. The funded term refers to whether an up-front payment is made for the credit derivative by the seller of protection. Commonly the unfunded element is ranked ahead of any funded element, and hence known as a *super-senior* swap.

The first synthetic deals were observed in the U.S. market, while the first deals in Europe were observed in 1998. Market growth has been rapid; the total value of cash and synthetic deals worldwide in 2001 approached $190 billion, and a growing share of this total has been of synthetic deals. Exhibit 7.4 illustrates market volume, while Exhibit 7.5 shows the breakdown of arbitrage CDOs, whether cash flow, market value or synthetic deals, in 2000 and 2001. Exhibit 7.5 appears to suggest that synthetic deals were a very small part of the market, but the total reflects the funded element of each transaction, which grew to 9% of all arbitrage deals in 2001. However, when the unfunded element of synthetic deals is included, we see that the synthetic deal share is substantially increased, shown at Exhibit 7.6. Market share volumes reported by say, the rating agencies generally include the note element, however as a measure of actual risk transferred by a vehicle, it is logical to include the unfunded super-senior swap element as well. This suggests that in 2001 similar amounts of synthetic and cash business were transacted.

The first synthetic deals were balance sheet CLOs, with underlying reference assets being commercial loans on the originator's balance sheet. Originators were typically banking institutions. Arbitrage synthetic CDOs have also been introduced, typically by fund management

EXHIBIT 7.5   Market Share of Arbitrage CDOs in 2000 and 2001

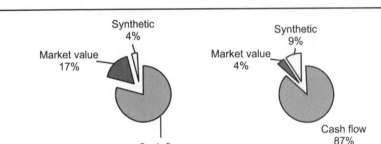

Source: UBS Warburg. Reproduced with permission.

EXHIBIT 7.6   Market Share of Arbitrage CDOs in 2001, Comparison when Unfunded Swap Element of Synthetic Deals is Included

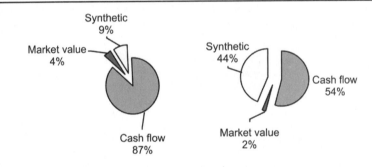

Source: UBS Warburg. Reproduced with permission.

institutions, and these involve sourcing credit derivative contracts in the market and then selling these on to investors in the form of rated notes, at the arbitrage profit. Within the synthetic market, arbitrage deals were the most frequently issued during 2002, reflecting certain advantages they possess over cash CDOs. A key advantage has been that credit default swaps for single reference entities frequently trade at a lower spread than cash bonds of same name and maturity, with consequent lower costs for the originator.

Motivations for Synthetic CDOs

Differences between synthetic and cash CDOs are perhaps best reflected in the different cost-benefit economics of issuing each type. The motivations behind the issue of each type usually also differ. A synthetic CDO can be seen as being constructed out of the following:

- A short position in a credit default swap (bought protection), by which the sponsor transfers its portfolio credit risk to the issuer.
- A long position in a portfolio of bonds or loans, the cash flow from which enables the sponsor to pay liabilities of overlying notes.

Synthetic deals can be unfunded, partially funded or fully funded. An *unfunded* CDO structure would be comprised wholly of credit default swaps, while *fully funded CDO structures* would be arranged so that the entire credit risk of the reference portfolio was transferred through the issue of credit-linked notes. We discuss these shortly.

The originators of the first synthetic deals were banks who wished to manage the credit risk exposure of their loan books, without having to resort to the administrative burden of true sale cash securitization. They are a natural progression in the development of credit derivative structures, with single-name credit default swaps being replaced by portfolio default swaps. Synthetic CDOs can be "delinked" from the sponsoring institution, so that investors do not have any credit exposure to the sponsor itself. The first deals were introduced (in 1998) at a time when widening credit spreads and the worsening of credit quality among originating firms meant that investors were sellers of cash CDOs which had retained a credit linkage to the sponsor. A synthetic arrangement also means that the credit risk of assets that are otherwise not suited to conventional securitization may be transferred, while assets are retained on the balance sheet. Such assets include bank guarantees, letters of credit or cash loans that have some legal or other restriction on being securitized. For this reason synthetic deals are more appropriate for assets that are described under multiple legal jurisdictions.

The economic advantage of issuing a synthetic versus a cash CDO can be significant. Put simply, the net benefit to the originator is the gain in regulatory capital cost, minus the cost of paying for credit protection on the credit default swap side. In a partially funded structure, a sponsoring bank will obtain full capital relief when note proceeds are invested in 0% risk weighted collateral such as U.S. Treasuries or U.K. gilts. In a *partially funded* structure, the majority of the credit risk of the pool of reference assets is transferred by means of the *super-senior swap*, which is a credit default swap. The remaining credit risk is transferred using credit linked notes, which is the "funded" element. The reason the swap is called "super-senior" is because the CDO is structured so that the most senior credit linked note is always rated AAA; the swap is rated senior to this, hence "super senior." It represents in fact catastrophe risk, because it

EXHIBIT 7.7   Cost Structure, Synthetic versus Cash Flow CDO

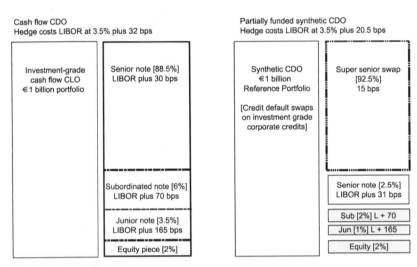

Cash flow CDO
Hedge costs LIBOR at 3.5% plus 32 bps

Investment-grade cash flow CLO €1 billion portfolio	Senior note [88.5%] LIBOR plus 30 bps
	Subordinated note [6%] LIBOR plus 70 bps
	Junior note [3.5%] LIBOR plus 165 bps
	Equity piece [2%]

Partially funded synthetic CDO
Hedge costs LIBOR at 3.5% plus 20.5 bps

Synthetic CDO €1 billion Reference Portfolio [Credit default swaps on investment grade corporate credits]	Super senior swap [92.5%] 15 bps
	Senior note [2.5%] LIBOR plus 31 bps
	Sub [2%] L + 70
	Jun [1%] L + 165
	Equity [2%]

Regulatory capital relief
Cash CDO
Capital charge on assets reduces from 8% (100% RW) to 2% (equity piece only now 100% RW)
Regulatory capital relief is 6%
Synthetic CDO
Capital charge on assets reduces from 8% (100% RW) to 3.48% (equity piece plus super senior swap at 20% RW)
Regulatory capital relief is 4.52%

would only expose the investor to a loss if the AAA piece below it experienced default—statistically a very low probability. The super senior swap portion will carry a 20% risk weighting.[4] In fact a moment's thought should make clear to us that a synthetic deal would be cheaper: where credit default swaps are used, the sponsor pays a basis point fee, which for AAA security might be in the range 10–30 bps, depending on the stage of the credit cycle. In a cash structure where bonds are issued, the cost to the sponsor would be the benchmark yield plus the credit spread, which would be considerably higher compared to the default swap premium. This is illustrated in the example shown in Exhibit 7.7, where we assume certain spreads and premiums in comparing a partially funded synthetic deal with a cash deal. The assumptions are:

■ That the super senior credit swap cost is 15 bps, and carries a 20% risk weight.
■ The equity piece retains a 100% risk weighting.

---

[4] This is as long as the counterparty is an OECD bank, which is invariably the case.

■ the synthetic CDO invests note proceeds in sovereign collateral that pays sub-LIBOR.

Mechanics

A synthetic CDO is so called because the transfer of credit risk is achieved "synthetically" via a credit derivative, rather than by a "true sale" to an SPV. Thus in a synthetic CDO the credit risk of the underlying loans or bonds is transferred to the SPV using credit default swaps and/or total return swaps (TRS). However the assets themselves are not legally transferred to the SPV, and they remain on the originator's balance sheet. Using a synthetic CDO, the originator can obtain regulatory capital relief and manage the credit risk on its balance sheet, but will not be receiving any funding.[5] In other words a synthetic CDO structure enables originators to separate credit risk exposure and asset funding requirements.

The credit risk of the asset portfolio, now known as the *reference portfolio*, is transferred, directly or to an SPV, through credit derivatives. The most common credit contracts used are credit default swaps. A portion of the credit risk may be sold on as credit-linked notes. Typically a large majority of the credit risk is transferred via the super-senior credit default swap, which is dealt with a swap counterparty, but usually sold to monoline insurance companies at a significantly lower spread over LIBOR compared with the senior AAA-rated tranche of cash flow CDOs. This is a key attraction of synthetic deals for originators. Most deals are structured with mezzanine notes sold to a wider set of investors, the proceeds of which are invested in risk-free collateral such as Treasury bonds or Pfandbriefe securities. The most junior note, known as the "first-loss" piece, may be retained by the originator. On occurrence of a credit event among the reference assets, the originating bank receives funds remaining from the collateral after they have been used to pay the principal on the issued notes, less the value of the junior note.

A generic synthetic CDO structure is shown in Exhibit 7.8. In this generic structure, the credit risk of the reference assets is transferred to the issuer SPV and ultimately the investors, by means of the credit default swap and an issue of credit-linked notes. In the default swap arrangement, the risk transfer is undertaken in return for the default swap premium, which is then paid to investors by the issuer. The note issue is invested in risk-free collateral rather than passed on to the originator. This is done in order to delink the credit ratings of the notes from the rating of the originator. If the collateral pool was not established, a

---

[5] This is because reference assets that are protected by credit derivative contracts, and which remain on the balance sheet, will, under Basel rules, attract a lower regulatory capital charge.

EXHIBIT 7.8 Synthetic CDO Structure

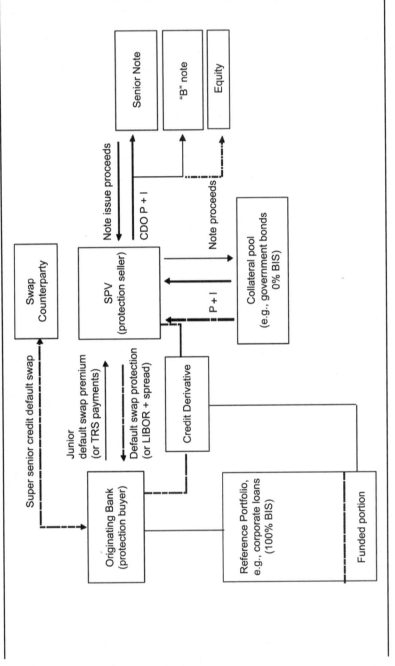

downgrade of the sponsor could result in a downgrade of the issued notes. Investors in the notes expose themselves to the credit risk of the reference assets, and if there are no credit events, they will earn returns at least the equal of the collateral assets and the default swap premium. If the notes are credit-linked, they will also earn excess returns based on the performance of the reference portfolio. If there are credit events, the issuer will deliver the assets to the swap counterparty and will pay the nominal value of the assets to the originator out of the collateral pool. Credit default swaps are unfunded credit derivatives, while CLNs are funded credit derivatives where the protection seller (the investors) fund the value of the reference assets upfront, and will receive a reduced return on occurrence of a credit event.

Funding Mechanics

As the super-senior piece in a synthetic CDO does not need to be funded, this provides the key advantage of the synthetic mechanism compared to a cash flow arbitrage CDO. During the first half of 2002, the yield spread for the AAA note piece averaged 45–50 bps over LIBOR,[6] while the cost of the super-senior swap was around 10–12 bps. This means that if the CDO collateral manager can reinvest in the collateral pool risk-free assets at LIBOR minus (say) 5 bps, it is able to gain from a savings of 28–35 bps on each nominal $100 of the structure that is not funded. This is a considerable gain. If we assume that a synthetic CDO is 95% unfunded and 5% funded, this is equivalent to the reference assets trading at approximately 26–33 bps cheaper in the market. There is also an improvement to the return on capital measure for the CDO collateral manager. Since typically the manager retains the equity piece, if this is 2% of the structure and the gain is 33 bps, the return on equity will be improved by [0.36/0.02] or 16.5%. In fact the deal economics that are modelled during the structuring of the transaction will play a part on how the deal is tranched: If there is investor appetite for more funded investments, a greater proportion of the deal will be in the form of credit-linked notes. The share of equity will also depend on market appetite for CDO equity.[7]

---

[6] Averaged from the yield spread on seven synthetic deals closed during January–June 2002, yield spread at issue, rate data from Bloomberg.

[7] There are pros and cons in the debate as to whether it is better for the CDO originator to retain some or all of the equity. One argument is that it motivates the originator to prudently manage the vehicle as it has an interest in its performance. The other side holds that as the equity piece return is variable and dependent on the surplus cash generated by the vehicle, it may tempt managers to trade recklessly.

Another benefit of structuring CDOs as synthetic deals is their potentially greater attraction for investors (protection sellers). Often, selling credit default swap protection on a particular reference credit generates a higher return than going long of the underlying cash bond. In general, as explained in Chapter 4, this is because the credit default swap price is greater than the asset swap price for the same name, for a number of reasons. For instance during the first half of 2002 the average spread of the synthetic price over the cash price as reported by Bloomberg was over 40 bps in the 5-year maturity area for BBB rated credits. The reasons why default swap spreads tend to be above cash spreads include:

- The credit risk covered by the default swap includes trigger events that are not pure default scenarios, such as restructuring.
- On occurrence of a credit event, the amount of loss is calculated assuming that the reference security was at an initial price of par, whereas in the cash market that security may have been bought at a discount to par. Assume we buy a security at a price discount to par of x, and that the obligor defaults: the physical security can be sold at the new defaulted-price of y, where $x > y$, resulting in a loss of $(x - y)$. If the investor had instead sold a credit default swap on the same name, the investor would pay the difference between par and y, which is a greater loss. Therefore the default swap price is higher to compensate for this.
- The bondholder is aware of the exact issue that they are holding in the event of default, however default swap sellers may receive potentially any bond from a basket of deliverable instruments that rank *pari passu* with the cash asset; this is the delivery option afforded the long swap holder. This applies to physically-settled default swaps and means the protections buyer will deliver the *cheapest-to-deliver* asset.
- The borrowing rate for a cash bond in the repo market may differ from LIBOR if the bond is to any extent *special*; this does not impact the default swap price which is fixed at inception.
- Certain bonds rated AAA (such as U.S. agency securities) sometimes trade below LIBOR in the asset swap market; however, a bank writing protection on such a bond will expect a premium (positive spread over LIBOR) for selling protection on the bond.
- Depending on the precise reference credit, the default swap may be more liquid than the cash bond, resulting in a lower default swap price, or less liquid than the bond, resulting in a higher price.
- Default swaps may be required to pay out on credit events that are technical defaults, and not the full default that impacts a cash bondholder; protection sellers may demand a premium for this additional risk.

Note however the existence of ongoing counterparty risk for the seller of a default swap is a factor that suggests that its price should be below the cash price!

Investor Risks in Synthetic Transactions

The key structural differences between a synthetic and conventional securitization are the absence of a true sale of assets and the use of credit derivatives. Investors must therefore focus on different aspects of risk that the synthetic CDO represents. Although it might be said that each securitization—irrespective of it being cash or synthetic—is a unique transaction with its own characteristics, synthetic deals are very transaction-specific because they can be tailor-made to meet very specific requirements. Such requirements can be with regard to reference asset type, currency, underlying cash flows, credit derivative instrument, and so on.

Investor risk in a synthetic deal centers on the credit risk inherent in the reference assets and the legal issues associated with the definition of credit events. Also, to a smaller extent, there is the counterparty credit risk associated with the credit default swap that transfers the credit risk to the CDO structure. The first risk is closely associated with securitization in general but synthetic securitization in particular. Remember that the essence of the transaction is credit risk transfer, and investors (protection sellers) desire exposure to the credit performance of reference assets. So investors are taking on the credit risk of these assets, be they conventional bonds, ABS securities, loans or other assets. The primary measure of this risk is the credit rating of the assets, taken together with any credit enhancements, as well as their historical ratings performance.

The second risk is more problematic and open to translation issues. In a number of deals the sponsor of the transaction is also tasked with determining when a credit event has taken place; as the sponsor is also buying protection there is scope for conflict of interest here. The more critical concern, and one which has given rise to litigation in past cases, is what exactly constitutes a credit event. A lack of clear legal definition can lead to conflict when the protection buyer believes that a particular occurrence is indeed a credit event and therefore the trigger for a protection payout, but this is disputed by the protection seller. Generally, the broader the definition of "credit event," the greater the risk there is of dispute. Trigger events should therefore be defined in the governing legal documentation as closely as possible.

This is of course key: Most descriptions of events defined as trigger events include those listed in the ISDA *Credit Derivatives Definitions* that were described in Chapter 3. They include circumstances that fall short of a general default, so that payouts can be enforced when the reference asset obligor is not in default. This means that the risk taken on by investors in a synthetic CDO deals is higher than that taken on in a cash CDO deal because the hurdle for a credit event may be lower than that for outright default. It is important for investors to be aware of this: Credit ratings for a bond issue will not reflect all the credit events that are defined by ISDA. This means that the probability of loss for a synthetic note of a specific rating may be higher than for a conventional note of the same reference name.

BISTRO: The First Synthetic Securitization

Viewed as the first synthetic securitization, Broad Index Secured Trust Offering (BISTRO) is a JPMorgan Chase vehicle brought to market in December 1997. The transaction was designed to remove the credit risk on a portfolio of corporate credits held on JPMorgan Chase's books, with no funding or balance sheet impact. The overall portfolio was $9.7 billion, with $700 million of notes being issued, in two tranches, by the BISTRO SPV. The proceeds of the note issue were invested in U.S. Treasury securities, which in turn were used as collateral for the credit default swap entered into between JPMorgan Chase and the SPV. This was a 5-year swap written on the whole portfolio, with JPMorgan Chase as the protection buyer. BISTRO, the protection seller, pays for the coupons on the issued notes from funds received from the collateral pool and the premiums on the credit default swap. Payments on occurrence of credit events are paid out from the collateral pool.

Under this structure JPMorgan Chase transferred the credit risk on $700 million of its portfolio to investors, and retained the risk on a first-loss piece and the residual piece. The first loss piece is not a note issue, but a $32 million reserve cash account held for the 5-year life of the deal. First losses are funded out of this cash reserve which is held by JPMorgan Chase. This is shown in Exhibit 7.9.

The asset pool is static for the life of the deal. The attraction of the deal for investors included a higher return on the notes compared to bonds of the same credit rating and a bullet-maturity structure, compared to the amortizing arrangement of other ABS asset classes.

Summary: Advantages of Synthetic Structures

The introduction of synthetic securitization vehicles was in response to specific demands of sponsoring institutions, and they present certain advantages over traditional cash flow structures. These advantages include:

- *Speed of implementation:* A synthetic transaction can, in theory, be placed in the market sooner than a cash deal, and the time from incep-

EXHIBIT 7.9   BISTRO Structure

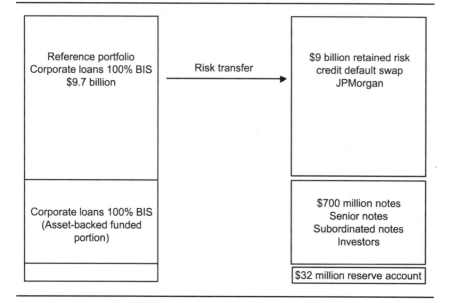

tion to closure can be as low as four weeks, with average execution time of 6–8 weeks compared to 3–4 months for the equivalent cash deal; this reflects the shorter ramp-up period noted above.

- No requirement to fund the super-senior element.
- For many reference names the credit default swap is frequently cheaper than the same name underlying cash bond.
- Transaction costs such as legal fees can be lower as there is no necessity to set up an SPV.
- Banking relationships can be maintained with clients whose loans need not be actually sold off the sponsoring entity's balance sheet.
- The range of reference assets that can be covered is wider, and includes undrawn lines of credit, bank guarantees and derivative instruments that would give rise to legal and true sale issues in a cash transaction.
- The use of credit derivatives introduces greater flexibility to provide tailor-made solutions for credit risk requirements.
- The cost of buying protection is usually lower as there is little or no funding element and the credit protection price is below the equivalent-rate note liability.

This does not mean that the cash CDO transaction is now an endangered species. It retains certain advantages of its own over synthetic deals, which include:

■ No requirement for an OECD bank (the 20% BIS risk-weighted entity) to act as the swap counterparty to meet capital relief requirements.

■ Lower capital relief available compared to the 20% risk weighting on the OECD bank counterparty.

■ Larger potential investor base, as the number of counterparties is potentially greater (certain financial and investing institutions have limitations on the degree of usage of credit derivatives).

■ Lower degree of counterparty exposure for originating entity. In a synthetic deal the default of a swap counterparty would mean cessation of premium payments or more critically a credit event protection payment, and termination of the credit default swap.

Investment banking advisors will structure the arrangement for their sponsoring client that best meets the latter's requirements. Depending on the nature of these, this can be either a synthetic or cash deal.

Variations in Synthetic CDOs

Synthetic CDOs have been issued in a variety of forms, labeled in generic form as arbitrage CDOs or balance sheet CDOs. Structures can differ to a considerable degree from one another, having only the basics in common with each other. The latest development is the *managed synthetic* CDO.

A synthetic arbitrage CDO is originated generally by collateral managers who wish to exploit the difference in yield between that obtained on the underlying assets and that payable on the CDO, both in note interest and servicing fees. The generic structure is as follows: A specially created SPV enters into a total return swap with the originating bank or financial institution, referencing the bank's underlying portfolio (the reference portfolio). The portfolio is actively managed and is funded on the balance sheet by the originating bank. The SPV receives the "total return" from the reference portfolio, and in return it pays LIBOR plus a spread to the originating bank. The SPV also issues notes that are sold into the market to CDO investors, and these notes can be rated as high as AAA as they are backed by high-quality collateral, which is purchased using the note proceeds. A typical structure is shown in Exhibit 7.10.

A balance sheet synthetic CDO is employed by banks that wish to manage regulatory capital. As before, the underlying assets are bonds, loans, and credit facilities originated by the issuing bank. In a balance sheet CDO, the SPV enters into a credit default swap agreement with the originator, with the specific collateral pool designated as the reference portfolio. The SPV receives the premium payable on the default swap, and thereby provides credit protection on the reference portfolio.

EXHIBIT 7.10 Generic Synthetic Arbitrage CDO Structure

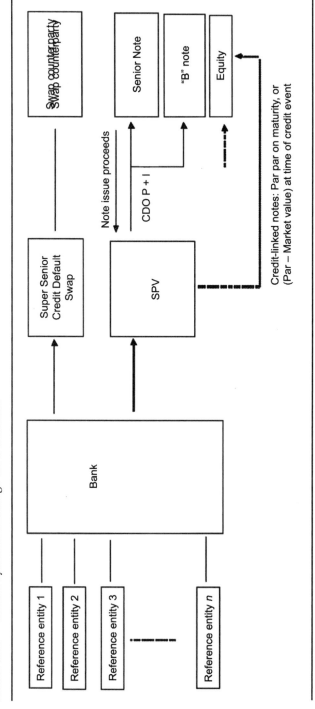

There are three types of CDO within this structure. A fully synthetic CDO is a completely *unfunded* structure which uses credit default swaps to transfer the entire credit risk of the reference assets to investors who are protection sellers. In a *partially funded* CDO, only the highest credit risk segment of the portfolio is transferred. The cash flow that would be needed to service the synthetic CDO overlying liability is received from the AAA rated collateral that is purchased by the SPV with the proceeds of an overlying note issue. An originating bank obtains maximum regulatory capital relief by means of a partially funded structure, through a combination of the synthetic CDO and what is known as a *super senior swap* arrangement with an OECD banking counterparty. A super senior swap provides additional protection to that part of the portfolio, the senior segment, that is already protected by the funded portion of the transaction. The sponsor may retain the super senior element or may sell it to a monoline insurance firm or credit default swap provider.

Some commentators have categorized synthetic deals using slightly different terms. For instance Boggiano, Waterson, and Stein define the following types:[8]

- Balance sheet static synthetic CDO
- Managed static synthetic CDO
- Balance sheet variable synthetic CDO
- Managed variable synthetic CDO

As described by Boggiano, Waterson, and Stein, the basic structure is as we described earlier for a partially funded synthetic CDO. In fact there is essentially little difference between the first two types of deal—in the latter a collateral manager rather than the credit swap counterparty selects the portfolio. However, the reference assets remain static for the life of the deal in both cases. For the last two deal types, the main difference would appear to be that an collateral manager, rather than the originator bank, trades the portfolio of credit swaps under specified guidelines. In our view, this is not a structural difference and so in this chapter we will consider them both as managed CDOs, which are described later.

A generic partially funded synthetic transaction is shown at Exhibit 7.11. It shows an arrangement whereby the issuer enters into two credit default swaps. The first swap with an SPV provides protection for losses

---

[8] Kenneth Boggiano, David Waterson, and Craig Stein, "Four Forms of Synthetic CDOs," *Derivatives Week*, 11, no. 23 (June 10, 2002).

up to a specified amount of the reference pool,[9] while the second swap is set up with the OECD bank or, occasionally, an insurance company.[10]

A *fully funded* CDO is a structure where the credit risk of the entire portfolio is transferred to the SPV via a credit default swap. In a fully funded (or just "funded") synthetic CDO the issuer enters into the credit default swap with the SPV, which itself issues credit-linked notes to the entire value of the assets on which the risk has been transferred. The proceeds from the notes are invested in risk-free government or agency debt such as U.S. Treasuries, U.K. gilts, German Bunds or Pfand-briefe, or in senior unsecured bank debt. Should there be a default on one or more of the underlying assets, the required amount of the collat-eral is sold and the proceeds from the sale paid to the issuer to recom-pense for the losses. The premium paid on the credit default swap must be sufficiently high to ensure that it covers the difference in yield between that on the collateral and that on the notes issued by the SPV. The generic structure is illustrated at Exhibit 7.12.

Fully funded CDOs are relatively uncommon. One of the advantages of the partially funded arrangement is that the issuer will pay a lower pre-mium compared to a fully funded synthetic CDO, because it is not required to pay the difference between the yield on the collateral and the coupon on the note issue (the unfunded part of the transaction). The downside is that the issuer will receive a reduction in risk weighting for capital purposes to 20% for the risk transferred via the super senior default swap.

The *fully unfunded* CDO uses only credit derivatives in its structure. The swaps are rated in a similar fashion to notes, and there is usually an "equity" piece that is retained by the originator. The reference portfolio will again be commercial loans, usually 100% risk-weighted, or other assets. The credit rating of the swap tranches is based on the rating of the reference assets, as well as other factors such as the diversity of the assets and ratings performance correlation. The typical structure is illus-trated in Exhibit 7.13. As well as the equity tranche, there will be one or more junior tranches, one or more senior tranches and super-senior tranche. The senior tranches are sold on to AAA-rated banks as a port-folio credit default swap, while the junior tranche is usually sold to an OECD bank. The ratings of the tranches will typically be:

- Super-senior: AAA
- Senior: AA to AAA

---

[9] In practice, to date this portion has been between 5% and 15% of the reference pool.
[10] An "OECD" bank, thus guaranteeing a 20% risk weighting for capital ratio pur-poses, under Basle I rules.

EXHIBIT 7.11 Partially Funded Synthetic CDO Structure

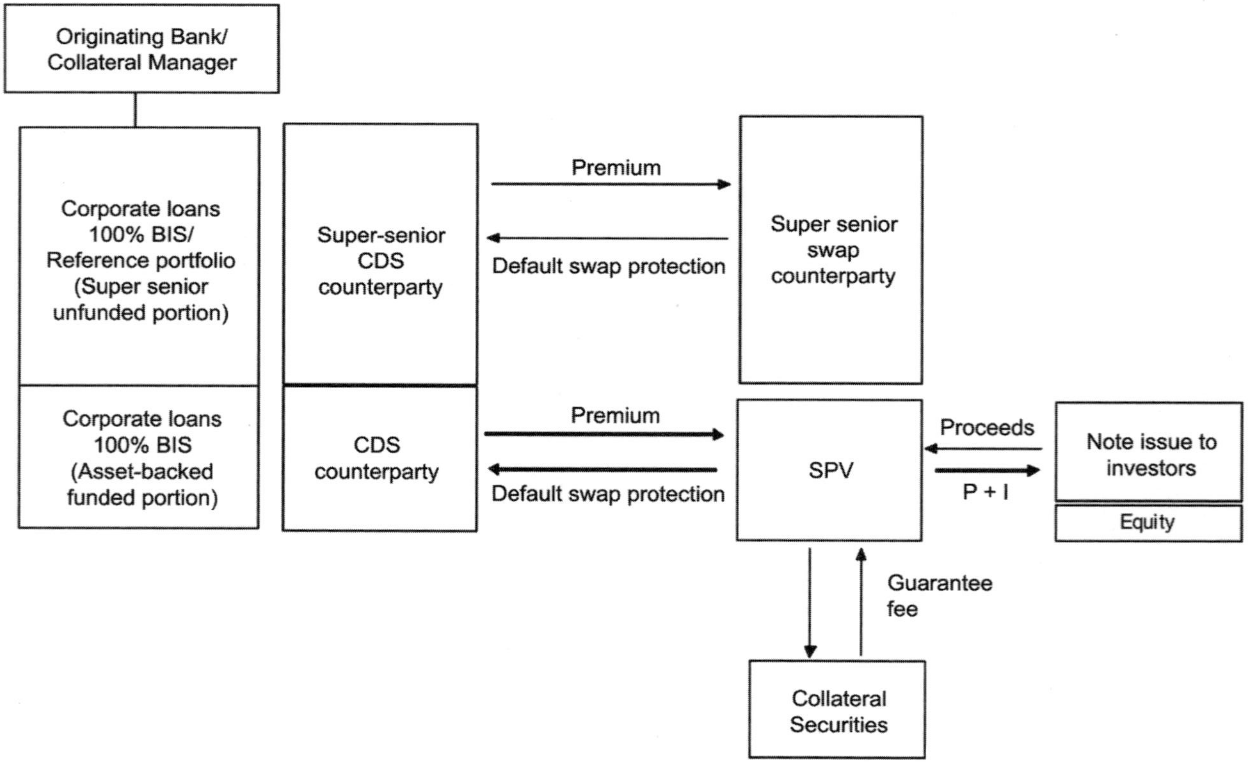

EXHIBIT 7.12   Fully Funded Synthetic Balance Sheet CDO Structure

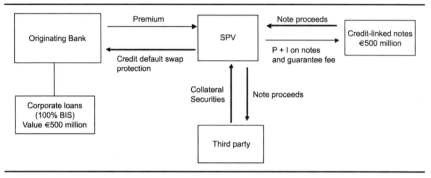

EXHIBIT 7.13   The Fully Synthetic or Unfunded CDO

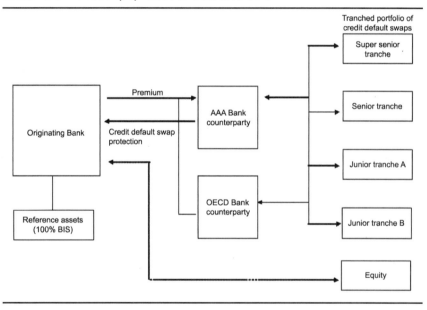

■ Junior: BB to A
■ Equity: unrated

The credit default swaps are not single-name swaps, but are written on a class of debt. The advantage for the originator is that it can name the reference asset class to investors to investors without having to disclose the name of specific loans. Default swaps are usually cash-settled and not physically settled, so that the reference assets can be replaced with other assets if desired by the sponsor.

Within the European market static synthetic balance sheet CDOs are the most common structure. The reasons that banks originate them are two-fold:

- *Capital relief:* Banks can obtain regulatory capital relief by transferring lower-yield corporate credit risk such as corporate bank loans off their balance sheet. Under Basle I rules all corporate debt carries an identical 100% risk-weighting; therefore with banks having to assign 8% of capital for such loans, higher-rated (and hence lower-yielding) corporate assets will require the same amount of capital, but will generate a lower return on that capital. A bank may wish to transfer such higher-rated, lower-yield assets from its balance sheet, and this can be achieved via a CDO transaction. The capital requirements for a synthetic CDO are lower than for corporate assets; for example, the funded segment of the deal will be supported by high quality collateral such as government bonds, and via a repo arrangement with an OECD bank would carry a 20% risk weighting, as does the super senior element;
- *Transfer of credit risk:* The cost of servicing a fully funded CDO, and the premium payable on the associated credit default swap, can be prohibitive. With a partially funded structure, the issue amount is typically a relatively small share of the asset portfolio. This lowers substantially the default swap premium. Also, as the CDO investors suffer the first loss element of the portfolio, the super senior default swap can be entered into at a considerably lower cost than that on a fully funded CDO.

Synthetic deals may be either static or managed. Static deals hold the following advantages:

- There are no ongoing management fees to be borne by the vehicle.
- The investor can review and grant approval to credits that are to make up the reference portfolio.

The disadvantage is that if there is a deterioration in credit quality of one or more names, then there is no ability to remove or offset this name from the pool and the vehicle continues to suffer from it. During 2001 a number of high profile defaults in the market meant that static pool CDOs performed below expectation. This explains partly the rise in popularity of the managed synthetic deal, which we consider next.

The Managed Synthetic CDO

Managed synthetic CDOs are the latest variant of the synthetic CDO structure.[11] They are similar to the partially funded deals we described earlier except that the reference asset pool of credit derivatives is actively traded by the sponsoring collateral manager. It is the maturing market in credit default swaps, resulting in good liquidity in a large number of synthetic corporate credits, that has facilitated the introduction of the managed synthetic CDO.

With this structure, originators can use credit derivatives to arbitrage cash and synthetic liabilities, as well as leverage off their expertise in credit trading to generate profit. The advantages for investors are the same as with earlier generations of CDOs, except that with active trading they are gaining a still-larger exposure to the abilities of the collateral manager. The underlying asset pool is again, a portfolio of credit default swaps. However these are now dynamically managed and actively traded, under specified guidelines. Thus, there is greater flexibility afforded to the sponsor, and the vehicle will record trading gains or losses as a result of credit derivative trading. In most structures, the collateral manager can only buy protection (short credit) in order to offset an existing sold protection default swap. For some deals, this restriction is removed and the collateral manager can buy or sell credit derivatives to reflect its view.

The structure of the managed synthetic is similar to the partially funded synthetic CDO, with a separate legally incorporated SPV. On the liability side there is an issue of notes, which note proceeds invested in collateral or *eligible investments* which is one or a combination of the following:

- A bank deposit account or guaranteed investment contract (GIC), which pays a prespecified rate of interest.[12]
- Risk-free bonds such as U.S. Treasury securities, German Pfandbriefe or AAA-rated bonds such as credit-card ABS securities.
- A repo agreement with risk-free collateral.
- A liquidity facility with a AA-rated bank.
- A market-sensitive debt instrument, often enhanced with the repo or liquidity arrangement described above.

---

[11] These are also commonly known as *collateralized synthetic obligations* or CSOs within the market. *RISK* magazine has called them *collateralized swap obligations*, which handily also shortens to CSOs. Boggiano, Waterson, and Stein refer to these structures as managed variable synthetic CDOs, although we have not come across this term elsewhere in the literature.

[12] A GIC has been defined either as an account that pays a fixed rate of interest for its term, or more usually an account that pays a fixed spread below LIBOR or EU-RIBOR, usually 3-month floating rolled over each interest period.

On the asset side, the SPV enters into credit default swaps and/or total return swaps, selling protection to the sponsor. The collateral manager can trade in and out of credit default swaps after the transaction has closed in the market.[13] The SPV enters into credit derivatives via a credit default swap to one swap counterparty, written on a portfolio of reference assets, or via multiple single-name credit swaps with a number of swap counterparties. The latter arrangement is more common and is referred to as a *multiple dealer* CDO. A percentage of the reference portfolio will be identified at the start of work on the transaction, with the remainder of the entities being selected during the ramp-up period ahead of closing. The SPV enters into the other side of the credit default swaps by selling protection to one of the swap counterparties on specific reference entities. Thereafter the collateral manager can trade out of this exposure in the following ways:

■ Buying credit protection from another swap counterparty on the same reference entity. This offsets the existing exposure, but there may be residual risk exposure unless premium dates are matched exactly or if there is a default in both the reference entity and the swap counterparty.
■ Unwinding or terminating the swap with the counterparty.
■ Buying credit protection on a reference asset that is outside the portfolio. This is uncommon as it will leave residual exposures and may affect premium spread gains.

The SPV actively manages the portfolio within specified guidelines, the decisions being made by the collateral manager. Initially the collateral manager's opportunity to trade may be extensive, but this will be curtailed if there are losses. The trading guidelines will extend to both individual credit default swaps and at the portfolio level. They may include:

■ Parameters under which the collateral manager (in the guise of the SPV) may actively close out, hedge or substitute reference assets using credit derivatives.
■ Guidelines under which the collateral manager can trade credit derivatives to maximize gains or minimize losses on reference assets that have improved or worsened in credit quality or outlook.

---

[13] This term is shared with other securitization structures: when notes have been priced, and placed in the market, and all legal documentation signed by all named participants, the transaction has *closed*. In effect this is the start of the transaction, and all being well the noteholders will receive interest payments during the life of the deal and principal repayment on maturity.

EXHIBIT 7.14 Generic Managed Synthetic CDO

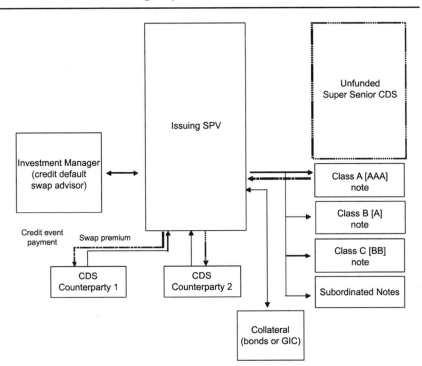

Credit default swaps may be cash settled or physically settled, with physical settlement being more common in a managed synthetic deal. In a multiple-dealer CDO, the legal documentation must be in place with all names on the counterparty dealer list, which may add to legal costs as standardization may be difficult.

Investors who are interested in this structure are seeking to benefit from the following advantages compared to vanilla synthetic deals:

- Active management of the reference portfolio and the trading expertise of the collateral manager in the corporate credit market.
- A multiple-dealer arrangement, so that the collateral manager can obtain the most competitive prices for default swaps.
- Under physical settlement, the collateral manager (via the SPV) has the ability to obtain the highest recovery value for the reference asset.

A generic managed synthetic CDO is illustrated at Exhibit 7.14.

CDO ANALYSIS

In this section we consider key issues for investors when analyzing CDO tranches.

Risk and Return Analysis for CDOs

The return analysis for CDOs performed by potential investors is necessarily different to that undertaken for other securitized asset classes. For CDOs the three key factors to consider are:

- Default probabilities and cumulative default rates
- Default correlations
- Recovery rates

Analysts make assumptions about each of these with regard to individual reference assets, usually with recourse to historical data. We consider each factor in turn.

Default Probability Rates

The level of default probability rates will vary with each deal. Analysts such as the rating agencies will use a number of methods to estimate default probabilities, such as individual reference credit ratings and historical probability rates. Since there may be as much as 150 or more reference names in a CDO's collateral pool, a common approach is to use the average rating of the reference portfolio. Rating agencies such as Moody's provide data on the default rates for different ratings as an "average" class, which can be used in the analysis.

Correlation

The correlation between assets in the reference portfolio of a CDO is an important factor in CDO returns analysis. A problem arises with what precise correlation value to use; these can be correlation between default probabilities, correlation between timing of default and correlation between spreads. The *diversity score* value of the CDO plays a part in this: it represents the number of uncorrelated bonds with identical par value and the same default probability.

Recovery Rates

Recovery rates for individual obligors differ by issuer and industry classification. Rating agencies such as Moody's publish data on the average prices of all defaulted bonds, and generally analysts will construct a database of recovery rates by industry and credit rating for use in modeling the expected recovery rates of assets in the collateral pool. Note that for synthetic CDOs with credit default swaps as assets in the portfolio, this factor is not relevant.

Analysts undertake simulation modeling to generate scenarios of default and expected return. For instance they may model the number of defaults up to maturity, the recovery rates of these defaults and the timing of defaults. All these variables are viewed as random variables, so they are modeled using a stochastic process. It is important to note that the recovery rates estimated by Moody's and other rating agencies are average recovery rates. The actual recovery rate can vary widely depending upon the current macroeconomic environment.

CDO Yield Spreads

Fund managers consider investing in CDO-type products as they represent a diversification in fixed-income markets, with yields that are comparable to credit-card or auto-loan ABS. A cash CDO also gives investors exposure to sectors in the market that may not otherwise be accessible to most investors—for example, credits such as small- or medium-sized corporate entities that rely on entirely bank financing. Also, the extent of credit enhancement and note tranching in a CDO means that they may show better risk/reward profiles than straight conventional debt, with a higher yield but incorporating asset backing and insurance backing. In cash and synthetic CDOs, the notes issued are often bullet bonds, with fixed term to maturity, whereas other ABS and MBS product are amortizing securities with only average (expected life) maturities. This may suit certain longer-dated investors.

An incidental perceived advantage of cash CDOs is that they are typically issued by financial institutions such as higher-rated banks. This usually provides comfort on the credit side but also on the underlying administration and servicing side with regard to underlying assets, compared to consumer receivables securitizations.

To illustrate yields in the European market, Exhibit 7.15 shows the spreads on a selected range of notes as at January 25, 2002 over the credit spectrum. Exhibit 7.16 shows a comparison of different asset classes in European structured products during February 2002. In Exhibit 7.17 we show the note spread at issue for a selected number of synthetic CDOs closed during 2001–2002. The regression of these and selected other AAA-rated note spreads against maturity shows an adjusted R^2 of 0.82, shown in Exhibit 7.18, which suggests that for a set of AAA rated securities, the term to maturity is not the only consideration.[14] Other factors that may explain the difference in yields include

---

[14] Calculated from 12 synthetic CDO senior (AAA-rated) notes issued in Europe during January–June 2002 based on yields obtained from Bloomberg.

EXHIBIT 7.15   Rating Spreads for Synthetic CDOs in the European Market as at January 2002 for Deals Issued During Last Quarter 2001

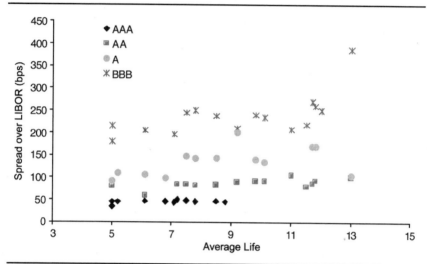

Source: Bloomberg Financial Markets.

EXHIBIT 7.16   Average Speads Over LIBOR for Various Securitization Asset Classes in February 2002

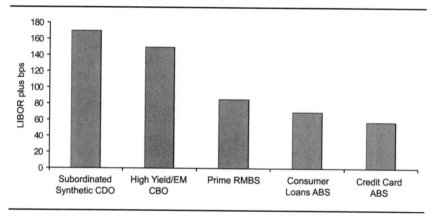

EXHIBIT 7.17 Selected Synthetic Deal Spreads at Issue

Deal Name plus Close Date	Moody's	S&P	Fitch	Spread (bps)	Index
Jazz CDO Mar-02					
Class A	Aaa	AAA		47	6m LIBOR
Class B	Aa2	AAA		75	6m LIBOR
Class C-1		A–		135	6m LIBOR
Class D		BBB		240	6m LIBOR
Robeco III CSO Dec-01					
Class A	Aaa			55	3m LIBOR/EURIBOR
Class B	Aa2			85	3m LIBOR
Class C	Baa1			275	3m LIBOR
Marylebone Road CBO III Oct-01					
Class A-1	Aaa	AAA		45	3m LIBOR
Class A-2	Aa1	AAA		65	3m LIBOR
Class A-3	A2	AAA		160	3m LIBOR
Brooklands € referenced linked notes Jul-01					
Class A	Aaa		AAA	50	3m LIBOR
Class B	Aa3		AA–	80	3m LIBOR
Class C	Baa2		BBB	250	3m LIBOR
Class D-1	n/a		BBB–	500	3m LIBOR
North Street referenced-linked notes 2000-2 Oct-00					
Class A			AAA	70	6m LIBOR
Class B			AA	105	6m LIBOR
Class C			A	175	6m LIBOR

Source: Bloomberg

EXHIBIT 7.18 AAA Spreads as at February 2002 (Selected European CDO Deals)

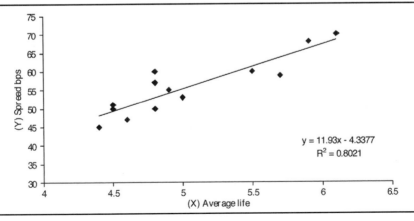

$y = 11.93x - 4.3377$
$R^2 = 0.8021$

perception of the collateral manager, secondary market liquidity. and the placing power of the arranger of the transaction.

CASE STUDIES

The latest manifestation of synthetic securitization technology is the managed synthetic collateralized debt obligation or collateralized synthetic obligation. In Europe these have been originated by fund managers, with the first example being issued in 2000. Although they are, in effect, investment vehicles, the disciplines required to manage what is termed a "structured credit product" is not necessarily identical to those required for a corporate bond fund. Investment bank arrangers are apt to suggest that a track record in credit derivatives trading is an essential prerequisite to being a successful CSO manager. There is an element of reputational risk at stake if a CDO suffers a downgrade. For example, during 2001 Moody's downgraded elements of 83 separate CDO deals, across 174 tranches, as underlying pools of investment-grade and high-yield corporate bonds experienced default.[15] Thus managing a CDO presents a high-profile record of a fund manager's performance.

In Europe fund managers that have originated managed synthetic deals include Robeco, Cheyne Capital Management, BAREP Asset Management, and Axa Investment Managers. In this section we look at four specific deals as case studies. These deals were issued during 2001 and 2002; we look at examples from the U.S., European, and Asian markets.

The deals discussed are innovative structures and a creative combination of securitization technology and credit derivatives. They show how a portfolio manager can utilize vehicles of this kind to exploit its expertise in credit trading as well as provide attractive returns for investors. Managed synthetic CDOs also present fund managers with a vehicle to build on their credit derivatives experience. As the market in synthetic credit, in Europe at least, is frequently more liquid than the cash market for the same reference names, it is reasonable to expect more transactions of this type in the near future.

Blue Chip Funding 2001-1 plc

Blue Chip Funding is a managed synthetic CDO originated by Dolmen Securities, which closed in December 2001. The deal has a €1 billion reference portfolio, with the following terms:

---

[15] *CreditFlux*, April 2002.

EXHIBIT 7.19   Blue Chip Funding Managed Synthetic CDO

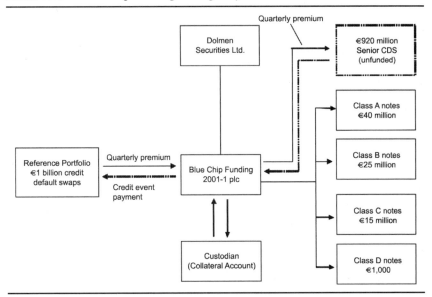

Source: Moody's, Pre-Sale Report, November 27, 2001. Used with permission.

Name	Blue Chip Funding 2001-1 plc
Manager	Dolmen Securities Limited
Arranger	Dolmen Securities Limited
	Dresdner Kleinwort Wasserstein
Closing date	December 17, 2001
Portfolio	€1 billion of credit default swaps
Reference assets	80 investment-grade entities
Portfolio Administrator	Bank of New York

The structure is partially funded, with €80 million of notes issued, or 8% of the nominal value. The share of the unfunded piece is comparatively high. The proceeds from the notes issue are invested in AAA securities, which are held in custody by the third-party agency service provider, which must be rated at AA– or higher. The diversity of the structure is reflected in there being 80 different credits, with a weighted average rating of A–, with no individual asset having a rating below BBB–. The structure is illustrated at Exhibit 7.19.

With this deal, the managers have the ability to trade the credit default swaps with a prespecified panel of dealers. The default swap counterparties must have a short-term rating of A-1+ or better. Trading will result in trading gains or losses. This contrasts with a static synthetic deal, where investors have not been affected by trading gains or losses that arise from pool substitutions. The deal was rated by Standard & Poor's, which in its rating report described the management strategy as "defensive trading" to avoid acute credit deteriorations. There are a number of guidelines that the manager must adhere to, such as:

- The manager may both sell credit protection and purchase credit protection; however, the manager may only short credit (purchase credit protection) in order to close out or offset an existing previous sale of protection.
- There is a discretionary trading limit of 10% of portfolio value.
- A minimum weighted average premium of 60 bps for swaps must be maintained.
- A minimum reinvestment test must be passed at all times. This states that if the value of the collateral account falls below €80 million, interest generated by the collateral securities must be diverted from the equity (Class C and D notes) to the senior notes until the interest cover is restored.

This deal has two residual equity tranches, the Class C and Class D notes. These can be considered as senior and junior equity pieces. Although they are both equity, the Class C note ranks above the Class D note in the priority of payments, and has a fixed coupon return. The Class D note has a variable return, based on the amount of surplus cash generated by the vehicle, which it receives. The Class A and B notes pay a floating spread over EURIBOR.

The issuer has sold protection on the reference assets. On occurrence of a credit event, the issuer will make credit protection payments to the swap counterparty (see Exhibit 7.19). If the vehicle experiences losses as a result of credit events or credit default swap trading, these are made up from the collateral account.

ALCO 1 Limited

The ALCO 1 CDO is described as the first rated synthetic balance sheet CDO from a non-Japanese bank.[16] It is a S$2.8 billion structure sponsored and managed by the Development Bank of Singapore (DBS). A summary of terms follows:

---

[16] Source: Moody's.

Name	ALCO 1 Limited
Originator	Development Bank of Singapore Ltd.
Arrangers	JPMorgan Chase Bank
	DBS Ltd.
Trustee	Bank of New York
Closing date	December 15, 2001
Maturity	March 2009
Portfolio	S$2.8 billion of credit default swaps (Singapore dollars)
Reference assets	199 reference obligations (136 obligors)
Portfolio Administrator	JPMorgan Chase Bank Institutional Trust Services

The structure allows DBS to shift the credit risk on a S$2.8 billion reference portfolio of mainly Singapore corporate loans to a special purpose vehicle, ALCO 1, using credit default swaps. As a result DBS can reduce the risk capital it has to hold on the reference loans, without physically moving the assets from its balance sheet. The structure is S$2.45 billion super-senior tranche—unfunded credit default swap—with S$224 million notes issue and S$126 million first-loss piece retained by DBS. The notes are issued in six classes, collateralized by Singapore government Treasury bills and a reserve bank account known as a "GIC" account. There is also a currency and interest-rate swap structure in place for risk hedging, and a put option that covers purchase of assets by arranger if the deal terminates before expected maturity date. The issuer enters into credit default swaps with specified list of counterparties. The default swap pool is static, but there is a substitution facility for up to 10% of the portfolio. This means that under certain specified conditions, up to 10% of the reference loan portfolio may be replaced by loans from outside the vehicle. Other than this though, the reference portfolio is static.

The first rated synthetic balance sheet deal in Asia, ALCO 1-type structures, have subsequently been adopted by other commercial banks in the region. The principal innovation of the vehicle is the method by which the reference credits are selected. The choice of reference credits on which swaps are written must, as expected with a CDO, follow a number of criteria set by the rating agency, including diversity score, rating factor, weighted average spread, geographical and industry concentration, among others.

Structure and Mechanics

The deal structure and note tranching are shown at Exhibit 7.20. The issuer enters into a portfolio credit default swap with DBS as the CDS

EXHIBIT 7.20   ALCO 1 Structure and Tranching

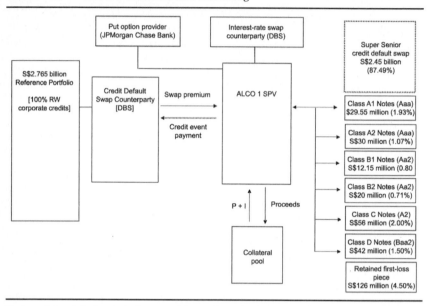

Source: Moody's Pre-Sale Report, November 12, 2001. Used with permission.

Class	Amount	Percent	Rating	Interest Rate
Super senior swap	S$2.450m	87.49%	NR	N/A
Class A1	US$29.55m	1.93%	Aaa	3m USD LIBOR + 50 bps
Class A2	S$30m	1.07%	Aaa	3m SOR + 45 bps
Class B1	US$12.15m	0.80%	Aa2	3m USD LIBOR + 85 bps
Class B2	S$30m	0.71%	Aa2	3m SOR + 80 bps
Class C	S$56m	2.00%	A2	5.20%
Class D	S$42m	1.50%	Baa2	6.70%

Source: Moody's.

counterparty to provide credit protection against losses in the reference portfolio. The credit default swaps are cash settled. In return for protection premium payments, after aggregate losses exceeding the S$126 million "threshold" amount, the issuer is obliged to make protection payments to DBS. The maximum obligation is the S$224 million note proceeds value. In standard fashion associated with securitized notes, further losses above the threshold amount will be allocated to overlying notes in their reverse order of seniority. The note proceeds are invested in collateral pool comprised initially of Singapore Treasury bills.

During the term of the transaction, DBS as the CDS counterparty is permitted to remove any eliminated reference obligations that are fully paid, terminated early or otherwise no longer eligible. In addition DBS has the option to remove up to 10% of the initial aggregate amount of the reference portfolio, and substitute new or existing reference names.

For this structure, credit events are defined specifically as:

- Failure to pay
- Bankruptcy

Note how this differs from European market CDOs where the list of defined credit events is invariably longer, frequently including restructuring and credit rating downgrade.

The reference portfolio is an Asian corporate portfolio, but with small percentage of loans originated in Australia. The portfolio is concentrated in Singapore (80%). The weighted average credit quality is Baa3/Ba1, with an average life of three years. The Moody's diversity score is low (20), reflecting the concentration of loans in Singapore. There is a high industrial concentration. The total portfolio at inception was 199 reference obligations amongst 136 reference entities (obligors). By structuring the deal in this way, DBS obtains capital relief on the funded portion of the assets, but at lower cost and less administrative burden than a traditional cash flow securitization, and without having to have a true sale of the assets.

Jazz CDO I B.V.

Jazz CDO I BV is an innovative CDO structure and one of the first *hybrid* CDOs introduced in the European market. A hybrid CDO combines elements of a cash flow arbitrage CDO and a managed synthetic CDO. Hence, the underlying assets are investment-grade bonds and loans, and synthetic assets such as credit default swaps and total return swaps.

The Jazz vehicle comprises a total of €1.5 billion of referenced assets, of which €210 million is made up of a note issue. A summary of terms follows:

Name	Jazz CDO I B.V.
Manager	Axa Investment Managers S.A.
Arrangers	Deutsche Bank AG
Closing date	March 8, 2002
Maturity	February 2011
Portfolio	€1.488 billion
Reference assets	Investment grade synthetic and cash securities
Portfolio Administrator	JPMorgan Chase Bank Institutional Trust Services

The hybrid arrangement of this deal enables the collateral manager to take a view on corporate and bank credits in both cash and synthetic markets; thus, a structure like Jazz bestows the greatest flexibility for credit trading on CDO originators. The vehicle is illustrated at Exhibit 7.21.

The main innovation of the structure is a design that incorporates both funded and unfunded assets as well as funded and unfunded liabilities. This arrangement means that the collateral manager is free to trade both cash and derivative instruments, thereby exploiting its experience and knowledge across the markets. At a time of increasing defaults in CDOs, during 2001 and 2002 (see Chapter 2), static pool deals began to be viewed unfavorably by certain investors, because of the inability to offload deteriorating or defaulted assets. Jazz CDO I is an actively managed deal, and its attraction reflects to a great extent the perception with which the collateral manager is viewed by investors. So the role of the collateral manager was critical to the ratings analysis of the deal. This covered:

- Experience in managing cash and synthetic assets.
- Its perceived strength in credit research.
- Previous experience in managing CDO vehicles.
- Infrastructure arrangements, such as settlement and processing capability.

These factors, together with the traditional analysis used for static pool cash CDOs, were used by the ratings agencies when assessing the transaction.

Structure

The assets in Jazz CDO I may be comprised of credit default swaps, total return swaps, bonds, and loans, at the collateral manager's discretion. The asset mix is set up by:

- Purchase of cash assets, funded by the proceeds of the note issue and the liquidity facility.
- Selling protection via credit default swaps.
- Buying protection via credit default swaps.
- Entering into total return swaps, whereby the total return of the reference assets is received by the vehicle in return for a payment of LIBOR plus spread (on the notional amount). This is funded via the liquidity facility.

The liability side of the structure is a combination of:

EXHIBIT 7.21 Jazz CDO I B.V. Structure Diagram

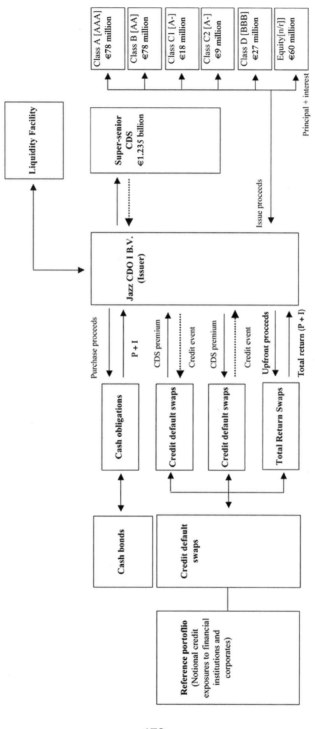

Source: S&P Post-sale report, February 2002. Used with permission.

■ The super-senior credit default swap.
■ Issued notes and equity piece (see Exhibit 7.21).

However, the asset and liability mix can be varied by the collateral manager at its discretion and can be expected to change over time. In theory the asset pool can comprise 100% cash bonds or 100% credit default swaps; in practice we should expect to see a mixture as shown in Exhibit 7.21.

Liquidity Facility

A liquidity facility of €1.7 billion is an integral part of the structure. It is used as a reserve to cover losses arising from credit default swap trading, occurrence of credit events, and to fund any purchases when the mix of cash versus synthetic assets is altered by the collateral manager. This can include the purchase of bonds and the funding of total return swaps. The facility is similar to a revolving credit facility and is provided by the arrangers of the transaction.

If the manager draws on the liquidity facility, this is viewed as a funded liability, similar to an issue of notes, and is in fact senior in the priority of payments to the overlying notes and the super-senior credit default swap.

Trading Arrangements

Hybrid CDOs are the latest development in the arena of managed synthetic CDOs. The Jazz CDO structure enables the portfolio manager to administer credit risk across cash and synthetic markets. The cash market instruments that may be traded include investment-grade corporate bonds, structured finance securities such as ABS or residential and commercial MBS, and corporate loans. The collateral manager may buy and sell both types of assets, that is, it may short credit in accordance with its view. In other words, the restriction that exists with the Blue Chip and Robeco III deals is removed in Jazz CDO. Therefore the collateral manager can buy protection in the credit derivative market as it wishes, and not only to offset an existing long credit position (sold protection). The only rules that must be followed when buying protection are that:

■ The counterparty risk is of an acceptable level.
■ There are sufficient funds in the vehicle to pay the credit derivative premiums.

The collateral manager may trade where existing assets go into default, or where assets have either improved or worsened in credit outlook (to take or cut a trading profit/loss). Another significant innovation is the ability of the SPV vehicle to enter into *basis trades* in the credit market. (We describe basis in credit default swaps in Chapter 4.) An example of such a trade would be to buy a cash bond and simultaneously purchase protection on that bond in the credit default swap market effectively shorting the bond to take advantage of mispricing opportunities. Similar to trades undertaken in the exchange-traded government bond futures market, this is an arbitrage-type strategy where the trader seeks to exploit price mismatches between the cash and synthetic markets.

The various combinations of trades that may be entered into are treated in different ways for counterparty risk and regulatory capital. For an offsetting position in a single name, the options are:

- Using only credit default swaps to cancel out an exposure, both credit default swaps traded with the same counterparty: this is netted out for risk purposes.
- Using credit default swaps only, but with different counterparties: there will be a set-aside for counterparty risk requirement exposure.
- Using credit default swap and cash bond: regarded as a AAA-rated asset for capital purposes.

The offering circular for the deal lists a number of trading guidelines that must be followed by the collateral manager. These include a limit of 20% by volume annual turnover level.

Channel CDO, Limited

Channel CDO is a U.S. market synthetic CDO that represents features of interest because it is another hybrid CDO structure. It is described as a managed hybrid transaction, with liabilities tranched into a super-senior swap element and a series of credit-linked notes. However the equity element of the structure are termed "Preference Shares." The CDO collateral manager is PIMCO, an investment advisory firm based in California. The deal closed in October 2002. The liability structure is shown at Exhibit 7.22.

The liabilities are referenced to a portfolio comprising a mixture of credit default swaps, corporate bonds and "eligible investments," which are typically money market instruments such as Treasury bills or straight bank deposits. The equity element is made up of $37.5 million of notes that pay out residual excess spread in the vehicle. The holders of the notes (preferred shares) bear the initial credit risk should any assets in the reference pool experience defaults or credit events. The deal is $60 million overcol-

EXHIBIT 7.22   Channel CDO Limited

Tranche	Amount ($ million)	Percent	Rating	Coupon or Spread
Super senior	840	82.76	[NR]	0.145%
Class A	90	8.87	Aaa	3m LIBOR + 0.5%
Class B	20	1.97	Aa3	3m LIBOR + 1.0%
Class C	15	1.48	A3	3m LIBOR + 2.25%
Class D	12.5	1.23	Baa2	3m LIBOR + 3.25%
Preference Shares	37.5	3.69	[NR]	Residual spread

Source: Moody's, *New Issue Report,* December 20, 2002. Used with permission.

lateralized, with this sum being placed in a reserve pool of cash. This pool is used to cover the first $60 million of credit losses.

In many CDO deals, the period when the originator acquires assets for placing into the SPV is known as the ramp-up phase. It is common for deals to be closed fully once the ramp-up period is over. An interesting feature of this transaction was that it was closed while the ramp-up phase was still in operation. As at October 2002 the vehicle was approximately 60% ramped-up. As described in the offering circular for this deal, the vehicle must be fully ramped up within a six-month period following the close date.

The deal was rated by Moody's. Under the terms of the rating agency criteria, as is common with CDOs, the portfolio manager must adhere to certain specified criteria with regard to the balance of the portfolio and investment decisions made subsequent to deal closure. These include restrictions on the amount of non-U.S. issuer reference credits, the amount of structured finance credits such as ABS securities, the number of zero-coupon bonds and the number of long-dated bonds. The Trustee to the deal, Wells Fargo Bank, monitors adherence to all the investment criteria during the life of the deal.

Conclusion of Case Studies

The four case studies we have described here are innovative structures and a creative combination of securitization technology and credit derivative instruments. We have seen that later structures have been introduced into the market that make use of total return swaps as well as credit default swaps, and also remove the restriction on shorting credit. Analysis of these SPVs shows how a collateral manager can utilize the arrangement to exploit its expertise in credit trading, and its experience of the credit derivatives market, to provide attractive returns for investors. The most flexible SPVs, such as Jazz CDO I, in theory allow more efficient portfolio risk management when compared to static or more restrictive deals. As the market in synthetic corporate credit is frequently more liquid than the cash market for the same reference names, it is reasonable to expect more transactions of this type in the near future.

CHAPTER 8

Credit Risk Modeling: Structural Models

To value credit derivatives it is necessary to be able to model credit risk. The two most commonly used approaches to model credit risk are structural models and reduced form models. In this chapter and the next, we will discuss these two approaches: structural models in this chapter and reduced form models in the next chapter.

The first structural model for default risky bonds was proposed by Fischer Black and Myron Scholes who explained how equity owners hold a call option on the firm. After that Robert Merton extended the framework and analyzed risk debt behavior with the model. Robert Geske extended the Black-Scholes-Merton model to include multiple debts. Recently many barrier models appear as an easy solution for analyzing the risky debt problem. We discuss each of these models in this chapter. In Chapter 10, we explain how to value credit default swaps.

COMPLEXITIES IN CREDIT RISK MODELING

Modeling credit risk is a difficult task. One form of credit risk, default risk, is a rare event. Historical data on default rates are discussed in Chapter 2. Default data are considerably less in comparison to the data available for the modeling of interest rate risk where time series of U.S. Treasury prices are available on a daily basis for many decades. Moreover, the sheer diversity of the corporations involved in terms of industrial sector, size, leverage, and quality of management makes it extremely difficult to use default data to draw any meaningful and possibly predictive conclusions about the likelihood of default.

Default has many different causes ranging from microeconomic factors (such as poor management) to macroeconomic factors (such as high interest rates and recession). These various causes make default very hard to predict. In these cases, default is a result of an inability to pay for corporate debtors. In the case of sovereign debt, default may not be a result of an inability to pay, but may be due to an unwillingness to pay that is driven by political motives (i.e., political risk).

In addition, default is not a universal concept. Countries have different laws dealing with defaults. In the United States, for example, the Bankruptcy Act of 1978 as amended sets forth the rights of the parties involved in a bankruptcy proceeding. Even where there are laws setting forth the priority of payments in a bankruptcy, the courts have not always followed them. For example, as explained in Chapter 2 when a company is liquidated, creditors receive distributions based on the "absolute priority rule" to the extent assets are available. The absolute priority rule is the principle that senior creditors are paid in full before junior creditors are paid anything. For secured creditors and unsecured creditors, the absolute priority rule guarantees their seniority to equityholders. In liquidations, the absolute priority rule generally holds. In contrast, there is a good body of literature that argues that strict absolute priority has not been upheld by the courts or the SEC. Studies of actual reorganizations under Chapter 11 have found that the violation of absolute priority is the rule rather the exception.[1]

Finally, adding to the complication of credit risk modeling is that the data collected regarding default rates are not necessarily consistent with the definition of credit events for determining a payout trigger for a credit default swap. For example, data on defaults by rating agencies do not include restructuring of debt obligations. Yet, in a trade the ISDA definition of credit events may include restructuring (old restructuring as defined by the 1999 ISDA definition and modified restructuring as defined by the 2001 ISDA definition). As a result, a debt restructuring due to a postponement of the principal repayment must be taken into account in modeling credit risk for evaluating a credit default swap but default data would not reflect such credit events.

OVERVIEW OF CURRENT MODELS

Models for credit risks have long existed in the insurance and corporate finance literature. Those models concentrate on default rates, credit ratings, and credit risk premiums. These traditional models focus on diver-

---

[1] See the references cited in Chapter 2.

sification and assume that default risks are idiosyncratic and hence can be diversified away in large portfolios. Models of this kind are along the line of portfolio theory that employs the *capital asset pricing model* (CAPM). In the CAPM, only the systematic risk, or market risk, matters.

For single isolated credits, the models calculate risk premiums as markups onto the risk-free rate. Since the default risk is not diversified away, a similar model to the CAPM called the *capital market line* is used to compute the correct markup for bearing the default risk. The *Sharpe ratio* is commonly used to measure how credit risks are priced.[2]

Modern credit derivative models can be partitioned into two groups known as structural models and reduced form models. *Structural models* were pioneered by Black and Scholes[3] and Merton.[4] The basic idea, common to all structural-type models, is that a company defaults on its debt if the value of the assets of the company falls below a certain default point. For this reason, these models are also known as *firm-value models*. In these models it has been demonstrated that default can be modeled as an option and, as a result, researchers were able to apply the same principles used for option pricing to the valuation of risky corporate securities. The application of option pricing theory avoids the use of risk premium and tries to use other marketable securities to price the option. The use of the option pricing theory set forth by Black-Scholes-Merton (BSM) provides a significant improvement over traditional methods for valuing default risky bonds. It also offers not only much more accurate prices but provides information about how to hedge out the default risk which was not obtainable from traditional methods. Subsequent to the work of BSM, there have been many extensions and these extensions are described in this chapter.

The second group of credit models, known as *reduced form models*, are more recent. These models, most notably the Jarrow-Turnbull[5] and Duffie-Singleton[6] models, do not look inside the firm. Instead, they model directly the likelihood of default or downgrade. Not only is the current probability of default modeled, some researchers attempt to

---

[2] Robert Merton, "Option Pricing When Underlying Stock Returns Are Discontinuous," *Journal of Financial Economics* 3 (1976), pp. 125–144.
[3] Fischer Black and Myron Scholes, "The Pricing of Options and Corporate Liabilities," *Journal of Political Economy* 81, no. 3 (1973), pp. 637–654.
[4] Robert Merton, "Theory of Rational Option Pricing," *Bell Journal of Economics* (Spring 1973), pp. 141–183, and Robert Merton, "On the Pricing of Corporate Debt: The Risk Structure of Interest Rates," *Journal of Finance* 29, no. 2 (1974), pp. 449–470.
[5] Robert Jarrow and Stuart Turnbull, "Pricing Derivatives on Financial Securities Subject to Default Risk," *Journal of Finance* 50, no. 1 (1995), pp. 53–86.
[6] Darrell Duffie and Kenneth Singleton, "Modelling the Term Structure of Defaultable Bonds," working paper, Stanford University (1997).

model a "forward curve" of default probabilities that can be used to price instruments of varying maturities. Modeling a probability has the effect of making default a surprise—the default event is a random event which can suddenly occur at any time. All we know is its probability. In the next chapter, we describe some of these approaches in detail.

There is no standard model for credit. Part of the reason why this is so is that each of the models has its own set of advantages and disadvantages, making the choice of which to use depend heavily on what the model is to be used for. A prescriptive discussion is provided in the next chapter.

THE BLACK-SCHOLES-MERTON MODEL

The earliest credit model that employed the option pricing theory can be credited to BSM. Black-Scholes, in the last section of their seminal option pricing paper, explicitly articulated that corporate liabilities can be viewed as a covered call: own the asset but short a call option. In the simplest setting where the company has only one zero-coupon debt, at the maturity of the debt, the debt holder either gets paid the face value of the debt—in such a case, the ownership of the company is transferred to the equity holder—or takes control of the company—in such a case, the equity holder receives nothing. The debt holder of the company therefore is subject to default risk for he or she may not be able to receive the face value of his or her investment. BSM effectively turned a risky debt evaluation into a covered call evaluation whereby the option pricing formulas can readily apply.

In BSM, the company balance sheet consists of issued equity with a market value at time t equal to $E(t)$. On the liability side is debt with a face value of K issued in the form of a zero-coupon bond which matures at time T. The market value of this debt at time t is denoted by $D(t,T)$. The value of the assets of the firm at time t is given by $A(t)$.

At time T (the maturity of the debt), the market value of the issued equity of the company is the amount remaining after the debts have been paid out of the firm's assets; that is,

$$E(T) = \max\{A(T) - K, 0\}$$

This payoff is identical to that of a call option on the value of the firm's assets struck at the face value of the debt. The payoff is graphed as a function of the asset value in Exhibit 8.1. The holders of the risky corporate debt get paid either the face value, K, under no default or take over the firm, A, under default. Hence the value of the debt on the maturity date is given by

EXHIBIT 8.1   Payoff Diagrams at Maturity for Equity, Risky Debt, and
Risk-Free Debt

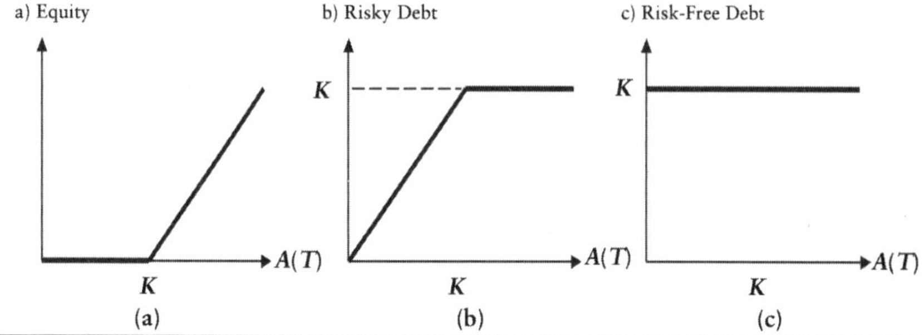

a) Equity   b) Risky Debt   c) Risk-Free Debt

(a)   (b)   (c)

$$D(T, T) = \min\{A(T), K\}$$
$$= A(T) - \max\{A(T) - K, 0\} \tag{8.1}$$
$$= K - \max\{K - A(T), 0\} \tag{8.2}$$

The equations provide two interpretations. Equation (8.1) decomposes the risky debt into the asset and a short call. This interpretation
was first given by Black and Scholes that equity owners essentially own
a call option of the company. If the company performs well, then the
equity owners should call the company; or otherwise, the equity owners
let the debt owners own the company. Equation (8.2) decomposes the
risky debt into a risk-free debt and a short put. This interpretation
explains the default risk of the corporate debt. The issuer (equity owners) can put the company back to the debt owner when the performance
is bad.[7] The default risk hence is the put option. These relationships are
shown in Exhibit 8.1. Exhibits 8.1(a) and 8.1(b) explain the relationship
between equity and risky debt and Exhibits 8.1(b) and 8.1(c) explain the
relationship between risky and risk-free debts.

Note that the value of the equity and debt when added together must
equal the assets of the firm at all times, i.e., $A(t) = E(t) + D(t,T)$. Clearly, at
maturity, this is true as we have

$$E(T) + D(T, T) = \max\{A(T) - K, 0\} + \min\{A(T), K\}$$
$$= A(T)$$

as required.

---

[7] A *covered call* is a combination of a selling call option and owning the same face
value of the shares, which might have to be delivered should the option expire in the
money. If the option expires in the money, a net profit equal to the strike is made. If
the option expires worthless, then the position is worth the stock price.

Since any corporate debt is a contingent claim on the firm's future asset value at the time the debt matures, this is what we must model in order to capture the default. BSM assumed that the dynamics of the asset value follow a lognormal stochastic process of the form

$$\frac{dA(t)}{A(t)} = rdt + \sigma dW(t) \tag{8.3}$$

where r is the instantaneous risk-free rate which is assumed constant, σ is the percentage volatility, and $W(t)$ is the Wiener process under the *risk neutral measure.*[8] This is the same process as is generally assumed within equity markets for the evolution of stock prices and has the property that the asset value of the firm can never go negative and that the random changes in the asset value increase proportionally with the asset value itself. As it is the same assumption as used by Black-Scholes for pricing equity options, it is possible to use the option pricing equations developed by BSM to price risky corporate liabilities.

The company can default only at the maturity time of the debt when the payment of the debt (face value) is made. At maturity, if the asset value lies above the face value, there is no default, else the company is in bankruptcy and the recovery value of the debt is the asset value of the firm. While we shall discuss more complex cases later, for this simple one-period case, the probability of default at maturity is

$$p = \int_{-\infty}^{K} \phi[A(T)]dA(T) = 1 - N(d_2) \tag{8.4}$$

where $\phi(\cdot)$ represents the log normal density function, $N(\cdot)$ represents the cumulative normal probability, and

$$d_2 = \frac{\ln A(t) - \ln K + (r - \sigma^2/2)(T - t)}{\sigma\sqrt{T - t}}$$

Equation (8.4) implies that the risk neutral probability of in the money $N(d_2)$ is also the *survival probability.* To find the current value of

---

[8] The discussions of the risk neutral measure and the change of measure using the Girsonav theorem can be found in standard finance texts. See, for example, Darrell Duffie, *Dynamic Asset Pricing* (Princeton, NJ: Princeton University Press, 2000), and John Hull, *Options, Futures, and Other Derivatives* (New York: Prentice Hall, 2002).

the debt, $D(t,T)$ (maturing at time T), we need to first use the BSM result to find the current value of the equity. As shown above, this is equal to the value of a call option:

$$E(t) = A(t)N(d_1) - e^{-r(T-t)}KN(d_2) \qquad (8.5)$$

where $d_1 = d_2 + \sigma\sqrt{T-t}$. The current value of the debt is a covered call value:

$$\begin{aligned} D(t, T) &= A(t) - E(t) \qquad (8.6) \\ &= A(t) - [A(t)N(d_1) - e^{-r(T-t)}KN(d_2)] \\ &= A(t)[1 - N(d_1)] + e^{-r(T-t)}KN(d_2) \end{aligned}$$

Note that the second term in the last equation is the present value of probability-weighted face value of the debt. It means that if default does not occur (with probability $N(d_2)$), the debt owner receives the face value K. Since the probability is risk neutral, the probability-weighted value is discounted by the risk-free rate. The first term represents the recovery value. The two values together make up the value of debt.

The yield of the debt is calculated by solving $D(t,T) = Ke^{-y(T-t)}$ for y to give

$$y = \frac{\ln K - \ln D(t, T)}{T - t} \qquad (8.7)$$

Consider the case of a company which currently has net assets worth $140 million and has issued $100 million in debt in the form of a zero-coupon bond which matures in one year. By looking at the equity markets, we estimate that the volatility of the asset value is 30%. The risk-free interest rate is at 5%. We therefore have

$$A(t) = \$140 \text{ million}$$
$$K = \$100 \text{ million}$$
$$\sigma = 30\%$$
$$T - t = 1 \text{ year}$$
$$r = 5\%$$

Applying equation (8.5), the equity value based upon the above example is

$$d_2 = \frac{\ln 140 - \ln 100 + (0.05 - 0.3^2) \times 1}{0.3\sqrt{1}} = 1.4382$$

$$d_1 = 1.4382 + 0.30 = 1.1382$$

$$E(t) = 140 \times N(1.1382) - e^{-0.05} \times 100 \times N(1.4382)$$
$$= \$46.48 \text{ million}$$

and market debt value, by equation (8.6) is

$$D(t, T) = A(t) - E(t) = 140 - 46.48 = \$93.52 \text{ million}$$

Hence, the yield of the debt is, by equation (8.7):

$$y = \frac{\ln 100 - \ln 93.52}{1} = 6.70\%$$

which is higher than the 5% risk-free rate by 170 bps. This "credit spread" reflects the 1-year default probability from equation (8.4):

$$p = 1 - N(1.4382) = 12.75\%$$

and the recovery value of

$$A(t)(1 - N(d_1)) = \$17.85$$

if default occurs.

From above, we can see that, as the asset value increases, the firm is more likely to remain solvent, the default probability drops. When default is extremely unlikely, the risky debt will be surely paid off at par, the risky debt will become risk free, and yield the risk-free return (5% in our example). In contrast, when default is extremely likely (default probability approaching 1), the debt holder is almost surely to take over the company, the debt value should be the same as the asset value which approaches 0.

Implications of BSM Model

As we can see from this example, the BSM model captures some important properties of risky debt; namely, the risky yield increases with the debt-to-asset leverage of the firm and its asset value volatility. Using the above equations, one can also plot the maturity dependency of the credit spread, defined as the difference between the risky yield and the risk-free rate.

What is appealing about this model is that the shapes of the credit spread term structures resemble those observed in the market. The highly leveraged firm has a credit spread which starts high, indicating that if the debt were to mature in the short term, it would almost certainly default with almost no recovery. However as the maturity increases, the likelihood of the firm asset value increasing to the point that default does not occur increases and the credit spread falls accordingly. For the medium leveraged firm, the credit spread is small at the short end—there are just sufficient assets to cover the debt repayment. As the maturity increases, there is a rapid increase in credit spread as the likelihood of the assets falling below the debt value rises. For the low-leveraged company, the initial spread is close to zero and so can only increase as the maturity increases and more time is allowed for the asset value to drop. The general downward trend of these spread curves at the long end due to the fact that on average the asset value grows at the riskless rate and so given enough time, will always grow to cover the fixed debt.

Empirical evidence in favor of these term structure shapes has been reported by Fons who observed similar relationships between spread term structure shapes and credit quality.[9] Contrary evidence was reported by Helwege and Turner who observed that the term structure of some low-quality firms is upward sloping rather than downward sloping.[10]

GESKE COMPOUND OPTION MODEL

If the company has a series of debts (zero coupon), then it is quite easy for the BSM model to characterize default at different times. The trick is to use the compound option model by Geske.[11] The main point is that defaults are a series of contingent events. Later defaults are contingent upon prior no-default. Hence, layers of contingent defaults build up a series of sequential compound options, one linking to the other.[12]

---

[9] Jerome Fons, "Using Default Rates to Model the Term Structure of Credit Risk," *Financial Analysts Journal* (September/October 1994), pp. 25–32.

[10] Jean Helwege and Christopher Turner, "The Slope of the Credit Yield Curve for Speculative-Grade Issuers," Federal Reserve Bank of New York Working Paper No. 97-25 (1997).

[11] See Geske, "The Valuation of Debt as Compound Options," and Robert Geske and Herbert Johnson, "The Valuation of Corporate Liabilities as Compound Options: A Correction," *Journal of Financial and Quantitative Analysis* 19, no. 2 (1984), pp. 231–232.

[12] A *compound option* is an option on another option.

For example, suppose there are two zero-coupon bonds expiring in one year and two years, respectively. Both bonds have a $100 face value. The asset value is $200 today and follows the diffusion process given by equation (8.3). If the asset value falls below the face value in year 1, the company is technically under default. The company may seek additional capital to keep it alive or the company may simply declare default and let the holders of the two debts liquidate the company. In this case we have

$$
\begin{aligned}
A(t) &= \$200 \text{ million} \\
K_1 &= \$100 \text{ million} \\
K_2 &= \$100 \text{ million} \\
\sigma &= 20\% \\
r &= 5\% \\
T_1 - t &= 1 \text{ year} \\
T_2 - t &= 2 \text{ years}
\end{aligned}
$$

The default point of a two-year model is the key to the problem. The recovery further complicates the problem. For example, the company may default when it fails to pay the first debt ($100); or the company may default if its asset value falls below the market value of the total debt, which is the face value of the first debt ($100) and the market value of the second debt. This happens at a situation where the second debt owner can audit the asset value of the firm. Furthermore, a fixed recovery of these debts simplifies the problem. But oftentimes recoveries of debts depend on claims on the assets at different priority levels.

Take a simple example where the company defaults when it fails to pay its first debt. In this case the default probability is

$$
d_2 = \frac{\ln 200 - \ln 100 + (5\% - 0.2^2/2) \times 1}{0.2 \sqrt{1}} = 3.6157
$$

$$
p = 1 - N(3.6157) = 0.015\%
$$

If we further assume that the first debt has a recovery rate of 0, then the debt value is

$$
D(t, T_1) = (1 - 0.015\%)e^{-5\% \times 1} \times 100 = 95.11
$$

If we calculate the yield as before, we find that the spread to the risk-free rate is 1.5 bps. If the recovery is the asset value, then we do need to follow equation (8.5) and the debt value is

$$d_2 = \frac{\ln 200 - \ln 100 + (0.05 - 0.2^2) \times 1}{0.2\sqrt{1}} = 3.6157$$

$$d_1 = 3.6157 + 0.2 = 3.8157$$

$$E(t) = 200 \times N(3.8157) - e^{-0.05} \times 100 \times N(3.6157)$$
$$= 104.877$$

$$D(t, T_1) = 200 - 104.8777 = 95.1223$$

The small difference in the two results is because the default probability is really small (only 0.015%). When the default probability gets bigger, the debt value difference will get larger.

The second bond is more complex to evaluate. It can be defaulted in $t = 1$ when the first debt is defaulted or $t = 2$ when only itself is defaulted. The retiring of the first debt can be viewed as the dividend of the stock. Under the lognormal model described above, we can write the firm value at the end of the two-year period as

$$A(t, T_2) = [A(t, T_1) - K_1]e^{(r-\sigma^2/2)(T_1-t)+\sigma W(T_1)}$$
$$= A(t)e^{(r-\sigma^2/2)(T_2-t)+\sigma W(T_2)}$$
$$- K_1 e^{(r-\sigma^2/2)(T_1-t)+\sigma W(T_1)}$$

where K_1 is the face value of the 1-year debt and

$$W(t) = \int_0^t dW(u)\,du$$

The default probability of the second debt is the sum of the first year default probability and the second year default probability as follows:

$$\Pr[A(T_1) < K_1] + \Pr[A(T_1) > K_1] \text{ and } (A(T_2) < K_2)$$

If the company survives the first period, it has to pay off the first debt, which clearly causes the asset price to be discontinuous. The discontinuity of the asset value makes the valuation of the second debt more difficult. Geske suggests that the if the firm issues equity to pay for the first debt, then the asset value should remain continuous and a closed-form solution can be achieved. In the appendix, we provide a simple valuation chart to demonstrate the intuition of the Geske model. Here, we simply show the result:

$$D(t, T_1) = e^{-r(T_1-t)}K_1 N(d_{11}^-) + A(t)[1 - N(d_{11}^+)]$$

$$\begin{aligned} D(t, T_2) = \; & A(t)[N(d_{11}^+) - M(d_{12}^+, d_{22}^+)] \\ & + e^{-r(T_2-t)}K_2 M(d_{12}^-, d_{22}^-) \\ & + e^{-r(T_1-t)}K_1[N(d_{12}^-) - N(d_{11}^-)] \end{aligned}$$

where

$$d_{ij}^\pm = \frac{\ln A(0) - \ln K_{ij} + (r \pm \sigma^2/2)}{\sigma\sqrt{T_{ij}}}$$

K_{12} is the internal solution to $E(T_1) = K_{11}$, which is given as the face value of the first debt (maturing at $t = 1$ year) and K_{22} is the face value of the second debt (maturing at $t = 2$). This formulation can be extended to include any number of debts, $T_{11} = T_{12} = T_1 = 1$ and $T_{22} = 2$. The correlation in the bivariate normal probability functions is the square root of the ratio of two maturity times. In this case, it is $\sqrt{1/2}$.

Note that the total debt values add to

$$\begin{aligned} & D(t, T_1) + D(t, T_2) \\ = \; & A(t)[1 - M(d_{12}^+, d_{22}^+)] + e^{-r(T_1-t)}K_1 N(d_{12}^-) \\ & + e^{-r(T_2-t)}K_2 M(d_{12}^-, d_{22}^-) \end{aligned}$$

which implies that the one-year survival probability is $N(d_{12}^-)$ and two-year is $M(d_{12}^-, d_{22}^-)$, which is a bivariate normal probability function with correlation $\sqrt{T_1/T_2}$. The equity value, which is the residual value:

$$\begin{aligned} E(t) = \; & A(t) - D(t, T_1) - D(t, T_2) \\ = \; & A(t)M(d_{12}^+, d_{22}^+) - e^{-r(T_1-t)}K_1 N(d_{12}^-) \\ & - e^{-r(T_2-t)}K_2 M(d_{12}^-, d_{22}^-) \end{aligned}$$

which is precisely the compound option formula derived by Geske. The two debt values in the example are $95.12 and $81.27, respectively. The equity is $23.61.

Using the information given in our earlier example, we solve for the "internal strike price"—the asset price at time 1 for $E(1) = K_{11}$ to be $195.12. In other words, if the asset price at time 1, $A(1)$, exceeds this value, the company survives; otherwise the company defaults. As a result, we can calculate the default probability of the first year to be:

$$Pr(A(T_1) < K_{12}) = 1 - N(d_{12}) = 1 - 0.6078 = 0.3922$$

The two-year total default probability is the one whereby the company defaults in year 1 or it survives the first year but defaults the second year:

$$Pr[A(T_1) < K_{12} \cup A(T_2) < K_{22}] = 1 - M(\overline{d}_{12}, \overline{d}_{22})$$
$$= 1 - 0.6077 = 0.3923$$

The default probability therefore between the first year and the second year is only 0.0001. In other words, the Geske model indicates that the majority default probability is in the first year, and then the company can survive with almost certainty.

In general, structural models are not easy to calibrate since information regarding the size and priority of claimants on a company's assets is not readily available. Typically companies only publish details of their balance sheets at most quarterly, and some companies, particularly those facing severe financial difficulties, do not disclose the full picture. Instead, practitioners tend to take equity volatility as a proxy for the asset value volatility.[13]

BARRIER STRUCTURAL MODELS

In addition to the Geske (compound option) model, another series of models have also evolved to extend the BSM model to multiple periods. Pioneered by Black and Cox,[14] these models view default as a knockout

---

[13] For example, KMV uses $\sigma_E = (A/E)N(d_1)\sigma_A$, where σ_E is the volatility of equity and σ_A is the volatility of the asset.
[14] Fischer Black and John Cox, "Valuing Corporate Securities: Some Effects of Bond Indenture Provisions," *Journal of Finance* 31, no. 2 (1976), pp. 351–367.

(down-and-out barrier) option[15] where default occurred the moment the firm value crossed a certain threshold.

More recently Longstaff and Schwartz[16] examined the effect of stochastic interest rates as did Briys and de Varenne[17] who modeled the default as being triggered when the forward price of the firm value hits a barrier. Few studies within the structural approach of credit risk valuation have incorporated jumps in the firm value process, because of lack of analytic tractability. Zhou[18] incorporates jumps into a setting used in Longstaff and Schwartz.[19] However, this model is very computation intensive.

Huang and Huang propose a jump-diffusion structural model which allows for analytically tractable solutions for both bond prices and default probabilities and is easy to implement.[20] The presence of jumps overcomes two related limitations of the BSM approach. First, it makes it possible for default to be a surprise since the jump cannot be anticipated as the asset value process is no longer continuous. Jumps also make it more likely that firms with low leverage can suddenly default in the short term and so enables them to have wider spreads at the short end than previously possible.

The barrier-based models all assume an exogenous barrier, crossing which triggers default. Given the firm value process described by equation (8.3), the probability of crossing a flat barrier is easy to compute.[21]

---

[15] A barrier option is a path dependent option. For such options both the payoff of the option and the survival of the option to the stated expiration date depends on whether the price of the underlying or the underlying reference rate reaches a specified level over the life of the option. Barrier options are also called down-and-out barrier options. Knockout options are used to describe two types of barrier options: knock-out options and knock-in options. The former is an option that is terminated once a specified price or rate level is realized by the underlying. A knock-in option is an option that is activated once a specified price or rate level is realized by the underlying.

[16] Francis Longstaff and Eduardo Schwartz, "A Simple Approach to Valuing Risky Fixed and Floating Rate Debt," *Journal of Finance* 50, no. 3 (1995), pp. 789–819.

[17] Eric Briys and Francois de Varenne, "Valuing Risky Fixed Rate Debt: An Extension," *Journal of Financial and Quantitative Analysis* 32, no. 2 (1997), pp. 239–248.

[18] Chunsheng Zhou, "An Analysis of Default Correlations and Multiple Defaults," *Review of Financial Studies* (2001), pp. 555–576.

[19] Longstaff and Schwartz, "A Simple Approach to Valuing Risky Fixed and Floating Rate Debt."

[20] Ming Huang and Jay Huang, "How Much of the Corporate-Treasury Yield Spread is Due to Credit Risk?" working paper, Stanford University (2002).

[21] The simple barrier option model can be found in Hull, *Options, Futures, and Other Derivatives.*

If the barrier is higher than the strike, that is, $H > K$, then the option value, which is the value of equity, is

$$
E(t) = A(t) \left\{ N(d^+) - \left[\frac{H}{A(t)} \right]^{-2q} N(b^+) \right\}
$$
$$
- e^{-r(T-t)} K \left\{ N(d^-) - \left[\frac{H}{A(t)} \right]^{2q-2} N(b^-) \right\}
$$

and the debt value is simply $A(t) - E(t)$:

$$
D(t, T) = A(t) \left\{ 1 - N(d^+) + \left[\frac{H}{A(t)} \right]^{2q} N(b^+) \right\}
$$
$$
+ e^{-r(T-t)} K \left\{ N(d^-) - \left[\frac{H}{A(t)} \right]^{2q-2} N(b^-) \right\}
$$

where

$$
d^{\pm} = \frac{\ln A(t) - \ln H}{\sigma \sqrt{T-t}} + (q - \tfrac{1}{2}) \sigma \sqrt{T-t} \pm \tfrac{1}{2} \sigma \sqrt{T-t}
$$

$$
b^{\pm} = \frac{\ln H - \ln A(t)}{\sigma \sqrt{T-t}} + (q - \tfrac{1}{2}) \sigma \sqrt{T-t} \pm \tfrac{1}{2} \sigma \sqrt{T-t}
$$

$$
q = r / \sigma^2 + \tfrac{1}{2} \sigma
$$

Note that the debt value consists of two parts, the coupon present value (second term) and recovery present value (first term). The coupon present value is the risk neutral survival probability (terms in brackets) times the coupon (K) times the risk-free discount factor:

$$
e^{-r(T_1 - t)}
$$

The survival probability is the probability of staying above barrier H at all times and also above strike K at maturity, which is equal to the probability of staying above the barrier at all times (first term in brackets) minus the probability of staying above the barrier but falls below the strike (second term in brackets). One minus such probability is the default probability, and for this condition the debt owner recovers the asset value.[22]

When $H < K$, then debt and equity values are:

$$E(t) = A(t)\left\{N(x^+) - \left[\frac{H}{A(0)}\right]^{2q}N(y^+)\right\}$$

$$-e^{-rT}K\left\{N(x^-) - \left[\frac{H}{A(0)}\right]^{2q-2}N(y^-)\right\}$$

$$D(t, T) = A(t)\left\{1 - N(x^+) + \left[\frac{H}{A(0)}\right]^{2q}N(y^+)\right\}$$

$$+ e^{-rT}K\left\{N(x^-) - \left[\frac{H}{A(0)}\right]^{2q-2}N(y^-)\right\}$$

where

$$x^{\pm} = \frac{\ln A(0) - \ln K + r(T-t)}{\sigma\sqrt{T-t}} \pm \tfrac{1}{2}\sigma\sqrt{T-t}$$

$$y^{\pm} = \frac{2\ln H - \ln A(t) - \ln K}{\sigma\sqrt{T-t}} + (q - \tfrac{1}{2})\sigma\sqrt{T-t} \pm \tfrac{1}{2}\sigma\sqrt{T-t}$$

The interpretation of the probabilities is the same.

---

[22] Note that

$$N(d^-) - \left[\frac{H}{A(t)}\right]^{2q-2}N(h^-)$$

and

$$N(d^+) - \left[\frac{H}{A(t)}\right]^{2q}N(h^+)$$

Both represent survival probability, but under different measures. For details, see Ren-Raw Chen, "Credit Risk Modelling: A General Framework," working paper Rutgers University (2003).

Usually the barrier is lower than the face value of the debt. Hence, we shall use the latter formulas to compute the values of debt and equity. To make the results of the barrier model comparable to those of Geske, we let the asset value be $200 and the face value also be $150. Also let the barrier be $150. The remaining information for the barrier model remains the same (as the Geske model): Volatility is 0.2, risk-free rate is 5%, and the time to maturity is two years.

Using above equations for $E(t)$ and $D(t,T)$, we obtain the equity value to be $62.65 and the debt value to be $200 - $62.65 = $137.35. This is slightly higher than the Geske result of $23.61. Clearly the two models cannot be directly comparable, since one assumes two discrete default points and one assumes continuous default; moreover, one assumes an endogenous barrier and one assumes exogenous barrier. The survival probability is

$$N(d^-) - \left[\frac{H}{A(t)}\right]^{2q-2} N(b^-) = 0.8905 - 0.2104 = 0.6801$$

Black and Cox propose a time-dependent, exponentially increasing barrier: $H(t) = e^{-r(T-t)}C$. In this case, the bond price is derived as

$$
\begin{aligned}
D(t, T) = {}& e^{-r(T-t)} P[N(z_1) - y^{2q-2} N(z_2)] \\
& + e^{-a(T-t)} A(0)[N(z_3) - y^{2q} N(z_4) \\
& + e^{a(T-t)} y^{\theta+\zeta} N(z_5) + e^{a(T-t)} y^{\theta+\zeta} N(z_6) \\
& - y^{\theta-\eta} N(z_7) - y^{\theta-\eta} N(z_8)]
\end{aligned}
$$

where

$$y = e^{-\gamma(T-t)} C / A(0)$$

$$\theta = (r - a - \gamma + \tfrac{1}{2}\sigma^2)/\sigma^2$$

$$\delta = (r - a - \gamma + \tfrac{1}{2}\sigma^2)^2 + 2\sigma^2(r - \gamma)$$

$$\zeta = \sqrt{\delta}/\sigma^2$$

$$\eta = \sqrt{\delta - 2\sigma^2 a}/\sigma^2$$

$$z_1 = [\ln A(0) - \ln K + (r - a - \tfrac{1}{2}\sigma^2)(T-t)]/\sqrt{\sigma^2(T-t)}$$

$$z_2 = [\ln A(0) - \ln K + 2\ln y + (r - a - \tfrac{1}{2}\sigma^2)(T-t)]/\sqrt{\sigma^2(T-t)}$$

$$z_3 = [\ln K - \ln A(0) - (r - a - \tfrac{1}{2}\sigma^2)(T-t)]/\sqrt{\sigma^2(T-t)}$$

$$z_4 = [\ln A(0) - \ln K + 2\ln y + (r - a + \tfrac{1}{2}\sigma^2)(T-t)]/\sqrt{\sigma^2(T-t)}$$

$$z_5 = [\ln y + \zeta\sigma^2(T-t)]/\sqrt{\sigma^2(T-t)}$$

$$z_6 = [\ln y - \zeta\sigma^2(T-t)]/\sqrt{\sigma^2(T-t)}$$

$$z_7 = [\ln y + \eta\sigma^2(T-t)]/\sqrt{\sigma^2(T-t)}$$

$$z_8 = [\ln y - \eta\sigma^2(T-t)]/\sqrt{\sigma^2(T-t)}$$

Following the same parameter values as in the flat barrier model and letting C be \$150 in the Black-Cox model and everything else is kept the same, we have the equity value of \$100.8. Hence the debt value is \$163.14.

Longstaff and Schwartz extend the flat barrier model to include an interest rate model of Vasicek.[23]

$$D(t, T) = P(t, T)\left(1 - w\sum_{i=1}^{n} q_i\right)$$

where

$$q_1 = N(a_1)$$

$$q_i = N(a_i) - \sum_{j=1}^{i-1} q_j N(b_{ij})$$

---

[23] Longstaff and Schwartz, "A Simple Approach to Valuing Risky Fixed and Floating Rate Debt."

$$a_i = \frac{-\ln A(0)/K - M(iT/n, T)}{\sqrt{S(iT/n)}}$$

$$b_{ij} = \frac{M(jT/n, T) - M(iT/n, T)}{\sqrt{S(iT/n) - S(jT/n)}}$$

$$M(t, T) = \left(\frac{\alpha - \rho\sigma\eta}{\beta} - \frac{\eta^2}{\beta^2} - \frac{\sigma^2}{2}\right)t + \left(\frac{\rho\sigma\eta}{\beta^2} - \frac{\eta^2}{2\beta^2}\right)e^{-\beta T}(e^{\beta t} - 1)$$

$$+ \left(\frac{r}{\beta} - \frac{\alpha}{\beta^2} - \frac{\eta^2}{\beta^3}\right)(1 - e^{-\beta t}) - \left(\frac{r}{\beta} - \frac{\alpha}{\beta^2} - \frac{\eta^2}{\beta^3}\right)(1 - e^{-\beta t})$$

The Vasicek model of the term structure of interest rates assumes the following interest rate process:

$$dr(t) = (\alpha - \beta r)dt + \eta dW$$

and gives the following discount bond pricing formula:

$$P(t, T) = e^{-r(t)F(t, T) - G(t, T)}$$

where

$$F(t, T) = \frac{1 - \exp(-\beta(T - t))}{\beta}$$

$$G(t, T) = \left(\alpha - \frac{\eta^2}{2\beta^2}\right)(T - t - F(t, T)) + \frac{\eta^2 F(t, T)^2}{4\beta}$$

The Longstaff-Schwartz model requires the Vasicek term structure model: $\beta = 1$, $\alpha = 0.06$, $\eta = 0.02$, and $\rho = 0$. Further, the recovery is assumed to be 0 (i.e., $w = 1$). With the same asset value ($r = 5\%$, $A(0) = 200$, and $K = 150$), the equity value can be computed as $98.14.

The BSM framework has been used by a number of credit software/consulting companies, including JPMorgan Chase's Credit Metrics (codeveloped with Reuters) and KMV. Both systems use the BSM approach to model defaults and are greatly helped by large databases of historical data. To make the BSM model operational, they define default as when the equity price falls below a certain barrier. This simplification is due to the fact that equity prices are much more available than asset values of the company. Credit Metrics goes further by modeling correlated defaults. If two equity prices are jointly lognormal, it is very straightforward to compute the joint default probability.

ADVANTAGES AND DRAWBACKS OF STRUCTURAL MODELS

Structural models have many advantages. First, they model default on the very reasonable assumption that it is a result of the value of the firm's assets falling below the value of its debt. In the case of the BSM model, the outputs of the model show how the credit risk of a corporate debt is a function of the leverage and the asset volatility of the issuer. The term structure of spreads also appear realistic and empirical evidence argues for and against their shape. Some of the more recent structural models have addressed many of the limitations and assumptions of the original BSM model.

However, structural models are difficult to calibrate and so are not suitable for the frequent marking to market of credit contingent securities. Structural models are also computationally burdensome. For instance, as we have seen, the pricing of a defaultable zero-coupon bond is as difficult as pricing an option. Just adding coupons transforms the problem into the equivalent of pricing a compound option. Pricing any subordinated debt requires the simultaneous valuation of all of the more senior debt. Consequently, structural models are not used where there is a need for rapid and accurate pricing of many credit-related securities.

Instead, the main application of structural models is in the areas of credit risk analysis and corporate structure analysis. As explained in the next chapter, a structural model is more likely to be able to predict the credit quality of a corporate security than a reduced form model. It is therefore a useful tool in the analysis of counterparty risk for banks when establishing credit lines with companies and a useful tool in the risk analysis of portfolios of securities. Corporate analysts might also use structural models as a tool for analyzing the best way to structure the debt and equity of a company.

APPENDIX: GESKE'S MODEL

As a demonstration, we derive a two-period Geske model. The general case of n periods is a straightforward (but tedious) extension of the result below.

$D_{01} = e^{-rt}\int_{K_1}^{\infty} K_1 f(A_1)dA_1 + e^{-rt}\int_0^{F_1} A_1 f(A_1)dA_1$ $= e^{-rt}K_1 N(d_{11}^-) + e^{-rt}\int_0^{\infty} A_1 f(A_1)dA_1 - e^{-rt}\int_{A_1}^{\infty} A_1 f(A_1)dA_1$ $= e^{-rt}K_1 N(d_{11}^-) + A_0 1 - N(d_{11}^+)$ $= e^{-rt}K_1 N(d_{11}^-)$ $D_{02} = e^{-2rt}\int_{K_{12}}^{\infty} E[\min A_2, K_2] + e^{-rt}\int_{K_1}^{K_{12}}(A_1 - K_1)$ $= e^{-2rt}\int_{K_{12}}^{\infty}\int_0^{K_2} A_2 + e^{-2rt}\int_{K_{12}}^{\infty}\int_{K_2}^{\infty} K_2$ $+ e^{-rt}\int_{K_1}^{\infty}(A_1 - K_1) - e^{-rt}\int_{K_{12}}^{\infty}(A_1 - K_1)$ $= A_0[N(d_{11}^+) - M(d_{12}^+, d_{22}^+)] + e^{-2rt}K_2 M(d_{12}^-, d_{22}^-)$ $+ e^{-rt}K_1[N(d_{12}^-) - N(d_{12}^-)]$	$\boxed{A_1 > K_1 + D_{12}(\equiv K_{12})}$ $D_{11} = K_1$ $D_{12} = e^{-rt}E[\min\{A_2, K_2\}]$ $E_1 = e^{-rt}\int_{K_2}^{\infty}(A_2 - K_2)f(A_2)dA_2$ $\boxed{K_1(\equiv K_{11}) < A_1 < K_1 + D_{12}(\equiv K_{12})}$ $D_{11} = K_1$ $D_{12} = A_1 - K_1$ $E_1 = 0$ $\boxed{A_1 < K_1(\equiv K_{11})}$ $D_{11} = A_1$ $D_{12} = 0$ $E_1 = 0$	$\boxed{A_2 > K_2(= K_{22})}$ $D_{22} = K_2$ $E_2 = \max\{A_2 - K_2, 0\}$ $\boxed{A_2 < K_2(\equiv K_{22})}$ $D_{22} = A_2$ $E_2 = 0$

CHAPTER 9

Credit Risk Modeling: Reduced Form Models

There are two approaches to modeling credit risk: structural models and reduced form models. The structural models in practice today are described in the previous chapter. In this chapter our focus is on reduced form models, although we briefly describe two other models (credit based spread models and hazard models).

The name *reduced form* was first given by Darrell Duffie to differentiate from the *structural form* models of the Black-Scholes-Merton (BSM) type. Reduced form models are mainly represented by the Jarrow-Turnbull[1] and Duffie-Singleton[2] models. Both types of models are arbitrage free and employ the risk-neutral measure to price securities. The principal difference is that default is endogenous in the BSM model while it is exogenous in the Jarrow-Turnbull and Duffie-Singleton models. As we will see, specifying defaults exogenously greatly simplifies the problem because it ignores the constraint of defining what causes default and simply looks at the default event itself. The computations of debt values of different maturities are independent, unlike in the BSM model that defaults of the later-maturity debts are contingent on defaults of earlier-maturity debts.

---

[1] Robert Jarrow and Stuart Turnbull, "Pricing Derivatives on Financial Securities Subject to Default Risk," *Journal of Finance* (March 1995), pp. 53–86.
[2] Darrell Duffie and Kenneth Singleton, "Modeling the Term Structure of Defaultable Bonds," working paper, Stanford University (1997).

THE POISSON PROCESS

The theoretical framework for reduced form models is the Poisson process. To see what it is, let us begin by defining a Poisson process that at time t has a value N_t. The values taken by N_t are an increasing set of integers 0, 1, 2, ... and the probability of a jump from one integer to the next occurring over a small time interval dt is given by

$$\Pr[N_{t+dt} - N_t = 1] = \lambda dt$$

where λ is known as the *intensity* parameter in the Poisson process.

Equally, the probability of no event occurring in the same time interval is simply given by

$$\Pr[N_{t+dt} - N_t = 0] = 1 - \lambda dt$$

For the time being we shall assume the intensity parameter to be a fixed constant. In later discussions and especially when pricing is covered in the next chapter, we will let it be a function of time or even a stochastic variable (known as a *Cox process*[3]). These more complex situations are beyond the scope of this chapter. It will be seen shortly that the intensity parameter represents the annualized instantaneous forward default probability at time t. As dt is small, there is a negligible probability of two jumps occurring in the same time interval.

The Poisson process can be seen as a counting process (0 or 1) for some as yet undefined sequence of events. In our case, the relationship between Poisson processes and reduced form models is that the event that causes the Poisson process to jump from zero to 1 can be viewed as being a default.

Another way to look at the Poisson process is to see how long it takes until the first default event occurs. This is called the *default time* distribution. It can be proven that the default time distribution obeys an *exponential distribution* as follows:

$$\Pr(T > t) = e^{-\lambda(T-t)}$$

This distribution function also characterizes the survival probability before time t:

$$Q(t, T) = \Pr(T > t) = e^{-\lambda(T-t)}$$

---

[3] David Lando, "On Cox Processes and Credit Risky Securities," *Review of Derivatives Research* 2 (1998), pp. 99–120.

THE JARROW-TURNBULL MODEL

The Jarrow-Turnbull model is a simple model of default and recovery based on the Poisson default process described in the previous section.[4] In their model, Jarrow and Turnbull assume that no matter when default occurs, the recovery payment is paid at maturity time T. Then the coupon bond value can be written as:

$$B(t) = P(t, T)R(T)\int_t^T -dQ(t, u)du + \sum_{j=1}^n P(t, T_j)c_j e^{-\lambda(T_j - t)}$$

$$= P(t, T)R(T)(1 - e^{-\lambda(T - t)}) + \sum_{j=1}^n P(t, T_j)c_j e^{-\lambda(T_j - t)}$$

where

$P(t,T)$	=	the risk-free discount factor
c_j	=	the j-th coupon
$Q(t,T)$	=	the survival probability up to time t
R	=	the recovery ratio

It is seen that the conditional default probability is integrated out and disappears from the final result. As a consequence, by assuming recovery payment to be at maturity, Jarrow and Turnbull assume away any dependency between the bond price and the conditional default probability.

It is worth noting that when the recovery rate is 0, for a zero-coupon bond the value of the intensity parameter is also the bond's forward yield spread. This is so because in any one-period interval in the binomial model, we have:

$$D(t, T) = P(t, T)e^{-\lambda(T - t)}$$
$$= p(t, T)Q(t, T)$$

This is known as the risky discount factor, which is the present value of $1 if there is no default.

The Jarrow-Turnbull model is usually modified when it is used in practice. One modification is to allow the Poisson intensity λ to be a function of time and the other is to allow recovery to be paid upon default. As a result the bond equation is modified as follows:

---

[4] Jarrow and Turnbull, "Pricing Derivatives on Financial Securities Subject to Default Risk."

$$B(t) = \int_t^T P(t, u)R(u)(-dQ(u)) + \sum_{j=1}^n P(t, T_j)c_jQ(t, T_j)$$

$$= \int_t^T P(t, u)R(u)\lambda(u)e^{-\int_t^u \lambda(w)dw} + \sum_{j=1}^n P(t, T_j)c_je^{-\int_t^{T_j} \lambda(w)dw}$$

To actually implement this equation, it is usually assumed that λ follows a step function. That is between any two adjacent time points, λ is a constant. Furthermore, it is also, as a matter of mathematical tractability, assumed that default can occur only at coupon times.[5] As a result of this further assumption, the above equation can be simplified as:

$$B(t) = \sum_{j=1}^n P(t, T_j)R(T_j)\lambda(T_j)e^{-\sum_{k=1}^j \lambda(T_k)} + \sum_{j=1}^n P(t, T_j)c_je^{-\sum_{k=1}^n \lambda(T_k)}$$

The major advantage of the Jarrow-Turnbull model is calibration. Since default probabilities and recovery are exogenously specified, one can use a series of risky zero-coupon bonds to calibrate out a default probability curve and hence a spread curve.

Calibration has become a necessary first step in fixed-income trading recently for it allows traders to clearly see *relative prices* and hence be able to construct arbitrage trading strategies. The ability to quickly calibrate is the major reason why reduced form models are strongly favored by real-world practitioners in the credit derivatives markets.

THE CALIBRATION OF JARROW-TURNBULL MODEL

Exhibit 9.1 best represents the Jarrow-Turnbull model.[6] The branches that lead to default will terminate the contract and incur a recovery payment. The branches that lead to survival will continue the contract which will then face future defaults. This is a very general framework to

---

[5] This assumption is not unreasonable because between two coupon times, if the company is not audited, the company should not have any reason to default.

[6] As recent articles by Ren-Raw Chen and Jinzhi Huang ["Credit Spread Bonds and Their Implications for Credit Spread Modeling," Rutgers University and Penn State University (2001)] and Ren-Raw Chen ["Credit Risk Modeling: A General Framework," working paper, Rutgers University (2003)] show, the binomial process is also applicable to structural models.

EXHIBIT 9.1   Tree Based Diagram of Binomial Default Process for a
Debt Instrument

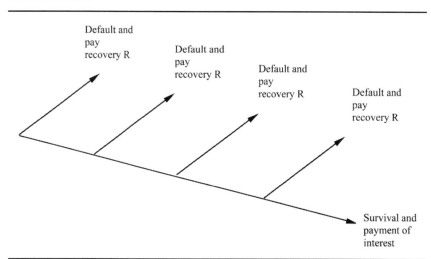

describe how default occurs and contract terminates. Various models
differ in how the default probabilities are defined and the recovery is
modeled.

Since a debt contract pays interest under survival and pays recovery
upon default, the expected payment is naturally the weighted average of
the two payoffs. For the ease of exposition, we shall denote the survival
probability from now to any future time as $Q(0,t)$ where t is some
future time. As a consequence, the difference between two survival
times, $Q(0,s) - Q(0,t)$ where $s > t$, by definition, is the default probability between the two future time points t and s.

The above binomial structure can be applied to both structural
models and reduced form models. The default probabilities can be easily
computed by these models. The difference resides in how they specify
recovery assumptions. In the Geske model, the asset value at the time is
recovered. In the Duffie-Singleton model, a fraction of the market debt
value is recovered. And in the Jarrow-Turnbull and other barrier models, an arbitrary recovery value is assumed (it can be beta distributed).[7]

From the observed bond prices, we can easily retrieve default probabilities from bond prices. Suppose there are two bonds, a 1-year bond
trading at $100 with a $6 annual coupon and a 2-year bond trading at
$100 with a $7 annual coupon. Assuming a recovery of $50 per $100
par value, the first bond price is calculated as

---

[7] For more details, see Chen, "Credit Risk Modeling: A General Framework."

$$100 = \frac{p(0, 1) \times 50 + 106 \times (1 - p(0, 1))}{1 + 5\%}$$

The default probability is then found by solving for $p(0,1)$:

$$105 = 106 - 56 \times p(0, 1)$$
$$p(0, 1) = 1.79\%$$

We use p_t to represent the forward/conditional default probability at time t. Hence, p_1 is the default probability of the first period. In the first period, the survival probability is simply 1 minus the default probability:

$$Q(0, 1) = 1 - p(0, 1) = 1 - 1.79\% = 98.21\%$$

and therefore

$$\lambda = -\ln 0.9821 = 1.8062\%$$

The second bond is priced, assuming a recovery of $20 out of $100:

$$100 = \frac{p(0, 1) \times 20 + Q(0, 1) \times \left[7 + \dfrac{p(1, 2) \times 20 + [1 - p(1, 2)] \times 107}{1.05} \right]}{1.05}$$

$$= \frac{1.79\% \times 20 + 98.21\% \times \left[7 + \dfrac{p(1, 2) \times 20 + [1 - p(1, 2)] \times 107}{1.05} \right]}{1.05}$$

Solving for the second-period default probability one obtains $p(1,2) = 14.01\%$.

The total survival probability till two years is surviving through the first year (98.21%) *and* the second year ($1 - 14.01\% = 85.99\%$):

$$Q(0, 2) = Q(0, 1)(1 - p(1, 2)) = 98.21\% \times (1 - 14.01\%) = 84.45\%$$

$$\lambda_1 + \lambda_2 = -\ln 0.8445 = 16.9011\%$$

$$\lambda_2 = 16.9011\% - \lambda_1 = 16.9011\% - 1.8062\% = 15.0949\%$$

EXHIBIT 9.2   Immediate Recovery

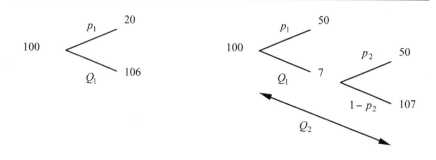

The total default probability is either defaulting in the first period (1.79%) *or* surviving through the first year (98.21%) *and* defaulting in the second (14.01%).

$$1.78\% + 98.21\% \times 14.01\% = 15.55\%$$

This probability can be calculated alternatively by 1 minus the 2-period survival probability:

$$1 - Q(0,2) = 1 - 84.45\% = 15.55\%$$

It should be noted that any forward default probability is the difference of two survivals weighted by the previous survival as shown below:

$$p(j-1, j) = \frac{Q(0, j-1) - Q(0, j)}{Q(0, j-1)} \qquad (9.1)$$

For example, the second period default probability is:

$$p(0,2) = 1 - Q(0,2)/Q(0,1)$$

To express this more clearly, let us examine a 2-period binomial tree shown in Exhibit 9.2. It should be clear how the recovery amount can change the default probabilities. Take the 1-year bond as an example. If the recovery were higher, the default probability would be higher. This is because for a higher recovery bond to be priced at the same price (par in our example), the default probability would need to be higher to compensate for it. If the default probability remains the same, then the bond should be priced above par.

So far we have not discussed any model. We simply adopt the spirit of the reduced form models and use the market bond prices to recover risk-neutral probabilities. This is very similar to the bootstrapping method in calibrating the yield curve. The probabilities are solved recursively.

No matter which model is used, the model has to match the default probabilities implied by the bond prices observed in the market. It can be seen in the above section that there is no closed-form solution. The reason is that the recovery amount is the liquidation value of the company and can change as time changes (so called "stochastic recovery").

Transition Matrix

The binomial structure can be extended to multinomial to incorporate various credit classes. It is as easy to specify n states (different credit ratings) instead of just two states (default and survival). The probabilities can always be given exogenously. Hence, instead of a single default for default (and survival), there can be a number of probabilities, each for the probability of moving from one credit rating to another credit rating. Based upon this idea, Jarrow, Lando, and Turnbull,[8] extend the Jarrow-Turnbull model to incorporate the so-called *migration risk*. Migration risk is different from default risk in that a downgrade in credit ratings only widens the credit spread of the debt issuer and does not cause default. No default means no recovery to worry about. This way, the Jarrow-Turnbull model can be more closely related to spread products, whereas as a model of default it can only be useful in default products. One advantage of ratings transition models is the ability to use the data published by the credit rating agencies. An example of a ratings transition matrix is shown in Chapter 2.

For a flavor of how a rating transition model can be obtained, consider a simple three-state model. At each time interval an issuer can be upgraded, downgraded or even jump to default. This process is shown in Exhibit 9.3. This time, the tree is more complex. From a "live" state, the issuer can be upgraded or downgraded, or even jump to default. The default state, on the other hand, is an absorbing barrier which cannot become live again. In terms of Exhibit 9.3, a movement from "good rating" to "middle rating" is downgrade, and vice versa.

To best describe the situation, we can establish the following transition matrix:

[8] Robert Jarrow, David Lando, and Stuart Turnbull, "A Markov Model for the Term Structure of Credit Spreads," *Review of Financial Studies* 10 (1997), pp. 481–532.

EXHIBIT 9.3   Multistate Default Process

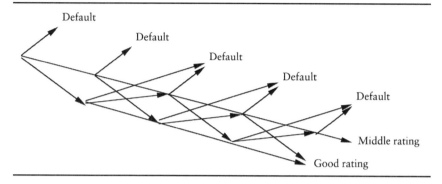

$$\begin{array}{c} \text{Future state} \\ \begin{array}{ccc} 2 & 1 & 0 \end{array} \\ \text{Current state } \begin{array}{c} 2 \\ 1 \\ 0 \end{array} \begin{bmatrix} p_{22} & p_{21} & p_{20} \\ p_{12} & p_{11} & p_{10} \\ 0 & 0 & 1 \end{bmatrix} \end{array}$$

where 0 is the default state, 1 is the middle credit rating state, and 2 is good credit rating state. p_{ij} is the transition probability to move from the current state i to future state j. The sum of the probabilities of each current state should be 1. That is,

$$\sum_{j=0}^{2} p_{ij} = 1$$

The last row of the matrix is all 0s except for the last column. This means that once the asset is in default, it cannot become live again and it will remain in default forever.

To make the model mathematically tractable, Jarrow-Lando-Turnbull assume that the transition matrix follows a Markov chain; that is, the n-period transition is the above matrix raised to the n-th power. The main purpose to derive such a matrix is that we can calibrate it to the historical transition matrix published by rating agencies. Note that the historical transition matrix consists of real probabilities which are different from the risk-neutral probabilities in the tree. Hence, Jarrow-Lando-Turnbull make a further assumption that the risk-neutral probabilities are *proportional* to the actual ones. For a risk averse investor, the risk-neutral default probabilities are larger than the actual ones because of the risk premium.

Since historical default probabilities are observable, we can then directly compute the prices of credit derivatives. For example, let the transition probability matrix for a 1-year period be:

$$
\begin{array}{c}
 & \text{Future state} \\
 & \begin{array}{ccc} 2 & 1 & 0 \end{array} \\
\text{Current state} \begin{array}{c} 2 \\ 1 \\ 0 \end{array} & \begin{bmatrix} 0.80 & 0.15 & 0.05 \\ 0.15 & 0.70 & 0.15 \\ 0 & 0 & 1 \end{bmatrix}
\end{array}
$$

Then, for a 1-year, 0-recovery coupon bond, if the current state is 1, it has 85% to receive the coupon and 15% to go into default in the next period. So the present value of the next coupon is

$$\frac{0.85 \times \$6}{1.06} = \$4.81$$

In the second period, the bond could be upgraded with probability of 15% or remain the same with probability of 70%. If it is at the good rating, then the probability of survival is 95% and if it is at the bad rating, the probability of survival is 85%. Hence, the total probability of survival is

$$0.15 \times 0.95 + 0.7 \times 0.85 = 0.7375 = 73.75\%$$

Therefore, the present value of the maturity cash flow (coupon and face value) is

$$\frac{0.7375 \times 106}{1.06^2} = \$69.58$$

The bond price today is

$$\$4.81 + \$69.58 = \$74.39$$

Similar analysis can be applied to the case where the current state is 2. In the above example, it is quite easy to include various recovery assumptions.

It is costly to include the ratings migration risk in the Jarrow-Turnbull model. It is very difficult to calibrate the model to the historical transition matrix. First of all, the historical probabilities computed by the rating agencies are *actual* probabilities while the probabilities that are used for computing prices must be *risk neutral* probabilities. The assumption by Jarrow, Lando, and Turnbull that there is a linear transformation does not necessarily provide a good fit to the data. Second, there are more variables to solve for than the available bonds. In other words, the calibration is an underidentification problem. Hence, more restrictive assumptions about the probabilities need to be made. In general, migration risk is still modeled by the traditional portfolio theory (non-option methodology). But the model by Jarrow, Lando, and Turnbull is a first attempt at using the option approach to model the rating migration risk.

THE DUFFIE-SINGLETON MODEL

Obviously, the Jarrow-Turnbull assumption that recovery payment can occur only at maturity is too far from reality. Although it generates a closed-form solution for the bond price, it suffers from two major drawbacks in reality: (1) recovery actually occurs upon (or soon after) default and (2) the recovery amount can fluctuate randomly over time.[9]

Duffie and Singleton take a different approach.[10] They allow the payment of recovery to occur at any time but the amount of recovery is restricted to be the proportion of the bond price at default time as if it did not default. That is,

$$R(t) = \delta D(t, T)$$

where R is the recovery ratio, δ is a fixed ratio, and $D(t,T)$ represents the debt value if default did not occur. For this reason the Duffie-Singleton model is known as a *fractional recovery model*. The rationale behind this approach is that as the credit quality of a bond deteriorates, the price falls. At default the recovery price will be some fraction of the final price immediately prior to default. In this way we avoid the contradictory scenario which can arise in the Jarrow-Turnbull model in which the recovery rate, being an exogenously specified percentage of the default-free payoff, may actually exceed the price of the bond at the moment of default.

The debt value at time t value is:[11]

---

[9] Recovery fluctuates because it depends on the liquidation value of the firm at the time of default.

[10] Duffie and Singleton, "Modeling the Term Structure of Defaultable Bonds."

[11] The probability, p, can be time dependent in a more general case.

$$D(t, T)$$

$$= \frac{1}{1 + r\Delta t}\{p\delta E[D(t + \Delta t, T)] + (1 - p)E[D(t + \Delta t, T)]\}$$

By recursive substitutions, we can write the current value of the bond as its terminal payoff if no default occurs:

$$D(t, T) = \left[\frac{1 - p\Delta t(1 - \delta)}{1 + r\Delta t}\right]^n X(T)$$

Note that the instantaneous default probability being $p\Delta t$ is consistent with the Poisson distribution,

$$\frac{-dQ}{Q} = p\Delta t$$

Hence, recognizing $\Delta t = T/n$,

$$D(t, T) = \frac{\exp(-p(1 - \delta)T)}{\exp(rT)}X(T) = \exp(-(r + s)T)X(T) \qquad (9.2)$$

When r and s are not constants, we can write the Duffie-Singleton model as:

$$D(t, T) = E_t\left[\exp\left(-\int_t^T [r(u) + s(u)]du\right)\right]X(T)$$

where $s(u) = p_u(1 - \delta)$. Not only does the Duffie-Singleton model have a closed-form solution, it is possible to have a simple intuitive interpretation of their result. The product $p(1 - \delta)$ serves as a spread over the risk-free discount rate. When the default probability is small, the product is small and the credit spread is small. When the recovery is high (i.e., $1 - \delta$ is small), the product is small and the credit spread is small.

Consider a two-year zero coupon bond. Assume that the probability of defaulting each year is 4%, conditional on surviving to the beginning of the year. If the bond defaults we assume that it loses 60% of its market value. We also assume that risk-free interest rates evolve as shown in Exhibit 9.4 where an up move and a down move have an equal probability of 50%. At any node on the tree the price is the risk-free dis-

EXHIBIT 9.4 Valuation of a Two-Year Defaultable Zero-Coupon Bond Using Duffie-Singleton

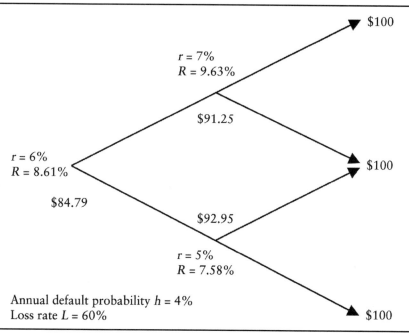

$r = 7\%$
$R = 9.63\%$

$91.25

$r = 6\%$
$R = 8.61\%$

$84.79

$92.95

$r = 5\%$
$R = 7.58\%$

Annual default probability $h = 4\%$
Loss rate $L = 60\%$

$100

$100

$100

counted expectation of the payoff at the next time step. Therefore, at the node where the risk-free rate has climbed to 7%, the value of the security is given by

$$\frac{1}{1.07}[(1 - 0.04) \times \$100 + 0.04 \times (\$100 - \$60)] = \$91.25$$

Using the relationship

$$\frac{1}{1+r+s} = \frac{1}{1+r}[p\delta + (1-p)]$$

this implies an effective discounting rate of $r + s = 9.63\%$ over the time step from the 7% node. In this way we can proceed to value the other nodes and roll back to calculate an initial price for the bond equal to $84.79. On each node in Exhibit 9.4 is also shown the effective discounting rate. Knowing these we can equally price the bond as though it were default free but discounted at $r + s$ rather than at the risk-free rate.

The Duffie-Singleton model has one very important advantage. The above result implies that it can be made compatible with arbitrage-free term structure models such as Cox-Ingersoll-Ross[12] and Heath-Jarrow-Morton.[13] The difference is that now the discounting is *spread adjusted*. Just like the yield curve for the risk-free term structure, the *spread curve* is added to the risk-free yield curve and we arrive at a *risky yield curve*. The spread curve is clearly based upon the *probability curve* (p_t for all t) and the recovery rate (δ).

Although the Duffie-Singleton model seems to be superior to the Jarrow-Turnbull model, it is not generic enough to be applied to all credit derivative contracts. The problem with the Duffie-Singleton model is that if a contract that has no payoff at maturity such as a credit default swap, their model implies zero value today, which is of course not true. Recall that credit default swaps pay nothing if default does not occur. If recovery is proportional to the no-default payment, then it is obvious that the contract today has no value. It is quite unfortunate that the Duffie-Singleton model is not suitable for the most popular credit derivative contracts. Hence, the proportionality recovery assumption is not very general.

The calibration of the Duffie-Singleton model is as easy as the Jarrow-Turnbull model. The two calibrations are comparable. However, there are significant differences. Note that in the Jarrow-Turnbull model, the recovery assumption is separate from the default probability. But this is not the case in the Duffie-Singleton model—the recovery and the default probability together become an instantaneous spread. While we can calibrate the spreads, we cannot separate the recovery from the default probability. On the other hand, in the Jarrow-Turnbull model, the default probability curve can be calibrated to *only if* a particular recovery assumption is adopted. Hence, the default probability is a function of the assumed recovery rate.

GENERAL OBSERVATIONS ON REDUCED FORM MODELS

While the reduced form models lay a solid theoretical foundation, as they attempt to model the underlying risk-neutral probability of default which is not a market observable, they are not as intuitive as one might like. They also suffer from the constraint that default is always a sur-

---

[12] John Cox, Jonathan Ingersoll, and Stephen Ross, "A Theory of the Term Structure of Interest Rates," *Econometrica* 53 (1985), pp. 385–407.
[13] David Heath, Robert Jarrow, and Andrew Morton, "Bond Pricing and the Term Structure of Interest Rates: A New Methodology," *Econometrica* 60 (January 1992), pp. 77–105.

prise. While this is true under some rare circumstances, Both Moody's and Standard & Poor's data show that there are very few defaults straight out of investment-grade quality bonds. Default is usually the end of a series of downgrades and spread widenings and so can be anticipated to a large extent. Hence, although more and more financial institutions are starting to implement the Jarrow-Turnbull and Duffie-Singleton models, spread-based diffusion models remain very popular.

The Jarrow-Turnbull and Duffie-Singleton models assume that defaults occur unexpectedly and follow the Poisson process. This assumption greatly reduces the complexity since the Poisson process has very nice mathematical properties. In order to further simplify the model, Jarrow-Turnbull and Duffie-Singleton respectively make other assumptions so that there exist closed-form solutions to the basic underlying asset.

OTHER MODELS

In addition to the models given above, there are a number of modeling approaches the industry uses to model credit risk: spread-based models and hazard models.

Spread-Based Models

In spirit, *spread-based models* are very similar to barrier structural models. The only difference is the use of a different state variable to detect default— a barrier structural model uses the market asset value and a spread-based model uses the bond spread. In both models, default barriers are exogenously given and need to be calibrated to real data. They also have in common that default is not a surprise (unless a jump is added).

Models that apply spread dynamics generally take par asset swap spreads as the fundamental spread variable. As explained in Chapter 4, par asset swap spreads are a spread over LIBOR (London interbank offered rate) which represents the credit quality of a specific security. While some triple-A corporate asset swap spreads can go below LIBOR, it is more reasonable for the spreads of corporates to remain positive. For this reason, coupled with the observation that credit spread distributions have long tails, a lognormal distribution may be a reasonable assumption for the evolution of the credit spread.

It is common to assume asset swap spreads follow a lognormal process of the following kind:

$$\frac{ds(t)}{s(t)} = \sigma dW(t)$$

where σ represents the percentage volatility of spread changes and $dw(t)$ represents a random Weiner process. In practice the spread is usually centered around its spot value so that

$$s(t) = s(0)\exp\left(-\frac{\sigma^2 t}{2} + \sigma W(t)\right)$$

The basic property of the above process can be found in Hull.[14]

To price default, we need to specify a default boundary in terms of a spread $K(t)$. This can be quite arbitrary and the boundary can be time dependent. However, some sort of methodology, such as relating the default spread to recovery rate, can be employed.

Implementations of this model, where not analytically tractable, are usually Monte Carlo-based and so are open to many variance reduction methods. Being Monte Carlo-based also makes them relatively easy to implement. The price of a digital default swap which pays out \$1 at maturity in the event of default and nothing otherwise is then given by

$$D(t, T) = E_t\left[\exp\left(-\int_t^T r(u)du\right)\Big|1_{s(u) > K(u)} \forall u\right]$$

When interest rates and spreads are independent, we can rewrite equation (9.1) as

$$D(t, T) = E_t\left[\exp\left(-\int_t^T r(u)du\right)\right]F(t, T)$$

where $F(t,T)$ is the price of a digital barrier option whose payoff equals the probability that the spread crosses the barrier at some time before maturity. Calibration of this model is then a process of determining the default boundary which reprices market instruments such as default swaps and digital default swaps. The problem with this approach is it is an ad hoc approach and lacks theoretical support. Any spread should be a result of default and cannot be itself a stochastic process. A direct analogy is that in the term structure literature, researchers have tried to model the long rate with a stochastic process and the model has been

---

[14] John Hull, *Options, Futures, and Other Derivatives* (Upper Saddle River, NJ: Prentice Hall, 2002).

proven to be internally inconsistent. An ad hoc spread model is doomed to be internally inconsistent.

Hazard Models

Shumway takes a different route in extending the BSM model.[15] He argues that a good default model should be an econometric model (i.e., let the data decide). He contends that many theoretical extensions only take care of some aspects of why default occurs, but not all. For example, he argues that accounting ratios, market size, and historical stock returns, have great value in predicting defaults, but are not considered in any of the theoretical models. Furthermore, he argues that those theoretical models usually generate inconsistent default probabilities.[16] As a result, he proposes a "hazard model" that incorporates both theoretical and "empirical" factors.

Define a survival function as

$$S(t, x; \theta) = 1 - \sum_{j < t} f(j, x; \theta)$$

where x is a collection of explanatory (empirical) variables and θ is a collection of parameters to be estimated. Hence, the hazard function is

$$h(t, x; \theta) = \frac{f(t, x; \theta)}{S(t, x; \theta)}$$

And then the maximum likelihood function (log) can be written as

$$L = \prod_{i=1}^{n} h(t_i, x_i; \theta)^{y_i} S(t_i, x_i; \theta)$$

where y_i is a dummy variable equal to 1 if default occurs at time t_i and 0 otherwise. The functional from of f is determined empirically by maximizing the likelihood function.

---

[15] Tyler Shumway, "Forecasting Bankruptcy More Accurately: A Simple Hazard Model," *Journal of Business* (January 2001), pp. 101–124
[16] For example, KMV, a service that uses BSM and barrier models, admits that its default probabilities are consistently underestimated.

SUMMARY AND EXTENSIONS

To summarize what we have demonstrated, our coverage of credit risk modeling in the previous chapter, the structural form models—led by Black-Scholes-Merton—have the advantage that the model is consistent with the reality of default. Not only are the default events endogenously determined, the recovery is also endogenously determined. The model is consistent with the capital structure of the company. The problem is that there is no easy way to compute credit derivative prices.

The reduced form models, led by Jarrow-Turnbull and Duffie-Singleton, make exogenous assumptions about defaults and recovery the models are therefore more mathematically tractable. However, independent default processes for different credit derivative contracts may generate conflict and correlated defaults are not as easy to describe as the Black-Scholes-Merton model.

Generally speaking, due to the nature of the two types of models, structural form models are more suitable for back office risk management while the reduced form models are more suitable for the front office trading. Risk management in the back office focuses more on capital structure, capital compliance, and balance sheet requirements. Also, back office, which does not require fast computations, can afford to use the Black-Scholes-Merton model to perform risk management tasks. On the other hand, front office traders need fast pricing models for determining fair value, prices and for hedges; therefore they rely more heavily on reduced form models as explained in the next chapter.

So far we have discussed various models in their simplest form. There have been numerous extensions on both the structural form and the reduced form models. As mentioned in the chapter, there have been efforts to simplify the recovery process, to employ exotic option techniques, and to use stock prices to substitute for asset values.

On the reduced form front, there have been efforts to randomize the intensity parameter of the Poisson process as suggested by Lando[17] and tie it to the value of the firm as suggested by Madan and Unal,[18] to incorporate term structure models as suggested by Das and Tufano,[19] and to randomize recovery rate as proposed by Madan and Unal. There have also been efforts to correlate multiple Poisson processes as pro-

---

[17] Lando, "On Cox Processes and Credit Risky Securities."

[18] Dilip Madan and Haluk Unal, "Pricing the Risks of Default," *Review of Derivatives Research* 2 (1998), pp. 121–160.

[19] Sanjiv Das and Peter Tufano, "Pricing Credit—Sensitive Debt When Interest Rates, Credit Ratings, and Credit Spreads are Stochastic," *Journal of Financial Engineering* 5, no. 2 (1996), pp. 161–198.

posed by Duffie and Singleton[20] and to reach out to credit portfolios such as collateralized debt obligations.

The problem with these extensions is that they tend to move in many different directions and there is no consistent framework under which all the extensions can be housed. However, which assumption to relax becomes problem-dependent or contract-dependent. There exists no good model that can be "universal" for all contracts in all situations.

Exhibit 9.5 provides a summary of the advantages, disadvantages, and applications of the structural and reduced form models discussed in this chapter and the previous one.

APPENDIX: CONTINUOUS TIME FORMALISM

In this appendix, we derive the continuous time counterparts of the discrete formulas in the chapter. The survival probability is labeled as:

$$Q(0, t) = E[1_{\{u > t\}}]$$

where 1 is the indicator function and u is the default time. Hence, the instantaneous default probability is

$$-dQ(0, t)$$

The total default probability is the integration of the per period default probabilities:

$$\int_0^T -dQ(0, t)dt = 1 - Q(0, T)$$

The "forward" default probability is a conditional default probability. Conditional on no default till time t, the default probability for the next instant is

$$\frac{-dQ(0, t)}{Q(0, t)}$$

In a Poisson distribution, defaults occur unexpectedly with intensity λ. Hence, the survival probability can be written as

---

[20] Darrell Duffie and Kenneth Singleton, "Simulating Correlated Defaults," working paper, Stanford University (September 1998).

EXHIBIT 9.5 Summary Table of Various Models

Model	Assumptions	Advantages	Disadvantages	Application
Black-Scholes-Merton (BSM) firm value model	•Default is triggered when the assets of the firm fall below a threshold •Assets evolve according to a lognormal distribution •Interest Rates are constant •Only one level of debt in capital structure	•Default can be anticipated •Spread curves appear realistic •Credit spread has realistic dependency on firm leverage and volatility •Useful for analysis of corporate structures •Can provide insight into causes of default	•Default is never a surprise •Difficult to calibrate •Difficult to price even basic securities	•Risk analysis of corporates •Analysis of corporate structures •Relative value pricing of corporate securities
Geske's compound option model	•Default barrier is market value of remaining debts	•Like BSM, default and recovery are both endogenous •A true structural model	•Computationally intensive, especially under random interest rates •Less flexible, difficult to calibrate	•Default prediction •Default probability curve construction
Barrier structural models (see text for references)	•Stochastic interest rates •Multiple levels of debt •Coupon paying bonds •Jump processes	•Can price whole capital structure •Understand effect of interest rate on default •Jumps make default a surprise	•Still difficult to calibrate •Still difficult to price simple securities	•Risk analysis of corporates •Analysis of corporate structures •Relative value pricing of corporate securities

EXHIBIT 9.5 (Continued)

Model	Assumptions	Advantages	Disadvantages	Application
Jarrow-Turnbull	•Default is a sudden event which occurs with a certain probability •We model probability of default	•Easy to fit to market •Easy to price many sorts of complex securities •Useful for relative value analysis	•Default is always a surprise •No insight about cause of default •Nonpredictive	•Risk-neutral pricing of many sorts of deals
Jarrow-Lando-Turnbull	•Model probability of ratings upgrade and downgrade as multistate default model	•Can use historical rating agency data to do predictive analysis	•Very difficult to implement •Very difficult to calibrate •Very few instruments with prices linked to rating changes	•Forward looking estimation of downgrade and default probability •Relative value analysis
Duffie-Singleton	•Fractional recovery model in which a bond loses a fraction of its face value each time it defaults which can be more than once	•Can implement using existing interest rate models (e.g., HJM) •Can have stochastic recovery rates •Correlations between hazard rate and interest rate possible •Easy to fit to market	•Cannot value instruments that pay nothing under no default—credit default swaps •Impossible to separate recovery from default probability, hence difficult to price recovery-only instruments	•Risk-neutral pricing of many types of structure
Spread-Based Model	•Model the credit spread where default corresponds to the spread crossing a certain barrier	•Intuitive •Can be calibrated to market •Can easily correlate with interest rates •Easy to implement	•Default is never a surprise •Ad hoc and lacking in academic rigor •Low spreads at short end •Adds no insight •Can create inconsistencies •Can be slow when using Monte Carlo	•Pricing simple spread-based deals where volatility and correlation play important role

$$Q(0, t) = \exp\left(-\int_0^t \lambda(u)du\right)$$

and the default probability is

$$-dQ(0, t) = Q(0, t)\lambda(t)dt$$

or the forward probability is

$$\frac{-dQ(0, t)}{Q(0, t)} = \lambda(t)dt$$

This result states that the intensity parameter in the Poisson process is also an annualized forward default probability.

Random Interest Rate and Hazard Rate

The "risky" discount factor is written as

$$E^{r, \lambda, \tau}\left[1_{(\tau > t)}\exp\left(-\int_0^t r(u)du\right)\right] = E^{r, \lambda}\left[E[1_{(\tau > t)}|r, \lambda]\exp\left(-\int_0^t r(u)du\right)\right]$$

If the default time, τ (conditional on λ), is uncorrelated with interest rate, r, then

$$E[1_{(\tau > t)}|r, \lambda] = E[1_{(\tau > t)}|\lambda] = \exp\left(-\int_0^t \lambda(u)du\right)$$

It is not unrealistic to assume that the default time is independent of the interest rate. It is generally accepted that the interest rate is correlated with the likelihood of default which is captured by the hazard rate. We now write the "risky" discount factor as

$$E^{r, \lambda, \tau}\left[1_{(\tau > t)}\exp\left(-\int_0^t r(u)du\right)\right] = E^{r, \lambda}\left[\exp\left(-\int_0^t r(u) + \lambda(u)du\right)\right]$$

Note that the interest rate and the hazard rate are correlated. Hence, the closed-form solution does not exist except for the case where both variables are normally distributed. Unfortunately, a normally distributed hazard rate is unacceptable since it may cause the survival probability to be greater than 1.

CHAPTER 10

Pricing of Credit Default Swaps

There are two approaches to pricing default swaps—*static replication* and *modeling*. The former approach is based on the assumption that if one can replicate the cash flows of the structure which one is trying to price using a portfolio of tradable securities, then the price of the structure should equal the value of the replicating portfolio. This is accomplished through an asset swap as discussed in Chapter 4. In that chapter we explained the limitations of asset swaps for pricing. In situations where either the nature of the instrument we are trying to price cannot be replicated or that we do not have access to prices for the instruments we would use in the replicating portfolio, it may become necessary to use a modeling approach.

Our focus in this chapter is on the modeling approach. We present a consistent pricing framework for valuing single-name credit default swaps drawing on our discussion of reduced form models in Chapter 8. In the second part of this chapter, we extend the model to valuing basket default swaps. In Chapter 11 we apply the basic model to pricing credit-related spread options.

PRICING SINGLE-NAME CREDIT DEFAULT SWAPS

Several models have been suggested for pricing single-name credit default swaps.[1] These products (before we take into account the valua-

---

[1] See, for example, John Hull and Alan White, "Valuing Credit Default Swaps I," working paper, University of Toronto (April 2000) and "Valuing Credit Default Swaps II: Counterparty Default Risk," working paper, University of Toronto (April 2000); and Dominic O'Kane, "Credit Derivatives Explained: Markets Products and Regulations," Lehman Brothers, Structured Credit Research (March 2001) and "Introduction to Default Swaps," Lehman Brothers, Structured Credit Research (January 2000).

tion of counterparty risk) are generally regarded as the "cash product" that can be directly evaluated off the *default probability* curves. No parametric modeling is necessary. This is just like the coupon bond valuation which is model free because the zero-coupon bond yield curve is all that is needed to price coupon bonds.

General Framework

To value credit derivatives it is necessary to be able to model credit risk. As explained in Chapters 8 and 9, the two most commonly used approaches to model credit risk are structural models and reduced form models. The latter do not look inside the firm. Instead, they model directly the likelihood of a default occurring. Not only is the current probability of default modeled, some researchers attempt to model a "forward curve" of default probabilities, which can be used to price instruments of varying maturities. Modeling a probability has the effect of making default a surprise—the default event is a random event that can suddenly occur at any time. All we know is its probability of occurrence.

Reduced form models are easy to calibrate to bond prices observed in the marketplace. Calibration has become a necessary first step in fixed-income trading for it allows traders to clearly see relative prices and hence be able to construct arbitrage trading strategies. The ability to quickly calibrate is the major reason why reduced form models are strongly favored by market practitioners in the credit derivatives market for pricing. As explained in the previous chapters, structural-based models are used more for default prediction and credit risk management.[2]

Both structural and reduced form models use risk-neutral pricing to be able to calibrate to the market. In practice, we need to determine the risk-neutral probabilities in order to reprice the market and price other instruments not currently priced. In doing so, we do not need to know or even care about the real-world default probabilities.

Since in reality, a default can occur any time, to accurately value a default swap, we need a consistent methodology that describes the following: (1) how defaults occur, (2) how recovery is paid, and (3) how discounting is handled.

---

[2] Increasingly, investors are seeking consistency between the markets that use different modeling approaches, as the interests in seeking arbitrage opportunities across various markets grows. Ren-Raw Chen has demonstrated that all the reduced form models described above can be regarded in a nonparametric framework. This nonparametric format makes the comparison of various models possible. Furthermore, as Chen contends, the nonparametric framework focuses the difference of various models on recovery. See Ren-Raw Chen, "Credit Risk Modeling: A General Framework," working paper, Rutgers University (2003).

Survival Probability and Forward Default Probability: A Recap

In the previous chapter we introduced two important analytical constructs: survival probability and forward default probability. We recap both below since we will need them in pricing credit default swaps.

Assume the risk-neutral probabilities exist. Then we can identify a series of risk-neutral default probabilities so that the weighted average of default and no-default payoffs can be discounted at the risk-free rate.

Let $Q(t,T)$ to be the survival probability from now t till some future time T. Then $Q(t,T) - Q(t,T + \tau)$ is the default probability between T and $T + \tau$ (i.e., survive till T but default at $T + \tau$). Assume defaults can only occur at discrete points in time, $T_1, T_2, ..., T_n$. Then the total probability of default over the life of the credit default swap is the sum of all the per period default probabilities:

$$\sum_{j=0}^{n} Q(t, T_j) - Q(t, T_{j+1}) = 1 - Q(T_n) = 1 - Q(T)$$

where $t = T_0 < T_1 < ... < T_n = T$ and T is the maturity time of the credit default swap. Note that the sum of all the per-period default probabilities should equal one minus the total survival probability.

The survival probabilities have a useful application. A \$1 "risky" cash flow received at time T has a risk-neutral expected value of $Q(t,T)$ and a present value of $P(t,T)Q(t,T)$ where P is the risk-free discount factor. A "risky" annuity of \$1 can therefore be written as

$$\sum_{j=1}^{n} P(t, T_j)Q(t, T_j)$$

This value represents the expected receipt of \$1 until default.

A "risky" bond with no recovery upon default and a maturity of n can thus be written as

$$B(t) = \sum_{j=1}^{n} P(t, T_j)Q(t, T_j) + P(t, T_n)Q(t, T_n)$$

This result is similar to the risk-free coupon bond where only risk-free discount factors are used. Due to this similarity, we can regard PQ as the "risky" discount factor.

The "forward" default probability is a conditional default probability for a forward interval conditional on surviving until the beginning of the interval. This probability can be expressed as

$$p(T_j) = \frac{Q(t, T_{j-1}) - Q(t, T_j)}{Q(t, T_{j-1})} \tag{10.1}$$

Credit Default Swap Value

A credit default swap takes the defaulted bond as the recovery value and pays par upon default and zero otherwise.

$$V = E\left[e^{-\int_0^u r(s)ds} 1_{u<T} [1 - R(u)] \right]$$

where u is default time.

Hence the value of the credit default swap (V) should be the recovery value upon default weighted by the default probability:

$$V = \sum_{j=1}^{n} P(t, T_j)[Q(t, T_{j-1}) - Q(t, T_j)][1 - R(T_j)] \tag{10.2}$$

where $P(\cdot)$ is the risk-free discount factor and $R(\cdot)$ is the recovery rate.

In equation (10.2) it is implicitly assumed that the discount factor is independent of the survival probability. However, as explained in the previous chapter, in reality, these two may be correlated—usually higher interest rates lead to more defaults because businesses suffer more from higher interest rates. Equation (10.2) has no easy solution.

From the value of the credit default swap, we can derive a spread (s) which is paid until default or maturity:

$$s = \frac{V}{\sum_{j=1}^{n} P(t, T_j)Q(t, T_j)} \tag{10.3}$$

Exhibit 10.1 depicts the general default and recovery structure. The payoff upon default of a default swap can vary. In general, the owner of the default swap delivers the defaulted bond and in return receives principal. Many default swaps are cash settled and an estimated recovery is

EXHIBIT 10.1   Payoff and Payment Structure of a Credit Default Swap

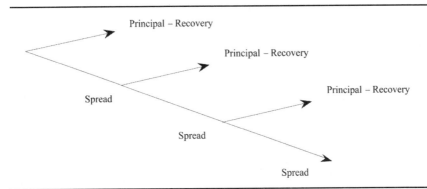

used. In either case, the amount of recovery is randomly dependent upon the value of the reference obligation at the time of default. Models differ in how this recovery is modeled.[3]

Illustration of Pricing a Credit Default Swap

To illustrate how to use the above formulation of credit default swap pricing, assume (1) there exists two "risky" zero-coupon bonds with one and two years to maturity and (2) no recovery upon default. From equation (10.1) we know the credit spreads of these two "risky" zeros are approximately their default probabilities. For example, the one-year zero has a spread of 100 bps and the two-year has a spread of 120. The survival probabilities can be computed from equation (10.1). For the one-year bond whose yield spread is 100 bps, the (one-year) survival probability is

$$1\% = -\ln Q(0, 1)$$
$$Q(0, 1) = e^{-1\%} = 0.9900$$

For the two-year zero-coupon bond whose yield spread is 120 bps, the (two-year) survival probability is

$$1.2\% \times 2 = -\ln Q(0, 2)$$
$$Q(0, 2) = e^{-1.2\% \times 2} = 0.9763$$

---

[3] In the appendix we provide an example where the two variables are independent and the defaults follow a Poisson process. In the example presented in the appendix the simple solution exists under the continuous time assumption.

These survival probabilities can then be used to compute forward default probabilities defined in equation (10.2):

$$p(1) = \frac{Q(0, 0) - Q(0, 1)}{Q(0, 0)} = \frac{1 - 99.00\%}{1} = 1.00\%$$

and

$$p(2) = \frac{Q(0, 1) - Q(0, 2)}{Q(0, 1)} = \frac{99.00\% - 97.63\%}{99.00\%} = 1.39\%$$

Since we assume a 5% flat risk-free rate for two years, the risk-free discount factors are

$$P(0, 1) = e^{-5\%}$$
$$P(0, 2) = e^{-5\% \times 2}$$

for one and two years, respectively. Assuming a 20% recovery ratio, we can then calculate using equation (10.3) the total protection value (V) that the default swap contract is providing:

$$\begin{aligned} V &= e^{-5\%}(1 - 0.99)(1 - 0.2) + e^{-5\% \times 2}(0.99 - 0.9763)(1 - 0.2) \\ &= 0.00761 + 0.010134 \\ &= 0.017744 = 177.44 \text{ bps} \end{aligned}$$

As mentioned, the default swap premium is not paid in full at the inception of the swap but paid in a form of spread until either default or maturity, whichever is earlier. From equation (10.3), we can compute the spread of the default swap as follows:

$$\begin{aligned} s &= \frac{0.017744}{0.99 \times \exp(-0.05) + 0.9763 \times \exp(-0.05 \times 2)} \\ &= \frac{0.017744}{1.824838} = 0.009724 \end{aligned}$$

which is 9.724 bps for each period, provided that default does not occur. This is a payment in arrears. That is, if default occurs in the first period, no payment is necessary. If default occurs in the second period, there is one payment; if default never occurs, there are two payments.

No Need For Stochastic Hazard Rate or Interest Rate

The analysis above demonstrates that to price a default swap, we only need a recovery rate, the risk-free yield curve (the P-curve), and the survival probability curve (the Q-curve). This implies that regardless of which model is used to justify the P-curve or the Q-curve, default swaps should be priced exactly the same. This further implies that there is no need to be concerned if the risk-free rate and the hazard rate are stochastic or not, because they do not enter into the valuation of the default swap. In other words, random interest rates and hazard rates are "calibrated out" of the valuation.[4]

Delivery Option in Default Swaps

As explained in Chapter 3, a credit default swap trade can specify a reference entity or a reference obligation. In the former case, the protection buyer has the option to deliver one of severable deliverable obligations of the reference entity. This effectively creates a similar situation to the well-known quality option for Treasury note and bond futures contracts where more than one bond can be delivered. In this case, the value of the credit default swap is

$$V = \sum_{j=1}^{n} P(t, T_j)[Q(t, T_{j-1}) - Q(t, T_j)][1 - \min R(T_j)]$$

The difference between the above equation and equation (10.1) is the recovery. The delivery of the lowest recovery bond, $\min\{R(T_j)\}$, for all j bonds is what the payoff is.

It is natural that the worst quality bond should be delivered upon default. For a credit default swap, the one with the lowest recovery should be delivered. Unlike Treasury bond and note futures, where the cheapest-to-deliver issue can change due to interest rate changes, recovery is mostly determined contractually and usually the lowest priority bond will remain the lowest priority for the life of the contract. The only uncertainty in determining the cheapest-to-deliver issue is the future introduction of new bonds. This is largely related to the capital structure of the company and beyond the scope of risk-neutral pricing. The model that can incorporate capital structure issues (i.e., using debt to optimize capital structure) needs to be a structural model with wealth maximization.[5]

---

[4] For the stochastic hazard rate model, see Daniel Lando, "On Cox Processes and Credit Risky Securities," *Review of Derivatives Research* (1998), pp. 99–120.

[5] Issues about optimal capital structure and default risk are discussed in Hayne E. Leland and Klaus Bjerre Toft, "Optimal Capital Structure, Endogenous Bankruptcy, and the Term Structure of Credit Spreads," *Journal of Finance* (July 1996), pp. 987–1019.

Default Swaps with Counterparty Risk

Counterparty risk is a major concern for credit default swap investors because major participants in the market are financial firms, which are themselves subject to default risk.[6] Most bank/dealer counterparties are single A or at most AA rated. If the reference entity name is a AAA rated company, then the default probability of the bank/dealer is so much higher than the reference entity that the bank/dealer may default well before the reference entity. In this case, the protection buyer in a credit default swap is more concerned with the counterparty default risk than the default risk of the reference entity. In this section, we shall extend the previous risk-neutral methodology to account for counterparty risk, with the assumption that the default of the reference entity and the default of the counterparty are uncorrelated.

We label the survival probability of the reference entity $Q_1(t,T)$ and that of the counterparty $Q_2(t,T)$. The default probabilities of the reference entity and counterparty in the jth period in the future are $Q_1(t,T_j) - Q_1(t,T_{j+1})$ and $Q_2(t,T_j) - Q_2(t,T_{j+1})$, respectively. The default of either one is

$$Q_1(t, T_j)Q_2(t, T_j) - Q_1(t, T_{j+1})Q_2(t, T_{j+1})$$

The above equation represents a situation that both the reference entity and counterparty jointly survive till T_j but not T_{j+1}. Hence one of them must have defaulted in the period (T_j, T_{j+1}). Subtracting the counterparty default probability from the probability of either default gives rise to the probability of the case that only the reference entity (but not the counterparty) defaults. Hence the total probability of only the reference entity defaulting is:

$$\sum_{j=0}^{n} [Q_1(t,T_j)Q_2(t,T_j) - Q_1(t,T_{j+1})Q_2(t,T_{j+1})] - [Q_2(t,T_j) - Q_2(t,T_{j+1})]$$

When recovery and discounting are included, we have the credit default swap value as

$$V = \sum_{j=0}^{n} P(t, T_j)[1 - R(T_j)][Q_1(t, T_j)Q_2(t, T_j) - Q_1(t, T_{j+1})Q_2(t, T_{j+1})] \\ -\{Q_2(t, T_j) - Q_2(t,T_{j+1})\}$$

---

[6] See also Hull and White, "Valuing Credit Default Swaps II: Counterparty Default Risk."

The default swap valued under the counterparty risk requires two default curves, one for the reference entity and one for the counterparty. This default swap should be cheaper than the default swap with only default risk for the reference entity. The difference is the value of the default swap that protects the joint default. An investor who buys such a default swap owns a default swap on the reference entity and has implicitly sold a default swap of joint default back to the counterparty.

When the defaults of the reference entity and the counterparty are correlated, the solution becomes much more complex. When the correlation is high, it is more likely that the counterparty should default before the reference entity, and the credit default swap should have very little value. On the other hand, when the correlation is low (negative), the situation where the reference entity defaults almost guarantees the survival of the counterparty. Consequently, in such instances the counterparty risk is not a concern.

VALUING BASKET DEFAULT SWAPS

In the previous section we presented a model for valuing single-name credit default swaps. Unlike a single-name credit default swap which provides protection for one bond, as explained in Chapter 3 a basket default swap provides protection against a basket of bonds. As with single-name credit default swaps, the protection buyer of a basket default swap makes a stream of spread payments until either maturity or default. In the event of default, the protection buyer receives a single lump-sum payment.

Default baskets have become popular because purchasing individual basket default swaps for a collection of bonds can be very expensive, especially considering how unlikely it is that all the bonds in a given basket will default simultaneously. Buying a basket default swap, instead, provides a much cheaper solution. Moreover, there has been increasing use of basket default swaps in the creation of structured credit products—credit-linked notes (see Chapter 6) and synthetic collateralized debt obligations (see Chapter 7). The most popular default basket swap contract is the first-to-default basket. In this contract, the seller pays (the default event occurs) when the first default is observed among the bonds in the basket.

In this section, we describe how to extend the model to basket default swaps. The key in the extension is estimating default correlations. We begin with the valuation model and then discuss how to model default correlations.

The Pricing Model

The number of issuers (or issues) contained in a default basket typically varies (three to five). As explained in Chapter 3, the payoff of a default basket contract can be a fixed amount or loss based. The first-to-default basket pays principal minus the recovery value of the first defaulted bond in the basket. Hence, for pricing the default basket, we can generalize the default swap valuation as follows:

$$V = E\left\{ e^{-\int_t^{\min(u_k)} r(s)ds} 1_{\min(u_k) < T}[1 - R_k(u_k)]\right\} \tag{10.4}$$

where 1 is the indicator function, u_j is the default time of the j-th bond, R_j is recovery rate of the j-th bond, and N_j is the notional of the j-th bond. The basket pays when it experiences the first default, i.e., min (u_j).[7]

Equation (10.4) has no easy solution when the default events (or default times, u_j) are correlated. For the sake of exposition, we assume two default processes and label the survival probabilities of the two credit names as $Q_1(t,T)$ and $Q_2(t,T)$. In the case of independence, the default probabilities at some future time t are $-dQ_1(t,T)$ and $-dQ_1(t,T)$ respectively. The default probability of either bond defaulting at time t is

$$-d[Q_1(t, T)Q_2(t, T)] \tag{10.5}$$

The above equation represents a situation wherein both credit names jointly survive until t, but not until the next instant of time; hence one of the bonds must have defaulted instantaneously at time t. Subtracting

---

[7] In either the default swap or default basket market, the premium is usually paid in a form of spreads. The spread is paid until either the default or maturity, whichever is earlier. From the total value of the default swap, we can convert it to a spread that is paid until default or maturity:

$$s = \frac{V}{\sum_{j=1}^{n} P(t, T_j)Q^*(t, T_j)}$$

where: $Q^*(t,T_j)$ is the survival probability of no default of all bond in the basket. Under independence assumption,

$$Q^*(t, T_j) = \prod_{k=1}^{N} Q_k(t, T_j)$$

where N is the number of bonds in the basket. When bonds are correlated, we need to use materials in the following section to compute Q^*.

the default probability of the first credit name from the probability of either defaulting gives rise to the probability that only the second name (but not the first) defaults:

$$
\begin{aligned}
\int_0^T &-d[Q_1(0, t)Q_2(0, t)] + dQ_1(0, t) \\
&= [1 - Q_1(0, T)Q_2(0, T)] - [1 - Q_1(0, T)] \\
&= Q_1(0, T)[1 - Q_2(0, T)]
\end{aligned}
\tag{10.6}
$$

This probability is equal to the probability of survival of the first name and default of the second name; thus, it is with this probability that the payoff to the second name is paid. By the same token, the default probability of the first name is $1 - Q_1(0,T)$, and it is with this probability that the payoff regarding to the first name is paid.

In a basket model specified in equation (10.5), the final formula for the price of an N bond basket under independence is

$$
V = \int_0^T \sum_{k=1}^N P(0, t) \left[-d \prod_{l=1}^k Q_l(0, t) + d \prod_{l=0}^{k-1} Q_l(0, t) \right][1 - R_k(t)]
\tag{10.7}
$$

where $Q_0(t) = 1$ and hence $dQ_0(t) = 0$. Equation (10.7) assumes that the last bond (i.e., bond N) has the highest priority in compensation, that is, if the last bond jointly defaults with any other bond, the payoff is determined by the last bond. The second-to-last bond has the next highest priority in a sense that if it jointly defaults with any other bond *but the last*, the payoff is determined by the second to last bond. This priority prevails recursively to the first bond in the basket.

Investment banks that sell or underwrite default baskets are themselves subject to default risks. If a basket's reference entities have a higher credit quality than their underwriting investment bank, then it is possible that the bank may default before any of the issuers. In this case, the buyer of the default basket is subject to not only the default risk of the issuers of the bonds in the basket, but also to that of the bank as well—that is, the counterparty risk. If the counterparty defaults before any of the issuers in the basket do, the buyer suffers a total loss of the whole protection (and the spreads that had been paid up to that point in time). We modify equation (10.7) to incorporate the counterparty risk by adding a new asset with zero payoff to the equation:

$$
V = \int_0^T \sum_{k=1}^{N+1} P(0, t) \left[-d \prod_{l=1}^k Q_l(0, t) + d \prod_{l=0}^{k-1} Q_l(0, t) \right][1 - R_k(t)]
\tag{10.8}
$$

where the first asset represents the counterparty whose payoff is zero. That is,

$$1 - R_1(t) = 0 \text{ for all } t \tag{10.9}$$

Note that the counterparty payoff has the lowest priority because the buyer will be paid if the counterparty jointly defaults with any issuer.

The default swap is a special case of the default basket with $N = 1$ discussed earlier. However, with a default swap, the counterparty risk is more pronounced than that with a basket deal. With only one issuer, equation (10.9) can be simplified to:

$$
\begin{aligned}
V &= \int_0^T P(0, t)\{-dQ_1(0, t)[1 - R_1(t)] \\
&\quad + [-dQ_1(0, t)Q_2(0, t) + dQ_1(0, t)][1 - R_2(t)]\} \\
&= \int_0^T P(0, t)\{[-dQ_1(0, t)Q_2(0, t) + dQ_1(0, t)][1 - R_2(t)]\} \tag{10.10}
\end{aligned}
$$

Equation 10.10 implies that the investor who buys a default swap on the reference entity effectively sells a default swap of joint default back to the counterparty.

When the defaults of the issuers (and the counterparty) are correlated, the solution to equation (10.7) becomes very complex. When the correlations are high, issuers in the basket tend to default together. In this case, the riskiest bond will dominate the default of the basket. Hence, the basket default probability will approach the default probability of the riskiest bond. On the other hand, when the correlations are low, individual bonds in the basket may default in different situations. No bond will dominate the default in this case. Hence, the basket default probability will be closer to the sum of individual default probabilities.

To see more clearly how correlation can impact the basket value, think of a basket that contains only two bonds of different issuers. In the extreme case where the default correlation is 1, the two bonds in the basket should default together. In this case, the basket should behave like a single bond. On the other extreme, if the correlation is −1 (the bonds are perfect compliments of one another), default of one bond implies the survival of the other and vice versa. In this case, the basket should reach the maximum default probability: 100%.

How to Model Correlated Default Processes[8]

Default correlation is not an easy concept to define or measure. Put in simple terms, it is a measurement of the degree to which default of one asset makes more or less likely the default of another asset. One can think of default correlation as being jointly due to (1) a macroeconomic effect which tends to tie all industries into the common economic cycle, (2) a sector-specific effect, and (3) a company-specific effect.

The first contribution implies that default correlation should in general be positive even between companies in different sectors. Within the same sector we would expect companies to have an even higher default correlation since they have more in common. For example, the severe fall in oil prices during the 1980s resulted in the default of numerous oil-producing industries. On the other hand, the fall in the price of oil would have made the default of oil-using industries less likely as their energy costs fell, thereby reducing their likelihood of default and reducing the default correlation. However the sheer lack of default data means that such assumptions are difficult to verify with any degree of certainty.

It is simple enough to define pure default correlation. Basically, this number must correspond to the likelihood that should one asset default within a certain time period, how more or less likely is another asset to also default. In the case of default correlation, it is important to specify the horizon which is being considered.

The pairwise default correlation between two assets A and B is a measure of how more or less likely two assets are to default than if they were independent.

Specifying Directly Joint-Default Distribution

Let two firms, A and B, follow the following joint Bernoulli distribution (letting superscripts denote complement sets):

		Firm A		
		0	1	
Firm B	0	$b(A^C \cap B^C)$	$p(A \cap B^C)$	$1 - p(B)$
	1	$b(A^C \cap B)$	$b(A \cap B)$	$p(B)$
		$1 - p(A)$	$p(A)$	1

where

---

[8] This discussion draws from Ren-Raw Chen and Ben J. Sopranzetti, "The Valuation of Default-Triggered Credit Derivatives," *Journal of Financial and Quantitative Analysis* (June 2003).

$$p(A^C \cap B) = p(B) - p(A \cap B)$$

$$p(A \cap B^C) = p(A) - p(A \cap B)$$

$$p(A^C \cap B^C) = 1 - p(B) - p(A \cap B^C)$$

The default correlation is

$$\frac{\text{cov}(1_A, 1_B)}{\sqrt{\text{var}(1_A)\text{var}(1_B)}} = \frac{p(B|A)p(A) - p(A)p(B)}{\sqrt{p(A)(1 - p(A)p(B))(1 - p(B))}}$$

For example, suppose that A is a large automobile manufacturer and B is a small auto part supplier. Assume their joint default distribution is given as:

		Firm A		
		0	1	
Firm B	0	80%	0%	80%
	1	10%	10%	20%
		90%	10%	100%

In this example where A defaults should bankrupt B but not vice versa, B contains A and

$$p(A \cap B) = p(A)$$

The dependency of the part supplier on the auto manufacturer is

$$p(B|A) = \frac{p(A \cap B)}{p(A)} = \frac{p(A)}{p(A)} = 100\%$$

and the dependency of the auto manufacturer on the part supplier is

$$p(A|B) = \frac{p(A \cap B)}{p(B)} = \frac{p(A)}{p(B)} = 50\%$$

The default correlation is

$$\frac{p(B|A)p(A) - p(A)p(B)}{\sqrt{p(A)(1 - p(A)p(B))(1 - p(B))}}$$

$$= \frac{10\% - 10\% \times 20\%}{\sqrt{10\% \times 90\% \times 20\% \times 80\%}}$$

$$= \frac{0.08}{\sqrt{0.0144}} = \frac{2}{3}$$

This examples demonstrates that perfect dependency does not imply perfect correlation. To reach perfect correlation, $p(A) = p(B)$. Similarly, perfectly negative dependency does not necessarily mean perfect negative correlation. To see that, consider the following example:

		Firm A		
		0	1	
Firm B	0	70%	10%	80%
	1	20%	0%	20%
		90%	10%	100%

It is clear that given A defaults, B definitely survives: $p(B^C|A) = 1$, and $p(B|A) = 0$. But the default correlation is only -0.25. To reach perfect negative correlation of -100%, $p(A) + p(B) = 1$.

The reason that perfect dependency does not result in perfect correlation is because correlation alone is not enough to identify a unique joint distribution. Only a normal distribution family can have a uniquely identified joint distribution when a correlation matrix is identified. This is not true for other distribution families.[9]

Having now defined default correlation, one can begin to show how it relates to the pricing of credit default baskets.

We represent the outcomes of the two defaultable assets A and B using a Venn diagram as shown in Exhibit 10.2. The left circle corresponds to all scenarios in which asset A defaults before time T. Its area is therefore equal to p_A, the probability of default of asset A. Similarly, the area within the circle labeled B corresponds to the probability of default of asset B and equals p_B. The area of the shaded overlap corresponds to all scenarios in which both assets default before time T. Its area is the probability of joint default, p_{AB}.

The probability of either asset defaulting is

---

[9] For an extension of the above two-company analysis to multiple companies, see Chen and Sopranzetti, "The Valuation of Default-Triggered Credit Derivatives."

EXHIBIT 10.2   Venn Diagram Representation of Correlated Default for Two Assets

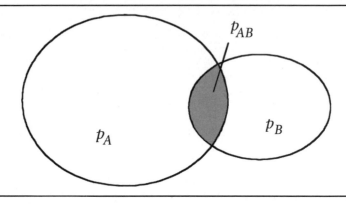

$$\Omega = p_A + p_B - p_{AB}$$

In the zero correlation limit, when the assets are independent, the probability of both assets defaulting is given by $p_{AB} = p_A p_B$. Substituting this into the above formula for the default correlation shows when the assets are independent, $\rho_D(T) = 0$ as expected (see Exhibit 10.3).

In the limit of high default correlation, the default of the stronger asset always results in the default of the weaker asset. In the limit the joint default probability is given by $p_{AB} = \min[p_A, p_B]$. This is shown in Exhibit 10.4 in the case where $p_A > p_B$. In this case we have a maximum default correlation of

$$\bar{\rho} = \frac{\sqrt{p_B(1-p_A)}}{\sqrt{p_A(1-p_B)}}$$

Once again, the price of a first-to-default basket is the area enclosed by the circles. In this case one circle encloses the other and the first-to-default basket price becomes the larger of the two probabilities:

$$\Omega_{\rho = \bar{\rho}} = p_A + p_B - p_{AB} = \max[p_A, p_B]$$

If p_A equals p_B then $p_{AB} = p_A$ and default of either asset results in default of the other. In this instance the correlation is at its maximum of 100%.

As correlations go negative, a point arrives at which there is zero probability of both assets defaulting together. Graphically, there is no

EXHIBIT 10.3   Independent Assets

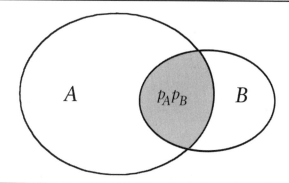

Outcome	In Venn Diagram	Probability
Both asset A and asset B default	Anywhere in overlap of both circles	p_{AB}
Asset B defaults and asset A does not default	Anywhere in B but not in overlap	$p_B - p_{AB}$
Asset A defaults and asset B does not default	Anywhere in A but not in overlap	$p_A - p_{AB}$
Neither asset defaults	Outside both circles	$1 - (p_A + p_B - p_{AB})$
Either asset A or asset B or both assets default	Anywhere within outer perimeter of circles	$p_A + p_B - p_{AB}$

EXHIBIT 10.4   Case of High Default Correlation

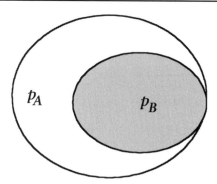

In the case default of the stronger asset is always associated with default of the weaker asset.

EXHIBIT 10.5 Negative Default Correlation Case

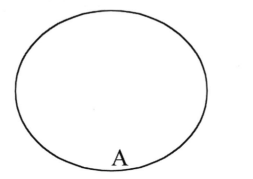

As the default correlation becomes negative, the two circles separate implying that the joint default probability has fallen to zero.

intersection between the two circles, as shown in Exhibit 10.5, and we have $p_{AB} = 0$. The correlation becomes

$$\rho = \frac{-\sqrt{p_A p_B}}{\sqrt{1 - p_A}\sqrt{1 - p_B}}$$

A negative correlation of –100% can only occur if $p_A = 1 - p_B$—that is, for every default of asset A, asset B survives and vice versa.

The price of the first-to-default basket is simply the area of the two nonoverlapping circles

$$\Omega_{\rho = \underline{\rho}} = p_A + p_B$$

This is when the default basket is at its most expensive.

We have seen above the price of a basket in the limits of low, high, and zero correlation. Given that $\Omega = p_A + p_B - p_{AB}$, we can write the price of a basket in terms of the default correlation as

$$\Omega = p_A + p_B - p_A p_B - \rho \sqrt{p_A - p_A^2} \sqrt{p_B - p_B^2}$$

As more assets are considered, more default combinations become possible. With just three assets we have the following eight possibilities:

■ No assets default

EXHIBIT 10.6   Venn Diagram for Three Issuers

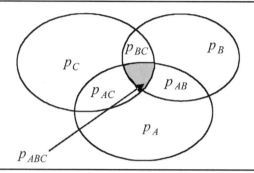

- Only Asset A defaults
- Only Asset B defaults
- Only Asset C defaults
- Asset A and Asset B default
- Asset B and Asset C default
- Asset A and Asset C default
- Asset A and Asset B and Asset C default

To price this basket we either need all of the joint probabilities or the pairwise correlations ρ_{AB}, ρ_{BC}, and ρ_{AC} (see Exhibit 10.6). The probability that the basket is triggered is given by

$$\Omega = p_A + p_B + p_C - p_{AB} - p_{BC} - p_{AC} + p_{ABC}$$

Joint Poisson Process

Recent evidence (for example, Enron, WorldCom, and Quest) demonstrated that severe economic hardship and publicity can cause chain defaults for even very large firms. Hence, incorporating default correlation is an important task in valuing credit derivatives.

As stated above, the period-end joint default probability by two reference entities is as follows:

$$\Pr(A \cap B) = E[1_{A \cap B}] = p_{AB}$$

where 1 is the indicator function.

The Black-Scholes-Merton (BSM) model, described in Chapter 8, is particularly useful in modeling correlated defaults. If two firms do business together, it is likely that the two firms may have a certain relationship between their defaults. The BSM model provides an easy explanation as to how that may be modeled:

$$\Pr(A_A(T) < K_A \cap A_B(T) < K_B)$$

A bivariate diffusion of firm A and firm B can easily provide what we need. Under the BSM model, logarithm of asset price is normally distributed. Hence, the previous equation is the tail probability of a bivariate normal distribution. The correlation between the two normally distributed log asset prices characterizes the default correlation. When the correlation in the bivariate normal is 100%, the distribution becomes a univariate normal distribution and the two firms default together. When the correlation is –100%, one firm defaulting implies the survival of the other firm; so there is always one that is live and one that is dead.

While the BSM model cleverly explains how default risk is priced in the corporate debt conceptually, as explained in Chapter 8 it remains a practical problem in that it cannot price today's complex credit derivatives. Hence, researchers recently have developed a series of reduced form models that simplify the computations of the prices.

Using Common Factors to Model Joint Defaults

There are two ways to model joint defaults in a reduced form model. One way, proposed by Duffie and Singleton, is to specify a "common factor."[10] When this common factor jumps, all firms default. Firms also can do so on their own. The model can be extended to multiple common factors: market factor, industry factor, sector factor, and so on to capture more sophisticated joint defaults.

Formally, let a firm's jump process be[11]

$$J_i = a_i q_M + q_i$$

where q_M is the market jump process and q_i is the idiosyncratic jump process. The coefficient a_i is to capture different correlation levels. The joint event is then

$$\text{corr}(J_i, J_j) = a_i a_j \text{var}[q_M]$$

---

[10] Darrell Duffie and Kenneth Singleton, "Econometric Modeling of Term Structure of Defaultable Bonds," *Review of Financial Studies* (December 1999), pp. 687–720.
[11] Darrell Duffie and Kenneth Singleton, unpublished lecture notes on credit derivatives and Darrell Duffie and Kenneth Singleton, "Simulating Correlated Defaults," working paper, Stanford University (September 1998).

Correlating Default Times

Before we discuss how the default correlation is introduced, we need to discuss how single-issuer default is modeled. The approach used is equivalent to the Jarrow-Turnbull model.[12] A hazard rate, $\lambda(t)$, is introduced where $\lambda(t)dt$ is the probability of defaulting in a small time interval dt. This leads to the definition of the survival probability:

$$Q(0, T) = \exp\left(-\int_0^T \lambda(s)ds\right)$$

The probability of surviving to a time T and then defaulting in the next instant is therefore given by the density function:

$$-dQ = \lambda(T)\exp\left(-\int_0^T \lambda(s)ds\right)dT$$

In the simple case when the hazard rate is constant over time so that $\lambda(t) = \lambda$ we have

$$-dQ = \lambda\exp(-\lambda T)dT$$

From this we see that the probability of defaulting at time T as given by $-dQ$ shows that default times are exponentially distributed. By extension, the average time to default is given by computing

$$\langle T \rangle = \lambda\int_0^\infty T\exp(-\lambda T)dT = \frac{1}{\lambda}$$

Knowing that defaults are normally distributed makes it easy to simulate default times for independent assets. We need to generate uniform random numbers in the range [0,1] and then given a term structure for the hazard rate, imply out the corresponding default time. For example, if we denote the uniform random draw by u, the corresponding default time T^* is given by solving

$$u = \exp(-\lambda T^*)$$

to give

---

[12] Robert Jarrow and Stuart Turnbull, "Pricing Derivatives on Financial Securities Subject to Default Risk," *Journal of Finance* 20, no. 1 (1995), pp. 53–86.

$$T^* = -\frac{\log(u)}{\lambda}$$

This is an efficient method for simulating default. Every random draw produces a corresponding default time. In terms of its usefulness, the only question is whether the default time is before or after the maturity of the contract being priced.

There are many ways to introduce a default correlation between the different reference entities in a credit default basket. One way is to correlate the default times. This correlation is defined as

$$\rho(T_A, T_B) = \frac{\langle T_A T_B \rangle - \langle T_A \rangle \langle T_B \rangle}{\sqrt{\langle T_A^2 \rangle - \langle T_A \rangle^2}\sqrt{\langle T_B^2 \rangle - \langle T_B \rangle^2}}$$

It is important to stress that this is not the same as the default correlation. Although correlating default times has the effect of correlating default, there are two reasons they are not equivalent. First, there is no need to define a default horizon when correlating default times. To measure this correlation we would observe a sample of assets over a long (infinite) period and compute the times at which each asset defaults. There is no notion of a time horizon for this correlation.

Second, since the default time correlation equals 100% when $T_j = T_i$ and when $T_j = T_i + \vartheta$, it is possible to have 100% default time correlation with assets defaulting at fixed intervals.

Under a Poisson assumption,

$$\langle T_A \rangle = \frac{1}{\lambda_A} \quad \text{and} \quad \langle T_B \rangle = \frac{1}{\lambda_B}$$

and

$$\sqrt{\langle T_A^2 \rangle - \langle T_A \rangle^2} = \frac{1}{\lambda_A} \quad \text{and} \quad \sqrt{\langle T_B^2 \rangle - \langle T_B \rangle^2} = \frac{1}{\lambda_B}$$

so we have

$$\rho(T_A, T_B) = \langle T_A T_B \rangle \lambda_A \lambda_B - 1$$

Copula Function

To generate correlated default times, we use the normal Copula function methodology as proposed by Li.[13] A Copula function is simply a specification of how the univariate marginal distributions combine to form a multivariate distribution. For example, if we have N-correlated uniform random variables $U_1, U_2, ..., U_N$ then

$$C(u_1, u_2, ..., u_N) = \Pr\{U_1 < u_1, U_2 < u_2, ..., U_N < u_N\}$$

is the joint distribution function which gives the probability that all of the uniforms are in the specified range.

In a similar manner we can define the Copula function for the default times of N assets

$$C(F_1(T_1), F_2(T_2), ..., F_N(T_N))$$
$$= \Pr\{U_1 < F_1(T_1), U_2 < F_2(T_2), ..., U_N < F_N(T_N)\}$$

where $F_i(T_i) = \Pr\{t_i < t\}$.

There are several possible choices but here we define the Copula function Θ to be the multivariate normal distribution function with correlation matrix ρ. We also define Φ^{-1} as the inverse of a univariate normal function. The Copula function is therefore given by

$$C(\mathbf{u}) = \Theta(\Phi^{-1}(u_1), \Phi^{-1}(u_2), \Phi^{-1}(u_3), \Phi^{-1}(u_4), ..., \Phi^{-1}(u_N), \boldsymbol{\rho})$$

where $\boldsymbol{\rho}$ is the correlation matrix.

What this specification says is that in order to generate correlated default times, we must first generate N-correlated multivariate gaussians denoted by $u_1, u_2, u_3, ..., u_N$—one for each asset in the basket. These are then converted into uniform random variables by cumulative probability functions.

Once we have the vector of correlated random uniforms $\mathbf{u}$ we can calculate the corresponding default times knowing that asset i defaults in trial n at time T given by

$$T_{in} = -\frac{\ln u_{in}}{\lambda_i}$$

---

[13] David X. Li, *Credit Metrics Monitor*, Risk Metrics Group (April 1999).

Comparing Default Correlation and Default Time Correlation

In addition to correlating default times, we could correlate default events. There is no simple way to do this directly. It is better to correlate the assets using some other mechanism and then measure the default correlation *a posteriori*. The question is: If we implement a model which correlates default times, how does the correlation relate to default correlation as defined above.

In common with the case of default correlation, it is only possible to have a 100% pairwise correlation in default times between two assets if both assets have the same default probabilities. Otherwise, the distributions are centered around different average default times and having equal default times and different average default times is not compatible.

If we assume that in both cases all assets have the same default probability, what is the difference between correlating default times and correlating default events. In the limit of zero correlation there is no difference as the assets default independently. In the limit of 100% correlation there is a fundamental difference: If default times have a 100% correlation then assets must default either simultaneously or with a fixed time difference.[14] However if there is 100% default correlation, then this means that the default of one asset within a certain horizon always coincides with the default of the other within the same horizon. In general, we would expect a 100% default correlation to imply that both assets default together, but this is not a strict requirement. In practice, the default of one asset may occur at any time and be followed by default of the other asset at the end of the horizon. Default correlation is 100% but default times have a lower correlation.

Consider also the effect of the default horizon. Given that default times are exponentially distributed, extending the default horizon makes it more likely for defaults to occur. Extending the default horizon therefore has the effect of increasing the measured default correlation. Indeed we must be careful to specify the horizon when we quote a default correlation. On the other hand, correlation of default times is independent of the trade horizon (i.e., the tenor of the default swap).

There is also a link between default correlation and the hazard rate. For a fixed horizon, increasing the hazard rate for all assets makes default more likely within that horizon. If the assets are correlated, the measured default correlation must increase. However the increase in default probability makes the distribution of default times more weighted towards earlier defaults. Yet, the default time correlation can remain unchanged.

---

[14] Since the default time correlation of 100% is preserved under translations of the form $T_j = T_i + \vartheta$.

The analysis below shows that the default correlation is always lower than the default time correlation. This can be understood in qualitative terms as follows: To have the same basket price we have the same number of defaults before maturity. As default correlation is a direct measurement of the likelihood of two assets to default within a fixed horizon, it is more closely linked with the pricing of a basket default swap than a correlation of default times. Indeed, as we have shown in the one-period model above, the value of the basket default swap is a linear function of the default correlation. Though a correlation of default times introduces a tendency for assets to default within a given trade horizon, it is an indirect way to do this. As a result, a simulation of defaults with a certain default time correlation will always tend to have a lower default correlation. In other words, less default correlation is required in order to have the same effect as a correlation of default times.

Numerical Examples

We now present numerical examples for valuing basket default swaps for a single-period case and a

Single Period Valuation

From equation (10.5), the closed-form solution for the basket default swap's value is

$$
\begin{aligned}
V &= P(t, T)p(A \cup B) \\
&= P(t, T)[p(A) + p(B) - p(B|A)p(A)]
\end{aligned}
\tag{10.11}
$$

where P is the risk-free discount factor. As can be seen, the basket value is linear in the conditional probability. We should note that the unconditional default correlation, which is calculated as follows:

$$
\rho(A, B) = \frac{p(B|A)p(A) - p(A)p(B)}{\sqrt{p(A)[1 - p(A)]p(B)[1 - p(B)]}}
\tag{10.12}
$$

is also linear in the conditional probability. It is easy to demonstrate that the basket value is a (negative) linear function of the default correlation. When the default correlation is small (or even negative), the issuers tend to default alternately: This increases the basket risk. When the correlation is large, the issuers tend to default together: This decreases the basket risk.

Using the above numerical example of the automobile manufacturer and the parts suppler, we show the relationship between the default correlation and the basket value in Exhibit 10.7.

EXHIBIT 10.7 Basket Value versus Default Correlation

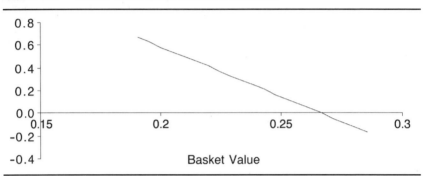

Note: Risk-free rate is 5%; default probability is 10% for the first bond and 20% for the second bond.

Multiperiod Valuation

Note that in multiple periods, default probabilities shall move over time randomly. The Bernoulli distribution for a single period can be extended to a Poisson process in continuous time. In a continuous time model, the above default correlation should be interpreted as the instantaneous default correlation. In a Poisson process, defaults occur unexpectedly with intensity λ (the hazard rate). Hence, the survival probability can be written as

$$Q(0, t) = \exp\left[-\int_0^t \lambda(u)du\right] \qquad (10.13)$$

Given equation (10.13), the instantaneous conditional forward default probability should become

$$p(t) = \frac{-dQ(0, t)}{Q(0, t)} = \lambda(t)dt \qquad (10.14)$$

The Poisson process intensity parameter can thus be interpreted as an annualized conditional forward default probability. The yield spread can also be represented by the intensity parameter:

$$s(t) = -\frac{\ln Q(0, t)}{t} = \int_0^t \lambda(u)du \qquad (10.15)$$

If default is governed by a Poisson process, then for any infinitesimally small period, the default event is a Bernoulli distribution. Thus, our single period analysis in the previous section can readily be generalized to continuous time. In multiple periods (continuous time), spreads change randomly but are correlated with one another; moreover, they are also correlated with changing interest rates. To accommodate this innovation, we randomize the hazard rate following the mathematical foundation established by Lando.[15]

For any issuer, the risky discount factor is written as

$$
\begin{aligned}
D(0, t) &= E^{r, \lambda, \tau}\left\{ 1_{(\tau > t)}\exp\left[-\int_0^t r(u)du\right]\right\} \\
&= E^{r, \lambda}\left\{ E[1_{(\tau > t)}|r, \lambda]\exp\left[-\int_0^t r(u)du\right]\right\}
\end{aligned}
\tag{10.16}
$$

where the interest rate, r, hazard rate, λ, and the default time, τ, are all random variables. In order to investigate the isolated impact of spread correlations on the value of default swaps and baskets, we assume that the default time, τ (conditional on λ), is uncorrelated with the interest rate, r. Thus the first term inside the expectation simplifies to

$$
E[1_{(\tau > t)}|r, \lambda] = E[1_{(\tau > t)}|\lambda] = \exp\left[-\int_0^t \lambda(u)du\right]
\tag{10.17}
$$

As a result, we can write the risky discount factor as

$$
\begin{aligned}
D(0, t) &= E^{r, \lambda, \tau}\left\{ 1_{(\tau > t)}\exp\left[-\int_0^t r(u)du\right]\right\} \\
&= E^{r, \lambda}\left\{ \exp\left[-\int_0^t r(u) + \lambda(u)du\right]\right\}
\end{aligned}
\tag{10.18}
$$

Note that the interest rate and the hazard rate are correlated. Hence, the closed-form solution does not exist except for the case where both variables are normally distributed. Unfortunately, a normally distributed hazard rate is infeasible since it may cause the survival probability to be greater than one (or the default probability to be negative).

Although the value of the risky discount factor in equation (10.18) is easy to obtain, the value of the default swap (and basket) is considerably

---

[15] David Lando "On Cox Processes and Credit Risky Securities," *Review of Derivatives Research* 2, no. 2/3 (1998), pp. 99–120.

more complex, since it requires the evaluation of a more complex integral where the risk-free discount factor is a function of the default time:

$$E^{r,\lambda,\tau}\left\{1_{\min\{\tau\}<T}\exp\left[-\int_0^{\min\{\tau\}}r(u)du\right](1-R_j)\right\} \qquad (10.19)$$

As mentioned in the previous section, Duffie[16] was the first to provide the valuation of the first-to-default basket. In order to show the impact of the spread correlation, we present an explicit example where the hazard rate follows a log normal process:

$$d\ln\lambda_j = \alpha(t)dt + \sigma dz_j \qquad (10.20)$$

where $j = 1, ..., N$ representing various issuers in the basket, dz is normal$(0, dt)$ and $\alpha(t)$ is a time dependent parameter used for calibrating the model to the default probability curve.[17] The correlations are defined as $\rho_{ij}dt = dz_i dz_j$.[18]

---

[16] Darrell Duffie, "First to Default Valuation," working paper, Stanford University (April 1998).

[17] The discrete version of equation (10.20) is as follows:

$$\lambda_{t+\Delta t} = \lambda_t\alpha_t e^{\sigma\sqrt{\Delta t}z_t}$$

where z is normal$(0,1)$ and $\alpha(t)$ is a time dependent parameter used for calibrating the following:

$$Q(0, t) = E_0\left[e^{-\int_0^t \lambda_s ds}\right]$$

In the simulation, we set a piece-wise flat a according to

$$Q(0, t+\Delta t) = E_0\left[e^{-\int_0^t \lambda_s ds}e^{-\lambda_{t+\Delta t}\Delta t}\right]$$

Every path in the simulation is a draw from an n-dimensional joint log normal distribution, each of which follows the process described as such. For every period, α is calculated for that period so that the forward probability curve is properly calibrated. Then, an *independent* random draw from an n-dimensional joint uniform is used to determine if any of the assets default.

Finally, the first-to-default protection value of a basket is the present value of the risk-neutral expectation of the payoff (notional value minus recovery value):

$$E\left[e^{-\int_0^t r_s ds}1_{(t<T)}\right]$$

where t is the default time, T is the maturity time of the basket, and 1 is the indicator function which returns a value of zero if its subscript is untrue and one if it is true. The valuation is achieved by calculating the average of the simulations.

[18] We follow Duffie and set the default correlations to zero.

EXHIBIT 10.8   Basket Value: Dynamic Spreads

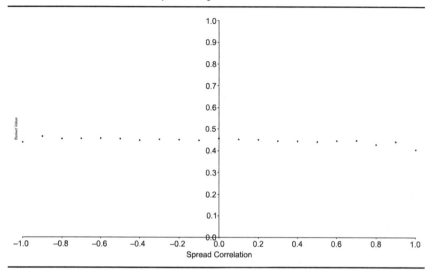

Note: The risk-free rate is 5%. The first (current) and second (forward) default probabilities are both 10% for the first issuer and 20% for the second issuer, $\sigma_1 = \sigma_2 = 100\%$.

We continue with our previous example of two issuers (the auto manufacturer and the supplier) that assume 10% and 20% default probabilities for the first period. For the second period, we assume the forward default probabilities are also 10% and 20%. The actual default probabilities are simulated according to equation (10.20) with $\sigma_1 = \sigma_2 = 100\%$ and any given correlation value. The simulated default probabilities are calibrated to the forward default probabilities. We assume a 5% risk-free interest rate for each period.

The impact of the spread correlation on the basket value is given in Exhibit 10.8.[19] As can readily be seen, the basket value fluctuates randomly around the 4% level. The standard error is around 0.18, which indicates that the fluctuation is mainly Monte Carlo noise. As a result, we find that the spread correlation has very little to say about the default probability. This is not so surprising, since basket default swaps are default sensitive claims, not spread sensitive claims—interdependence among issuer default within the basket is more important than interdependence between their individual spreads. Since the spread correlation has no impact on default probability in even a simple two-period setting, it is trivial to extend the results to the case of multiple periods.

---

[19] The exhibit is based on 10,000 simulations. We simulation 5,000 independent paths, and then use antithetic technique to generate the other 5,000 paths.

SUMMARY

In this chapter we present a model for valuing single-name and basket credit default swaps. The pricing model we present is sufficiently general so as to be consistent with both structural and reduced form models. In other words, the pricing model we present is model-free. The rationale is that default swaps and default baskets are "cash" products which do not rely on any modeling assumptions but only cash default probability curves. However, because reduced form models are easier than structural models for extracting default probabilities, with recovery exogenously specified, we demonstrate our model using the reduced form approach. The pricing of default basket swaps are very sensitive to correlation risk. The sensitivity is largely attributed to default correlation rather than spread correlation. We provide popular methods in modeling default correlation in this chapter.

APPENDIX

Continuous Time Formalism

In this appendix we derive the continuous time counterparts of the discrete formulas in the text. The survival probability is labeled as

$$Q(0, t) = E[1_{(u > t)}]$$

where 1 is the indicator function and u is the default time. Hence the instantaneous default probability is $-dQ(0, t)$.

The total default probability is the integration of the per period default probabilities:

$$\int_0^T -dQ(0, t)dt = 1 - Q(0, T)$$

The "forward" default probability is a conditional default probability. Conditional on no default till time t, the default probability for the next instant is

$$\frac{-dQ(0, t)}{Q(0, t)}$$

In a Poisson distribution, defaults occur unexpectedly with intensity λ. Hence, the survival probability can be written as

$$Q(0, t) = \exp\left(-\int_0^t \lambda(u)du\right)$$

and the default probability is

$$-dQ(0, t) = Q(0, t)\lambda(t)dt$$

or the forward probability is

$$\frac{-dQ(0, t)}{Q(0, t)} = \lambda(t)dt$$

This result states that the intensity parameter in the Poisson process is also an annualized forward default probability.

In the case of constant λ, constant interest rate, and constant recovery rate, the credit default swap value can be simplified to give the following result:

$$V = (1 - R)\lambda \int_0^T e^{-(r+\lambda)u}du$$

$$= (1 - R)\frac{\lambda}{r + \lambda}e^{-(r+\lambda)T}$$

In a general case, the equation looks like

$$V = \int_0^T [1 - R(\tau)]p(\tau)[-dQ(\tau)]$$

which is a continuous time counterpart of equation (10.3). After considering the delivery option, the equation becomes

$$V = \int_0^T \{1 - E[\min R_j(\tau)]\}p(\tau) - [dQ(\tau)]$$

Where the counterparty risk is considered, the recovery is paid only when the reference entity defaults but not the counterparty. Hence, the instantaneous default probability of this kind is

$$d[Q_1(0, t)Q_2(0, t)] - dQ_1(0, t)$$

Since we assume independence between the reference entity and the counterparty, $Q_1(0, t)$ is the survival probability of the reference entity and $Q_1(0, t)Q_2(0, t)$ is the probability that both survive. Hence, $dQ_1(0, t)$ is the default probability of the reference entity and $d[Q_1(0, t)Q_2(0, t)]$ is the default probability of either reference entity or counterparty. Subtracting the default of the counterparty from the default of either gives the default of only the reference entity but not the counterparty.

When we assume Poisson processes for the defaults with constant intensity parameters for the reference entity and the counterparty, we can write the result in the text as

$$dQ_2(0, t) = -e^{-\lambda_2 t}\lambda_2$$
$$d[Q_1(0, t)Q_2(0, t)] = -e^{-(\lambda_1 + \lambda_2)t}(\lambda_1 + \lambda_2)$$

and the result is

$$\int_0^T (\lambda_1 + \lambda_2)e^{-(\lambda_1 + \lambda_2)t} - \lambda_2 e^{-\lambda_2 t}\, dt = -e^{-\lambda_1 T}(1 - e^{-\lambda_2 T})$$

This result confirms that the first term is the survival of the counterparty and the second term is the default of the reference entity. Since both are independent, the product is the desired result.

The integrand states that when the counterparty risk is considered, the buyer of the credit default swap actually sells back a credit default swap to the counterparty.

When discount is considered, the integral becomes

$$\int_0^T (\lambda_1 + \lambda_2)e^{-(\lambda_1 + \lambda_2 + r)t} - \lambda_2 e^{-(\lambda_2 + r)t}\, dt$$

CHAPTER 11

Options and Forwards on Credit-Related Spread Products

In this chapter we will look at option and forward contracts where the underlying is a credit-related spread product. We begin with a discussion of the various types of credit-related spreads. At the end of this chapter, we describe how these credit derivative products are priced.

CREDIT-RELATED SPREADS

The term "spread" is frequently used in the market to represent the difference between two interest rates.[1] The spread reflects the differences between the risk associated with two securities. These risks include credit risk, option risk, liquidity risk, and exchange rate risk.

The following spread measures are typically used in the market:

- Bond yield spread
- Quoted margin and discount margin
- Interest rate swap spread
- Asset swap spread
- Credit default swap spread

In Chapter 3 we discussed single-name credit default swaps. The credit default swap spread is the spread paid by the protection buyer to the protection seller for credit protection. In Chapter 4 we covered asset swaps

---

[1] Of course, the term *spread* is also used by market participants in referring to the difference between a bid and offer price, a measure of market liquidity.

and the asset swap spread. The asset swap spread is the spread to LIBOR received by a party to an asset par swap who synthetically creates a floating rate security. The other three measures are explained below.

Bond Yield Spread

Traditional analysis of the spread for a credit-risky bond involves calculating the difference between the credit-risky bond's yield to maturity (or yield to call) and the yield to maturity of a comparable maturity Treasury coupon security. The spread is called is the *bond yield spread*.

For example, consider the following 10-year bonds:

Issue	Coupon	Price	Yield to maturity
Treasury	6%	$100.00	6.00%
Credit-risky bond	8%	$104.19	7.40%

The bond yield spread for the credit-risky bond as traditionally computed is 140 bps (7.4% minus 6%). Market participants also refer to this traditional yield spread as the *nominal spread*.

The drawbacks of the nominal spread are (1) for both bonds the yield fails to take into consideration the term structure of the spot rates; and (2) in the case of callable or putable bonds, interest rate volatility may alter the cash flow of the credit-risky bond. Overcoming the first problem leads to the zero-volatility spread measure; the option-adjusted spread measure overcomes the second problem.

Zero-Volatility Spread

The *zero-volatility spread* is a measure of the spread that the investor would realize over the entire Treasury spot rate curve if (1) the bond is held to maturity and (2) the spot rates do not change. It is not a spread off one point on the Treasury yield curve, as is the nominal spread. The zero-volatility spread, also called the *static spread*, is calculated as the spread that will make the present value of the cash flow from the credit-risky bond, when discounted at the Treasury spot rate plus the spread, equal to the credit-risky bond's full price. A trial-and-error procedure is required to determine the zero-volatility spread.

To illustrate how this is done, let's use the credit-risky bond in our previous illustration and the Treasury yield curve in Exhibit 11.1. Hypothetical Treasury spot rates are in the fourth column of the exhibit. The third column in the exhibit is the cash flow for the 8% 10-year credit-risky bond. The goal is to determine the spread that when added to all the Treasury spot rates will produce a present value for the cash flow of the credit-risky bond equal to its market price of $104.19. The

EXHIBIT 11.1   Determination of the Zero-Volatility Spread for the 8%, 10-Year Credit-Risky Bond Selling at 104.19 to Yield 7.4%

Period	Years	Cash Flow ($)	Spot Rate (%)	Present Value Spread 100 bp ($)	Present Value Spread 125 bp ($)	Present Value Spread 146 bp ($)
1	0.5	4.00	3.0000	3.9216	3.9168	3.9127
2	1.0	4.00	3.3000	3.8334	3.8240	3.8162
3	1.5	4.00	3.5053	3.7414	3.7277	3.7163
4	2.0	4.00	3.9164	3.6297	3.6121	3.5973
5	2.5	4.00	4.4376	3.4979	3.4767	3.4590
6	3.0	4.00	4.7520	3.3742	3.3497	3.3293
7	3.5	4.00	4.9622	3.2565	3.2290	3.2061
8	4.0	4.00	5.0650	3.1497	3.1193	3.0940
9	4.5	4.00	5.1701	3.430	3.0100	2.9826
10	5.0	4.00	5.2772	2.9366	2.9013	2.8719
11	5.5	4.00	5.3864	2.8307	2.7933	2.7622
12	6.0	4.00	5.4976	2.7255	2.6862	2.6537
13	6.5	4.00	5.6108	2.6210	2.5801	2.5463
14	7.0	4.00	5.6643	2.5279	2.4855	2.4504
15	7.5	4.00	5.7193	2.4367	2.3929	2.3568
16	8.0	4.00	5.7755	2.3472	2.3023	2.2652
17	8.5	4.00	5.8331	2.2596	2.2137	2.1758
18	9.0	4.00	5.9584	2.1612	2.1148	2.0766
19	9.5	4.00	6.0863	2.0642	2.0174	1.9790
20	10.0	104.00	6.2169	51.1833	49.9638	48.9630
			Total	107.5414	105.7165	104.2145

last column of the exhibit shows the present value when a 146 bp spread is tried. The present value ($104.21) is almost equal to the credit-risky bond's price. Therefore 146 bps is the zero-volatility spread, compared to the nominal spread of 140 bps.

Typically, for standard coupon-paying bonds with a bullet maturity (i.e., a single payment of principal) the zero-volatility spread and the nominal spread will not differ significantly. In our example it is only 6 bps (146 bps versus 140 bps). For short-term bullet issues, there is little divergence. The main factor causing any difference is the shape of the yield curve. The steeper the yield curve, the greater the difference. Moreover, the difference between the zero-volatility spread and the nominal spread is greater for issues in which the principal is repaid over time (i.e., an amortizing structure) rather than only at maturity (i.e., a bullet structure). Thus, the difference between the nominal spread and the zero-volatility spread will be considerably greater for sinking fund bonds, mortgage-backed securities, and asset-backed securities in a steep yield curve environment.

Option-Adjusted Spread

For a credit-risky bond with an embedded option such as a call or put option, a portion of the nominal spread and zero-volatility spread reflects compensation for the value of the embedded option. For example, in our previous illustration the zero-volatility spread is 146 bps. The *option-adjusted spread* (OAS) adjusts the spread to reflect the value of the embedded option.

Suppose that our credit-risky bond is a callable issue and the value of the embedded call option is determined to be 46 bps. The OAS is 100 bps—the 146 bps reduced by the 46 bp value for the call option. If instead, the credit-risky bond is putable and the value of the put option is estimated to be 24 bps, then this value would be added to the zero-volatility spread. The OAS would be 170 bps.

The OAS is computed by using a model for valuing bonds with embedded options. For valuing callable and putable corporate and sovereign bonds, the lattice model is used. For residential nonagency mortgage-backed securities and asset-backed securities backed by residential mortgage loans (i.e., home equity loans and manufactured housing loans), the model most commonly used in practice is Monte Carlo simulation.[2]

Par Floater Spread

The coupon rate for a floating-rate security changes periodically according to a reference interest rate. The coupon reset formula is the reference rate plus or minus a spread. The spread in the coupon formula is referred to as the *quoted margin*.

Since the future value for the reference rate is unknown, it is not possible to determine the cash flows. This means that a yield to maturity cannot be calculated. Instead, there are several conventional measures referred to as margin or spread measures cited by market participants for floaters. These include spread for life (or simple margin), adjusted simple margin, adjusted total margin, and discount margin. The most

---

[2] For a description of the lattice and Monte Carlo models, see Chapters 5 and 8 in Frank J. Fabozzi, *The Valuation of Fixed Income Securities and Derivatives* (New Hope, PA: Frank J. Fabozzi Associates, 1998).

commonly used of these measures is *discount margin*, so we will discuss this measure and its limitations below. This measure estimates the average margin over the reference rate that the investor can expect to earn over the life of the security. The procedure for calculating the discount margin for a credit-risky bond is as follows:

Step 1. Determine the cash flows assuming that the reference rate does not change over the life of the security.

Step 2. Select a margin.

Step 3. Discount the cash flows found in Step 1 by the current value of the reference rate plus the margin selected in Step 2.

Step 4. Compare the present value of the cash flows as calculated in Step 3 to the price plus accrued interest. If the present value is equal to the security's price plus accrued interest, the discount margin is the margin assumed in Step 2. If the present value is not equal to the security's price plus accrued interest, go back to Step 2 and try a different margin.

For a par floater (i.e., a floating-rate security selling at par), the discount margin is simply the quoted margin in the coupon reset formula. The quoted margin for a par floater is called the *par floater spread*.

To illustrate the calculation, suppose that the coupon reset formula for a 6-year credit-risky floating-rate security selling for $99.3098 is 6-month LIBOR plus 80 bps. The coupon rate is reset every six months. Assume that the current value for the reference rate is 10%.

Exhibit 11.2 shows the calculation of the discount margin for this security. The second column shows the current value for 6-month LIBOR. The third column sets forth the cash flows for the security. The cash flows for the first 11 periods are equal to one-half the current 6-month LIBOR (5%) plus the semiannual assumed margin of 40 bps multiplied by $100. At the maturity date (i.e., period 12), the cash flow is $5.4 plus the maturity value of $100. The top row of the last five columns shows the assumed margin. The rows below the assumed margin show the present value of each cash flow. The last row gives the total present value of the cash flows.

For the five assumed margins, the present value is equal to the price of the floating-rate security ($99.3098) when the assumed margin is 96 bps. Therefore, the discount margin is 96 bps. Notice that the discount margin is 80 bps, the same as the quoted margin, when the security is selling at par.

EXHIBIT 11.2   Calculation of the Discount Margin for a Floating-Rate Credit-Risky Security

Maturity	= 6 years
Price	= 99.3098
Coupon formula	= LIBOR + 80 bps
	Reset every six months

			Present value ($) at assumed margin of[b]				
Period	LIBOR (%)	Cash flow ($)[a]	80 bp	84 bp	88 bp	96 bp	100 bp
1	10	5.4	5.1233	5.1224	5.1214	5.1195	5.1185
2	10	5.4	4.8609	4.8590	4.8572	4.8535	4.8516
3	10	5.4	4.6118	4.6092	4.6066	4.6013	4.5987
4	10	5.4	4.3755	4.3722	4.3689	4.3623	4.3590
5	10	5.4	4.1514	4.1474	4.1435	4.1356	4.1317
6	10	5.4	3.9387	3.9342	3.9297	3.9208	3.9163
7	10	5.4	3.7369	3.7319	3.7270	3.7171	3.7122
8	10	5.4	3.5454	3.5401	3.5347	3.5240	3.5186
9	10	5.4	3.3638	3.3580	3.3523	3.3409	3.3352
10	10	5.4	3.1914	3.1854	3.1794	3.1673	3.1613
11	10	5.4	3.0279	3.0216	3.0153	3.0028	2.9965
12	10	105.4	56.0729	55.9454	55.8182	55.5647	55.4385
		Present value	100.0000	99.8269	99.6541	99.3098	99.1381

[a] For periods 1–11: Cash flow = $100 (0.5) (LIBOR + Assumed margin)
  For period 12: Cash flow = $100 (0.5) (LIBOR + Assumed margin) + $100
[b] The discount rate is found as follows. To LIBOR of 10%, the assumed margin is added. Thus, for an 88 bp assumed margin, the discount rate is 10.88%. This is an annual discount rate on a bond-equivalent basis. The semiannual discount rate is then half this amount, 5.44%. It is this discount rate that is used to compute the present value of the cash flows for an assumed margin of 88 bps.

Interest Rate Swap Spread

As explained in Chapter 4, in an interest rate swap there are two parties who exchange payments based on some notional amount of principal. In the most common type of interest rate swap, one party pays a fixed interest rate and the other party pays a floating interest rate. The party that pays the fixed interest rate over the life of the swap pays an interest rate equal to a yield spread above the Treasury rate at the inception of the swap. More specifically, it is the yield spread above the on-the-run Treasury rate with the same maturity as the term of the swap. So, if the swap is a 5-year swap, the fixed-rate payer pays the 5-year Treasury rate plus a yield spread. The yield spread is the *swap spread*. The fixed-rate payer receives a floating rate, typically LIBOR.

LIBOR reflects the credit risk of international banks. So, if the swap is a 5-year swap and the swap spread is 80 bps, this means that the fixed-rate payer pays the 5-year Treasury rate plus 80 bps to receive LIBOR. The swap spread effectively reflects general corporate credit risk, as well as other factors. Historically, swap spreads have been highly correlated with nominal spreads on corporate bonds.

The other factors in addition to the general level of credit risk in the market that affect the size of the swap spread are (1) the supply of Treasury securities relative to the supply of credit spread products; (2) the liquidity premium demanded by the market; (3) market psychology toward spread products and the expected direction in interest rates; and (4) the risk appetite of dealer desks.[3]

CREDIT-RELATED SPREAD OPTIONS

Credit-related spread options are options in which the underlying is one of the following:

- A credit spread for a bond
- An asset swap spread
- A credit default swap spread

Option on the Credit Spread for a Bond

An option on the credit spread for a bond is an option whose value/pay-off depends on the change in credit spreads for a reference obligation. It is critical in dealing with such options to define what the underlying is. The underlining can be either:

- The level of the credit spread for a reference obligation, o.
- A reference obligation that is a credit-risky bond.

Option on a Bond Yield Spread

When the underlying is the level of the credit spread for a reference obligation, we refer to this option as an *option on a bond yield spread* or an

---

[3] These factors are explained in more detail in Richard Gordon, "The Truth About Swap Spreads," in Frank J. Fabozzi (ed.), *Professional Perspectives on Fixed Income Portfolio Management: Volume 1* (New Hope, PA: Frank J. Fabozzi Associates, 2000).

option on a credit spread. For an option on a bond yield spread, a reference obligation and a reference benchmark are specified. The payoff function for an option on a bond yield spread depends on:

1. The bond yield spread at the exercise date of the option.
2. The strike bond yield spread.
3. The notional amount of the contract.
4. A risk factor.

The risk factor is equal to:

$$\text{Risk factor} = 10,000 \times \left[\begin{array}{l} \text{Percentage price change for a 1 bp change} \\ \text{in rates for the reference obligation} \end{array} \right]$$

By including the risk factor, a bond yield spread option overcomes the problem we will identify below, where the underlying is a reference obligation rather than a bond yield spread. For such options described later, the payoff depends on both changes in the level of interest rates (the yield on the referenced benchmark) and the bond yield spread. For an option on a bond yield spread the payoff is only dependent upon the change in the bond yield spread. Therefore, fluctuations in the level of the referenced benchmark's interest rate will not affect the value of the option.

The payoff functions are the greater of zero and the value from the formula below:

Bond yield spread call option:

Payoff = (Bond yield spread at exercise – Strike bond yield spread)
     × Notional amount × Risk factor

Bond yield spread put option:

Payoff = (Strike bond yield spread – Bond yield spread at exercise)
     × Notional amount × Risk factor

The strike bond yield spread (in decimal form) is fixed at the outset of the option. The bond yield spread at exercise (in decimal form) is the yield spread over a referenced benchmark at the exercise date.

To illustrate the payoff, suppose that the current bond yield spread for a bond yield spread call option is 300 bps and the investor wants to protect against a bond yield spread widening to more than 350 bps. Accordingly, suppose that a strike bond yield spread of 350 bps is selected. Then assuming that the risk factor is 5 and the notional amount is $10 million, then the payoff for this option is

Payoff = (Bond yield spread at exercise − 0.035) × $10,000,000 × 5

If at the exercise date the bond yield spread is 450 bps, then the payoff is

Payoff = (0.045 − 0.035) × $10,000,000 × 5 = $500,000

The profit realized from this option is $500,000 less the cost of the option.

Note from the above example that a bond yield spread *call* option is used to protect against an increase in the credit spread.

Option on a Credit-Risky Bond

As an alternative to an option on a bond yield spread for a specific bond, the underlying can be the bond itself with the strike price based on a fixed credit spread. We refer to this option as an *option on a credit-risky bond* or an *option on a defaultable bond*.

A put and a call option on a credit risk bond are defined as follows:

Put option: An option that grants the option buyer the right, but not the obligation, to sell a reference obligation at a price that is determined by a strike credit spread over a referenced benchmark at the exercise date.

Call option: An option that grants the option buyer the right, but not the obligation, to buy a reference obligation at a price that is determined by a strike credit spread over a referenced benchmark at the exercise date.

Both a put option and a call option on a defaultable bond can be settled in cash or by physical delivery. The price for the reference obligation (i.e., the credit-risky bond) is determined by specifying a strike credit spread over the referenced benchmark, typically a default-free government security. For example, suppose that the reference obligation is an 8% 10-year bond selling to yield 8%. That is, the bond is selling at par. Suppose further that the benchmark is a 10-year U.S. Treasury bond that is selling to yield 6%. Then the current credit spread is 200 bps. Assume that a strike credit spread of 300 bps is specified and that the option expires in six months. At the end of six months, suppose that the 9.5-year Treasury rate is 6.5%. Since the strike credit spread is 300 bps, then the yield used to compute the strike price for the reference obligation is 9.5% (the Treasury rate of 6.5% plus the strike credit spread of 300 bps). The price of a 9.5-year 8% coupon bond selling to yield 9.5% is $90.75 per $100 par value.

The payoff at the expiration date would then depend on the market price for the reference obligation. For example, suppose that at the end of six months the reference obligation is trading at 82.59. This is a yield of 11% and therefore a credit spread of a 350 bps over the 9.5-year Treasury yield of 6.5%.

For a credit spread put option, the buyer can sell the reference obligation with a market value of 82.59 for a the strike price of 90.75. The payoff from exercising is 8.16. This payoff is reduced by the cost of the option to determine the profit. For a credit spread call option, the buyer will not exercise the option and will allow it to expire worthless. There is a loss equal to the cost of the option.

Notice the following payoff before taking into account the option cost when the underlying for the a credit spread option is the reference obligation:

Type of option	Positive payoff if at expiration
Put	Credit spread at expiration > Strike credit spread
Call	Credit spread at expiration < Strike credit spread

Consequently, to protect against credit spread risk, an investor can buy a credit spread *put* option where the underlying is a reference obligation.

There is one problem with using a credit spread option on a credit-risky bond as just described. It is dependent upon the value of the reference obligation, which is affected by both the change in the level of interest rates (as measured by the referenced benchmark) and the change in the credit spread. For example, suppose in our illustration that the 9.5-year Treasury at the exercise date is 4.5% (instead of 6.5%) and the credit spreads increases to 350 bps. This means that the reference obligation is trading at 8% (4.5% plus 350 bps). Since it is an 8% coupon bond with 9.5-years to maturity selling at 8%, the price is par. In this case, the credit spread put option would have a payoff of zero because the price of the reference obligation is 100 and the strike price is 90.74. Thus, there was no protection against credit spread risk because the interest rate for the referenced benchmark fell enough to offset the increase in the credit spread. This problem does not occur for an option on a bond yield spread, hence explaining their greater use as a credit derivative.

Option on an Asset Swap Spread

In the interest rate swap market, there are options on interest rate swaps. These derivative instruments are referred to as swaptions. There are two types of swaptions. A *pay fixed swaption* (also called a *payer swaption*) entitles the option buyer to enter into an interest rate swap in which the buyer of the option pays a fixed rate and receives a floating rate. For example, suppose that a European-style pay fixed swaption has a strike rate equal to 6%, a term of three years, and expires in two years. This means that at the end of two years the buyer of this pay fixed swaption has the right to enter into a 3-year interest rate swap in which the buyer pays 6% (the swap fixed rate which is equal to the strike rate) and receives the reference rate.

In a *receive fixed swaption* (also called a *receiver swaption*) the buyer of the swaption has the right to enter into an interest rate swap that requires paying a floating rate and receiving a fixed rate. For example, if the strike rate is 5.75%, the swap term is four years, and the option expires in one year, the buyer of this receiver fixed swaption has the right at the end of the next year (assuming a European-style option) to enter into a 4-year interest rate swap in which the buyer receives a swap fixed rate of 5.75% (i.e., the strike rate) and pays the reference rate.

As explained in Chapter 4, an asset swap spread is a specialized type of interest rate swap. Consequently, an option on an asset swap spread is nothing more than a swaption. The swaption can be a pay fixed asset swaption (or payer asset swaption) or a receive fixed asset swaption (or receiver asset swaption).

Option on a Credit Default Swap Spread

While an option on a credit default swap spread is not commonly traded as of this writing, this option is similar to any swaption. That is the buyer of the call (payer) option obtains a right to lock in a cheaper credit default swap spread. A cancellable credit default swap spread option can be viewed as a vanilla credit default swap with a put (receiver) option.

Pricing of Options on Credit-Spread Related Products

The pricing of a spread option (European) is no different from the pricing of an equity option where an expectation (risk neutral) is taken over the payoff function. Hence, the key to a pricing formula is the distribution of the spread. In the Black-Scholes case, where the log stock price is normally distributed, the option has a closed-form solution. In this chapter, we have introduced options on a number of different spreads. Theoretically, these spreads are all distributed differently and, for that reason, their option pricing formulas are all different. However, complex pricing formulas are not welcomed by practitioners, mostly due to computational issues. As a result, it is quite popular to assume that all spreads, regardless of their true distributions, are log normally distributed and the Black-Scholes model is used for pricing the option. In this section, we first use a simple example (zero-coupon, zero-recovery bond) to demonstrate how a spread can be derived and its distribution determined. Then we show how to price various spread options.

In Chapter 10 we explained how credit default swaps are priced. We know that the distribution of a bond's yield spread is derived from assumptions regarding the default and recovery processes. We will use the notation in Chapter 10 to demonstrate to show how the price of an option on a bond yield spread is determined.

Let's take a simple example of a zero recovery, zero-coupon bond, and the Poisson process of default. In this case, the survival probability is

$$Q(t, T) = E\left[\exp\left(-\int_t^T \lambda(u)du\right)\right]$$

As explained in Chapter 10, the spread is given by

$$s(t, T) = -\frac{\ln Q(t, T)}{T - t}$$

As a result, if the intensity parameter of the Poisson process, $\lambda(t)$, is deterministic, then the spread, $s(t,T)$, should also be deterministic:

$$s(t, T) = -\frac{\ln Q(t, T)}{T - t} = \frac{1}{T - t}\exp\left(-\int_t^T \lambda(u)du\right)$$

But if the intensity, $\lambda(t)$, is stochastic, then the distribution of the spread depends on the distribution of the survival probability, $Q(t,T)$, which is a solution to the exponential of the integral of $\lambda(t)$. To arrive at a simple distribution for the spread, one can assume a normally distributed $\lambda(t)$.[4] As a result, $Q(t,T)$ will be log normally distributed.[5] Then it is straightforward to see that the spread is normally distributed. However, it is incorrect to assume a normally distributed $\lambda(t)$ because it implies that the survival probability $Q(t,T)$ can exceed 100% (i.e., when

---

[4] For example, λ can follow an mean reverting Gaussian (Ornstein-Uhlenbeck) process as follows:

$$d\lambda = \alpha(\mu - \lambda)dt + \sigma dW$$

where α, μ, and α are all constants.

[5] The solution to $Q(t,T)$ is identical to the term structure solution provided in Oldrich Vasicek, "An Equilibrium Characterization of the Term Structure," *Journal of Financial Economics* 5 (1977), pp. 177–188. For the detailed derivation of the option formula see Farshid Jamshidian, "An Exact Bond Option Formula," *Journal of Finance* 44 (1989), pp. 205–209.

$\lambda(t)$ is negative). This is a direct violation of the no-arbitrage condition since no probabilities are allowed to be more than 100%. Some researchers propose the square root process for $\lambda(t)$.[6] While there is a closed-form for the survival probability, the distribution of the survival probability is unknown. As a result, the distribution of the spread is then unknown. In fact, because the spread is a log transformation of the survival probability, other than log normally distributed survival probability, no known distribution can lead to a closed-form distribution for the spread.

The spread of a zero-coupon bond of the structural Merton model described in Chapter 8 is[7]

$$s(t, T) = -\ln \frac{D(t, T)}{P(t, T)}$$

$$= -\ln\{A(t)[1 - N(d_1)] + P(t, T)KN(d_2)\} + \ln P(t, T)$$

where $A(t)$ is the asset price at time t, K is the face value of debt (no coupon), and

$$d_1 = \frac{\ln A(t) - \ln K - \ln P(t, T) + V/2}{\sqrt{V}}$$

$$d_2 = d_1 - \sqrt{V}$$

$$V = \text{var } [\ln A(T)]$$

Clearly, the spread variable has no closed-form solution for its distribution.

Without the closed-form distribution for the spread, it is not possible to derive an easy solution to the spread option. On the other hand, for practical purposes, quick and fast solutions are needed for pricing spread options. As mentioned in Chapter 9, where we explained

---

[6] This follows the Cox-Ingersoll-Ross model (John Cox, Jonathan Ingersoll, and Stephen Ross, "A Theory of the Term Structure of Interest Rates," *Econometrica* 53 (1985), pp. 385–408) for the term structure where the short rate (now intensity) follows the square root process:

$$d\lambda = \alpha(\mu - \lambda)dt + \sigma\sqrt{\lambda}dW$$

The option model is also derived in the same article by Cox, Ingersoll, and Ross.
[7] Note that in the Merton model, the recovery is endogenous and cannot be assumed to be 0.

reduced form models, the industry has been using a "spread based" model where a stochastic process is directly assigned to the spread:[8]

$$\frac{ds(t, T)}{s(t, T)} = \sigma dW(t)$$

However, modeling the spread directly like this may generate internal inconsistency.[9]

Various Spreads and the Pricing Model

To price spread options, we first need to know what spread the option is written on (i.e., the underlying spread). In the previous section, we used the zero-coupon, zero-recovery bond as an example. For this simplest contract, we have already seen that there is no closed-form solution in a rigorous manner. We either have to (1) assume a normally distributed intensity parameter, but then violate no-arbitrage; or (2) we adopt an industry practice to directly assume a log normally distributed spread that may generate internal inconsistency. For the spreads on more complex contracts, the hope for an easy solution for the option seems unlikely.

Options can be written on many spreads: bond spreads, credit default swap spreads, and asset swap spreads. Each spread is distributed differently, if the default and recovery follow a chosen model. In this chapter, we adopt the "spread based" model for pricing the options. All spreads are assumed to follow a log normal process given above. Note that the spread should be driftless, a process similar to the one for the futures (or forward) price. A spread call option is assumed to have the following payoff:

$$\max\{s(u, T) - K, 0\}$$

where $t < u < T$ and K is the strike of the option. The option formula is identical to the Black model for futures:[10]

---

[8] Here, we use $s(t,T)$ instead of $s(t)$. Note that any spread is a "term" spread that is the spread of some underlying asset (zero-coupon zero recovery bond here) that has an expiration date. In Chapter 10, we use the short-hand notation for convenience or we can regard $s(t)$ as an "instantaneous spread."

[9] The better known examples are the Brennan-Schwartz model (Michael Brennan and Eduardo Schwartz, "A Continuous Time Approach to the Pricing of Bonds," *Journal of Banking and Finance* 3 (1979), pp. 133–155 and the Ball-Torous model (Clifford A. Ball and Walter N. Torous, "Bond Price Dynamics and Options," *The Journal of Financial and Quantitative Analysis* 18, no. 4. (December 1983), pp. 517–531).

$$C(t) = e^{-r(u-t)}[s(t, T)N(d_1) - KN(d_2)]$$

where

$$d_1 = \frac{\ln s(t, T) - \ln K + \sigma(u-t)/2}{\sigma\sqrt{u-t}}$$

$$d_2 = d_1 - \sigma\sqrt{u-t}$$

Pricing Options on Swap Spreads

Options on asset swaps or credit default swaps are embedded options in swaps. If a payer asset swap (pay fixed and receive floating) can be canceled at a future fixed date (European), a wider spread will trigger exercise since the new asset swap will have a higher floating rate due to the higher spread. It is beneficial for the payer swap to cancel it and engage a new one to receive more from the floating one. Such an option is called a "put." It is more in the money when the spread is wider. It gives the right to cancel the payer swap (or enter a receiver swap with the strike spread being the same as the existing payer).

On the other hand, for a receiver swap (pay floating), a narrower spread will trigger the cancellation because the new swap will have a lower floating rate due to the lower spread. This option is called a "call." It is more in the money when the spread is narrower. It gives the right to cancel the receiver swap (or enter a payer swap).

When a call option is exercised, the option holder pays K instead of s to the counterparty of the swap. As a result, the benefit is a series of differences between the contract spread and the strike spread:

$$\max\left\{\sum_{j=1}^{n}(s_j - K)a_j P_j, 0\right\}$$

where a_j is the j-th accrued period and $s_j = s(u, T_j)$ and $P_j = P(u, T_j)$ are the spread and the discount factor observed at the option expiration time u for swap coupon time T_j. In general, there is no closed-form solution to this problem. But a simple lattice model can be carried out easily.

---

[10] Fischer Black, "The Pricing of Commodity Contracts," *Journal of Financial Economics* 3 (1976), pp. 167–179.

Summary on Option Pricing Models for Spread Options

Strictly speaking, there is no easy solution to price any spread option. To avoid complex computation, the industry generally uses a simplistic approach—assuming a log normal spread, to price spread options. For options on swaps (asset swaps or credit default swaps), we need a usual lattice model to price the option.

CREDIT SPREAD FORWARD CONTRACTS

A *credit spread forward contract* requires an exchange of payments at the settlement date based on a spread existing on that date. As with credit-related spread options, the underlying spread can be a bond yield spread, an asset swap spread, or a credit default swap spread. The payoff depends on the spread at the settlement date of the contract. The payoff is positive (i.e., the party receives cash) if the spread moves in favor of the party at the settlement date. The party makes a payment if the spread moves against the party at the settlement date.

For example, suppose that an asset manager has a view that the bond yield spread will increase to more than the current 250 bps in one year for an issue of ABD Corporation. Then the payoff function for this spread forward contract would be

(Bond yield spread at settlement date − 250) × Notional amount
  × Risk factor

Assuming that the notional amount is $10 million and the risk factor is 5, then if the yield spread at the settlement date is 325 bps, then the amount that will be received by the asset manager is:

$$(0.035 - 0.025) \times \$10{,}000{,}000 \times 5 = \$500{,}000$$

Instead, suppose that the bond yield spread at the settlement date decreased to 190 bps, then the asset manager would have to pay out $300,000 as shown below:

$$(0.019 - 0.025) \times \$10{,}000{,}000 \times 5 = -\$300{,}000$$

The fact that the asset manager can make or lose money on the credit forward demonstrates the symmetry of forward contracts in contrast to the asymmetry of option contracts where the maximum loss is limited to the option premium.

In general, if an asset manager takes a position in a spread forward contract to benefit from an increase in the spread, then the payoff would be as follows:

(Bond yield spread at settlement date – Yield spread in contract)
× Notional amount × Risk factor

For an asset manager taking a position that the bond yield spread will decrease, the payoff is:

(Bond yield spread in contract – Yield spread at settlement date)
× Notional amount × Risk factor

Pricing of Credit Spread Forward Contracts

Like any forward contract, the forward contract for a credit spread allows buyers to "lock in" a desired credit spread for the contract they are interested in acquiring. Hence, buyers can buy a forward spread contract on a credit default swap spread, an asset swap spread, a bond yield spread, or a LIBOR spread.

Just like the option pricing for a credit spread, it is difficult to derive the forward prices for the above-mentioned spreads under a consistent default model. Again, take a zero-coupon, zero-recovery bond as an example. The price of the bond today is

$$D(t, T) = P(t, T)Q(t, T)$$

and the spread is

$$s(t, T) = -\frac{\ln Q(t, T)}{T - t}$$

The bond price in a future time, u, is similarly defined as

$$D(u, T) = P(u, T)Q(u, T)$$

and the spread is

$$s(u, T) = -\frac{\ln Q(u, T)}{T - t}$$

which is random. Let us assume there exists a forward contract on the bond $D(u,T)$ with the forward price $F(t,u,T)$. Then the following two strategies must be identical:

Strategy #1: Buy a T-maturity bond

Strategy #2: Buy a fraction equal to the forward price of a u-maturity bond and a forward contract $G(t,u,T)$.

At time u, if $D(t,u)$ and $D(t,T)$ both do not default, then $\$G(t,u,T)$ is paid and it is used to acquire the bond $D(u,T)$, which is identical to holding a bond $D(t,T)$ from the start. If both bonds $D(t,u)$ and $D(t,T)$ default at time u, then both pay nothing. Then one is again indifferent between Strategy #1 and Strategy #2. By the law of one price, the cost of Strategy #1 must be equal to the cost of Strategy #2, and as a result:

$$G(t,u,T) = \frac{D(t,T)}{D(t,u)} = \frac{P(t,T)Q(t,T)}{P(t,u)Q(t,u)}$$
$$= F(t,u,T)\frac{Q(t,T)}{Q(t,u)}$$

which is equal to the risk-free forward price, $F(t,u,T)$, times the ratio of two survival probabilities. Hence, the spread of the forward contract is

$$-\frac{1}{T-u}\ln\frac{G(t,u,T)}{F(t,u,T)} = -\frac{1}{T-u}\ln\frac{Q(t,T)}{Q(t,u)}$$
$$= \frac{1}{T-u}[s(t,T)(T-t)-s(t,u)(u-t)]$$

which is equal to the difference in two spot spreads, a result that is identical to the risk-free forward rate (i.e., equal to the difference between two spot risk-free rates).

With recovery, the story is different. Consider the same two strategies, only that this time bonds recover a nonzero value. At time u, if $D(t,u)$ and $D(t,T)$ both survive, then $\$G(t,u,T)$ is paid and it is used to acquire the bond $D(u,T)$, which is identical to holding a bond $D(t,T)$ from the start. But if both bonds $D(t,u)$ and $D(t,T)$ default at time u, then $D(t,u)$ pays R_1 and $D(t,T)$ pays R_2. Unless $R_1 = R_2$ received at the same time and the forward contract also defaults, there will be a difference in payoffs between Strategy #1 and Strategy #2 and there exists no easy solution for the forward price.

To make the matter simple, we assume both R_1 and R_2 are paid at maturity. Then, under the default path, Strategy #1 pays $R_1[1 - Q(t,T)]$ and Strategy #2 pays $R_2[1 - Q(t,T)]$. Under the survival path, both strategies deliver $D(u,T)Q(t,u)$. Hence the difference is $(R_1 - R_2)[1 - Q(t,T)]P(t,T)$. As a result, the cost of Strategy #1 should be higher than the cost of Strategy #2 by an amount equal to

$$D(t, T) - (R_1 - R_2)[1 - Q(t, T)]P(t, T) = D(t, u)G(t, u, T)$$

yielding the following forward price:

$$G(t, u, T) = \frac{1}{D(t, u)}[D(t, T) - (R_1 - R_2)[1 - Q(t, T)]P(t, T)]$$

and the forward spread has no easy solution. Clearly this result converges to the previous result if $R_1 = R_2$.

We have seen that even for the zero-coupon bond, as long as recovery is considered (even it the simplest form as described in Jarrow and Turnbull[11]), there can be no easy solution to the forward spread.

Credit Default Swap Forward Spread

Recall that credit default swap market spread (breakeven spread) is computed as

$$s(t) = \frac{V(t)}{\displaystyle\sum_{j=1}^{n} P(t, T_j)Q(t, T_j)}$$

where

$$V(t) = \int_{t}^{T} [1 - R(w)]P(t, w)[-dQ(t, w)]$$

To lock in a forward credit default swap spread, it must be the case that the expected loss and gain are equal. In other words, the forward spread, K, needs to be set so that the expected gain or loss from the market credit default swap spread at the forward settlement time, T_k, $s(T_k)$, and the forward spread, K, is 0:

---

[11] Robert Jarrow and Stuart Turnbull, "Pricing Derivatives on Financial Securities Subject to Default Risk," *Journal of Finance* 50, no. 1 (1995), pp. 53–86.

$$\hat{E}_t\left[\exp\left(-\int_t^{T_k} r(u)du\right)\sum_{j=1}^m [s(T_k)-K]P(T_k, T_{k+j})Q(T_k, T_{k+j})\right] = 0$$

Rearranging the equation:

$$K = \frac{\hat{E}_t\left[\exp\left(-\int_t^{T_k} r(u)du\right)\sum_{j=1}^m s(T_k)P(T_k, T_{k+j})Q(T_k, T_{k+j})\right]}{\hat{E}_t\left[\exp\left(-\int_t^{T_k} r(u)du\right)\sum_{j=1}^m P(T_k, T_{k+j})Q(T_k, T_{k+j})\right]}$$

It can be seen that the forward spread, K, is a weighted average of "discounted survival probabilities." A simpler expression can be obtained if we adopt specific interest rate and credit risk models.

CHAPTER 12

Accounting for Credit
Derivatives

Accounting for derivative transactions is governed by two Financial Accounting Standards: SFAS 133 (*Accounting for Derivative Instruments and Hedging Transactions*) and SFAS 138 (*Accounting for Certain Derivative Instruments and Certain Hedging Instruments*). SFAS 133 was originally introduced in 1998, with a scheduled application date of June 15, 1999. However, the Statement was so cumbersome and costly to implement that the Financial Accounting Standards Board (FASB) formed the Derivatives Implementation Group (DIG) to help resolve the many issues surrounding the application of SFAS 133.

The DIG recommended an amendment to SFAS 133, and SFAS 138 was born. SFAS 138 was drafted specifically as an amendment to SFAS 133 to clarify many of the implementation issues. The introduction of SFAS 138 took more time to digest, and the required adoption date of the two Statements was delayed until January 1, 2001.

Still, this was not enough. In July 2002, FASB released yet another amendment to SFAS 133 with an implementation date of January 2003. On top of this, the DIG has released 176 Implementation Issue Statements on SFAS 133 that provide guidance on everything from the definition of a derivative to analysis of hedging techniques. These Implementation Issue Statements are each two to several pages long, adding another several hundred pages of derivative accounting rules and guidance. The two amendments to SFAS 133 and the many DIG Implementation Issue Statements demonstrate that accounting for derivative instruments is a difficult task.

In a nutshell, SFAS 133 requires all derivative instruments to be booked on the balance sheet and adjusted to fair value every reporting quarter. Sounds simple, but there are many devilish details. In this chapter, we provide a brief overview of SFAS 133 and 138. We also provide several examples of when and where SFAS 133 and 138 apply to credit derivatives.

AN OVERVIEW OF SFAS 133

SFAS 133 establishes the accounting rules (and SFAS 138 establishes the amendments to those rules) and reporting standards for all derivative transactions and instruments used by U.S. companies and reporting entities. SFAS 133 represents a decade long struggle by FASB to produce a comprehensive approach to recording and reporting derivative instruments and transactions.

SFAS 133 presents a shift by FASB from issuing accounting rules for specific parts of the derivatives markets such as currency hedging (SFAS 52, *Foreign Currency Translation*) and commodities (SFAS 80, *Accounting for Futures Contracts*) to issuing a comprehensive approach that addresses both risk hedging and income generation of derivatives. SFAS 133 also replaces prior FASB Statements that generated a piecemeal reporting approach for derivatives such as SFAS 119 (*Disclosure about Derivative Financial Instruments and Fair Value of Financial Instruments*). In sum, SFAS 133 is a sweeping approach by FASB to bring any type of derivative transaction and every type of reporting disclosure under one guiding statement.

The trade-off is a complicated accounting rule. Simplicity is not one of SFAS 133's advantages. At 245 pages of detailed text, it is one of the lengthiest and most complicated of accounting standards. Add another 69 pages of amendments from SFAS 138, and over 70 pages for the July 2002 amendment to SFAS 133, and you have a large book of accounting dedicated to derivatives. All told, SFAS 133, its amendments, and the 176 DIG Implementation Issue Statements provide about 900 pages of accounting rules and regulations for derivatives.

With so much to cover, we first examine the basics of SFAS 133 before providing examples of its application.

The Basic Provisions

SFAS 133 requires a reporting entity to recognize all derivative contracts and instruments as either assets or liabilities in the statement of financial position (balance sheet) and measure those instruments at their fair market value. SFAS 133 breaks derivative instruments down into four categories:

1. *Those derivative instruments that have no hedging designation.* The change in value associated with a derivative instrument that is used for income generation and not as a hedge of a financial asset or transaction must be recorded in current earnings. Bottom line: These derivative instruments will impact immediately the net income of the organization.

2. *Those derivatives that hedge the fair value of an instrument.* The gain or loss for a derivative designated as a fair value hedging instrument as well as the offsetting loss or gain on the hedged item must be recognized in current income. To the extent that the gain or loss from the hedging derivative instrument exactly offsets the loss or gain from the hedged item, there will be no net impact on net income. However, if the hedge is inexact, that is, changes in the value of the derivative instrument are not synchronized with changes in the value of the hedged asset, gain or loss will be recorded in the income statement for that quarter.

3. *Those derivatives that hedge a cash flow transaction.* The effective portion of the gain or loss on a derivative instrument used to hedge a cash flow transaction shall be reported as a component of *Other Comprehensive Income* (a new category on the balance sheet) and reclassified into the income statement in the period during which the hedged forecasted transaction affects earnings. In other words, the gains and losses associated with a derivative instrument designated as a cash flow hedge are not immediately recorded in the income statement. Rather, these gains and losses are accumulated on the balance sheet until such time as the forecasted transaction is completed. Then the full amount of the gains and losses from the hedge are transferred back to the income statement and are used to offset the change in cash flows associated with the hedged transaction. Any excess gain or loss flows down to net income.

4. *Those derivatives that are used for a foreign currency hedge.* Essentially derivatives used to hedge the fair value of a foreign currency-denominated asset are recorded as a gain or loss to income as discussed above for fair value hedges. For derivatives used to hedge a foreign currency-denominated transaction, the cash flow accounting rules discussed above apply.

Credit derivatives fall into the first two categories, either for income enhancement or to protect against a loss of value. In addition, certain credit derivatives are embedded within credit-risky securities. These derivatives require another set of rules. In the examples provided in this chapter, we will focus on these three provisions of SFAS 133.

What Constitutes a Derivative?

As a threshold question, we should ask whether credit derivatives fall within the definition of a derivative under SFAS 133 such that they must follow the new accounting rules. The answer, unfortunately, is yes and no. We will see that most credit derivative transactions fall within the scope of SFAS 133 while others are exempted from its application.

Paragraph 6 of SFAS 133 defines a derivative broadly to be an instrument that has all three of the following characteristics:

1. It has one or more underlyings and one or more notional amounts or payment provisions of both. Those terms determine the amount of the settlement or settlements, and, in some cases, whether or not a settlement is required.
2. If it is an option-based contract, it has an initial net investment equal to the fair value of the option component. If it is not an option-based contract, it requires an initial net investment that is less than 5% of the fully prepaid amount.[1]
3. Its terms require or permit net settlement, it can readily be settled net by a means outside the contract, or it provides for the delivery of an asset that puts the recipient in a position not substantially different from net settlement.

This broad definition encompasses credit default swaps, credit-based asset swaps, credit-linked notes with embedded derivatives, credit options, and credit forward contracts.

However, like all rules, there are exceptions. For example, Paragraph 10(d) of SFAS 133 specifically exempts from its provisions certain financial guarantee contracts. SFAS 133 does not classify as derivatives those financial guarantee contracts that provide for payments to be made to a credit protection buyer for a loss incurred when an underlying debtor fails to pay when payment is due, either at prespecified payment dates or because of an event of default occurred.

Consider Exhibit 12.1. This is a basic credit default swap. The credit protection buyer pays a swap premium to the protection seller in return for the right to receive a payment in the event of a default by the underlying debtor. This is similar to a credit insurance contract. If the underlying debtor fails to pay when payment is due, the credit protection seller will pay to the credit protection buyer the amount of the default, or a prespecified amount. This type of credit derivative transac-

---

[1] Part 2 to of the definition of a derivative was added by the July 2002 Amendment to SFAS 133.

EXHIBIT 12.1   A Credit Default Swap

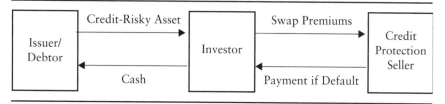

EXHIBIT 12.2   Value of a Credit Put Option

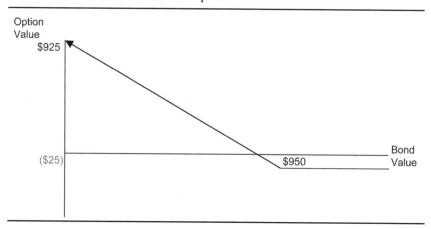

tion is exempt from the definition of a derivative under SFAS 133, and therefore, not bound by the accounting requirements of SFAS 133.

The key criteria is that the credit protection buyer must suffer a loss from the default. It is not sufficient that the credit protection buyer suffers a decline in value on the underlying asset. There must be a failure to pay by the debtor. It is not enough for the underlying debtor to incur a credit downgrade that causes the underlying asset to suffer a decline in value. A credit rating downgrade reflects a probability statement about a debtor's ability to pay but it does not mean that the debtor will default.

Consider Exhibit 12.2. This is a credit put option that pays off at maturity based on the declining value of an underlying credit-risky asset. Assume that the option is set at a strike price of $950 on a $1,000 bond, with a cost of the option at $25 dollars. This credit put option comes into the money when the high-yield bond price declines below $950. At this point any further decline in value will result in a positive payout to the credit protection buyer (with a maximum net payout of $925). At maturity of the option, the credit protection buyer will receive the difference between the high-yield bond price and the strike price. Therefore, the credit protection buyer receives a payment even though the underlying debtor has not defaulted on the bond. This credit derivative must be accounted as a fair value hedge under SFAS 133 as discussed below.

SFAS 138 Amendments to SFAS 133

We briefly cover the major amendments to SFAS 133 promulgated under SFAS 138. Fortunately, these amendments do not include within their scope credit derivatives. We provide a short summary of the amendments for completeness of the new accounting regulations.

SFAS 138 amends SFAS 133 for the following circumstances:

1. The normal purchases and sales exception under paragraph 10(b) of SFAS 133 may be applied to contracts that implicitly or explicitly permit net settlement, and have a market mechanism to allow net settlement. Under SFAS 133, this exception did not apply to a contract that had net settlement procedures because SFAS 133 automatically assumed that such a contract would be a derivative instrument instead of a purchase or sale within the normal course of business.
2. SFAS 138 reduces the confusion regarding the definition of interest rate risk. The amendment divides the risk associated with fixed income assets into two buckets: interest rate risk and credit risk. It is a popular practice to have a hedging instrument (the derivative) and the hedged item to be based on two different indices. Previously, SFAS 133 would not recognize the derivative instrument as a hedge because of the differences in benchmarks. SFAS 138 changed this rule and broadened the scope of qualifying hedges to include LIBOR-based derivative contracts that hedge financial securities that are benchmarked to U.S. Treasury rates.
3. SFAS 138 allows the joint hedging of interest rate and foreign exchange risk in one derivative instrument. Under SFAS 133, such cross-currency hedging was not allowed as either a fair value or cash flow hedge—meaning that all changes in value of the derivative instrument had to be charged to the income statement.
4. SFAS 138 allows for intercompany derivative transactions to be hedging instruments in either cash flow or fair value hedges.

ACCOUNTING FOR DERIVATIVE INSTRUMENTS UNDER SFAS 133

Under SFAS 133 all derivative instruments must be recognized in an entity's statement of financial position (i.e., balance sheet) as either an asset or liability. Also, all derivative instruments must be measured at their fair value; historical cost basis is no longer allowed. This means that a reporting entity must mark to market its derivative instrument holdings on a quarterly basis. Changes in value to those derivatives eventually make their way to the income statement depending upon whether the derivative instrument is held for hedging purposes or not.

With respect to credit derivatives, we focus on three aspects of SFAS 133 that apply: (1) derivative instruments with no hedging designation; (2) fair value hedges; and (3) embedded derivatives.

Derivative Instruments that Have No Hedging Designation

Derivative instruments that have no hedging designations are the easiest type of derivative instrument to account for under SFAS 133 and its amendments. The change in market value for this type of derivative instrument must be recorded in current income as either a gain or loss.

Consider Exhibit 12.3. This is a total return swap with respect to a pool of credit-risky assets. The asset pool could be a portfolio of high-yield bonds, leveraged loans, or a pool of asset-backed securities. The purpose of the credit swap from the investor's point of view is to receive the economic exposure of the underlying credit-risky assets. This transaction has no hedging component for the investor. Its purpose is to acquire credit exposure, not hedge it. The change in value of the swap to the investor over time must be recorded in current income as either a gain or loss.[2]

EXHIBIT 12.3   Total Return Swap on a Credit-Risky Asset

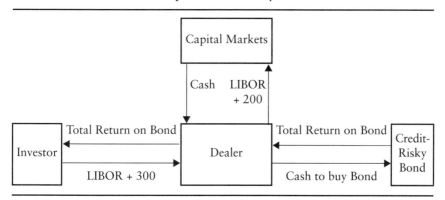

---

[2] Note that in Exhibit 12.3 all of the cash flows net out except for an extra 100 bps—the difference between the rate at which the dealer borrows from the capital markets and the rate that the dealer charges to the Investor. This is the dealer's fee and is calculated as the 100 bps times the notional value of the swap.

At the time an asset swap is entered into by both parties in Exhibit 12.3, the fair value of the swap is zero. That is, the swap is a fair bargain to both parties at the outset of the swap agreement because the present value of expected payments promised by one party is equal to the present value of expected payments promised by the counterparty. Therefore, the net present value of the swap to both parties is zero. However, during the life of a swap its value can change such that the swap may have positive or negative value to either counterparty.

Also, at the outset of a swap agreement there is no exchange of cash flows. Instead, both parties obligate themselves to make future payments. As a result, no accounting entry is required at the time the swap is initiated because there are no cash flows to record. However, at the end of one period, the swap payments will be netted and one party will reflect a net inflow, while another party will record a net outflow of cash. Under usual accounting practices, the inflow is recorded as income while the outflow is a charge against earnings.

SFAS 133 comes into play at the end of the first period (and every period thereafter) to recognize the change in value of the swap agreement to the counterparties. At the end of one period, the swap will most likely have a positive value to one party and a negative value to the counterparty. The reason is that market variables such as interest rates can, and do, change over time. In fact, even the simple amortization of swap payments can result in positive and negative swap values.[3] Consequently, after one period, the swap will have a positive value to one party that and a negative value to the counterparty. This change in value must be recorded in current income.

Let's put some number to an example. Exhibit 12.4 presents the details for a total return swap on a high-yield bond. The bond has a face value of $1,000, matures in three years, has a coupon of 8%, and has a current value of $970. An investor enters into this asset swap with a dealer with a notional value of $1,000 whereby the investor will receive the total return on the high-yield bond, and the dealer will receive LIBOR + 300.

At the top of Exhibit 12.4, we present the zero-coupon yield curve for 1, 2, and 3 year U.S. Treasury strips, the 1-year forward rates implied by the zero-coupon yield curve, and the expected 1-year forward rates for LIBOR. One-year forward rates are calculated through a bootstrapping method.[4]

---

[3] It is possible that after one period the swap will still have a net present value of zero to both parties. However, this occurrence is more by chance when changes in market variables exactly offset the amortization of the swap payments.

[4] For example the 1-year forward rate between years one and two may be calculated as $(1.04) \times (1.04)/1.03 = 1.05$. The 1-year forward rate is then 5%.

EXHIBIT 12.4 Calculations for an Asset Swap on a Credity Risky Bond

Zero-Coupon Treasury Curve		Implied 1-Year Forward Rates		Expected 1-Year LIBOR Forward Rates	
1 year	3%			Year 1	5%
2 years	4%	Year 1 to 2	5%	Year 2	6%
3 years	4.50%	Year 2 to 3	5.50%	Year 3	7%

$t = 0$

Present Value of Asset Swap to Investor
$\$90/1.03 + \$90/(1.04)^2 + \$90/(1.045)^3 = \$249$

Present Value of Asset Swap to Dealer
$\$80/1.03 + \$90/(1.04)^2 + \$100/(1.045)^3 = \$249$

Net present value of swap to Investor = $\$249 - \$249 = 0$

$t = 1$

Present Value of Asset Swap to Investor
$\$90/1.05 + \$90/(1.05)(1.055) = \$166.96$

Present Value of Asset Swap to Dealer
$\$90/1.05 + \$100/(1.05)(1.055) = \$175.99$

Current value of the swap to Investor = $\$166.96 - \$175.99 = -\$9.03$

$t = 2$

Present Value of Asset Swap to Investor
$\$90/1.055 = \$85.30$

Present Value of Asset Swap to Dealer
$\$100/1.055 = \$94.79$

Current value of swap to Investor = $\$85.30 - \$94.79 = -\$9.49$

Change in Swap Value = $(-\$9.49) - (-\$9.03) = -\$0.46$

With respect to the total return on the high-yield bond, the investor expects to receive the annual coupon of 8% plus any capital appreciation. Since the bond is currently trading at a discount of $30, the investor would expect the bond price to roll up the maturity curve by this amount over the next three years. We assume, in fact, that the high-yield bond will roll up by $10 each year until maturity. Therefore, the expected total return on the bond is $90 each year. Using the zero-coupon yield curve for discount rates, the present value of these future cash flows to the investor is $249.

For the dealer, the value of the swap is the present value of the LIBOR payments. The investor's payments to the dealer will vary depending on how LIBOR rates change.[5] Using the expected 1-year forward LIBOR rates, the investor will pay $80, $90, and $100 at the end of years one, two, and three, respectively. Exhibit 12.4 presents the present value of these swap payments.

In Exhibit 12.4, we see that at the beginning of the swap the present value of expected payments to the investor equals the present value of expected payments to the dealer. Therefore, at $t = 0$, there is no net expense or gain recorded by either the investor or the dealer. Consequently, there are no accounting entries at the outset of the swap.

However, at $t = 1$, there will be accounting entries to reflect the net swap payments between the investor and the dealer and the to record any change in swap value. At $t = 1$ the investor receives a total return of $90 while the dealer receives $80. Netting these payments results in a net cash inflow for the investor that is recorded in earnings. Exhibit 12.5 presents the accounting entries under SFAS 133 for the Investor.

In addition there is a change in the value of the swap for the investor and the dealer. In Exhibit 12.4, we calculate the present value of the swap for the investor at the end of the first and second years. At $t = 1$, we can see that the swap has a negative value, –$9.03, to the investor (we use the one-year forward rates to discount the expected swap payments). This change in swap value must be recorded in the income statement of the investor as a charge against earnings. This is demonstrated in Exhibit 12.5.

At the end of year of the second year, the payments between the investor and the dealer net to zero (both pay each other $90). However, the swap has changed in value again. The current value of the swap to the investor is now a –$9.49. This is a change in value of –$0.46 from the end of the first year, and this amount must be charged to income at the end of the second year. Notice that $9.49 is the present value of the investor's expected payment to be made next year to the dealer.

Finally, at the end of the third year, the investor must record a net outflow of $10 ($90 – $100). At the end of year three, the swap matures,

---

[5] The discount rate used to determine the present value of the swap cash flows should represent the riskiness of those cash flows. Generally, the market convention is to assume that an appropriate discount rate is one that corresponds to the risk level of the floating rate payment underlying a swap. This is a common assumption that allows the floating rate to be used as the discount rate. In our example, we assume that both counterparties are of high credit quality and apply the zero-coupon Treasury curve as the discount rate. We also acknowledge that there is a rounding error in our example of 99 cents. Our purpose is to demonstrate the accounting technique for a credit swap rather than illustrate the precision of swap payments.

EXHIBIT 12.5   Application of SFAS 133 for a Total Return Swap on a Credit-Risky Asset for an Investor

	Debit	Credit
Time $t = 0$		
No accounting entries at the outset of swap		
Time $t = 1$		
Cash	$10.00	
Earnings		$10.00
To record net swap payment from Dealer		
Earnings	$9.03	
Swap Value		$9.03
To reflect change in swap value		
Time $t = 2$		
Earnings	$0.46	
Swap Value		$0.46
To reflect change in swap value		
(note that net swap payment is $0)		
Time $t = 3$		
Earnings	$10.00	
Cash		$10.00
To record net swap payment to Dealer		
Swap Value	$9.49	
Earnings		$9.49
To reflect change in swap value		

and its present value again becomes zero because there are no further cash flows to be paid. Therefore, the investor will record a positive change in swap value from a –$9.49 to zero. These accounting entries are also reflected in Exhibit 12.5.

Fair Value Hedges

A reporting entity may designate a derivative instrument as a hedge of the fair value of either an asset or liability or a portion of a hedged item that is attributable to a particular risk. Assets and liabilities that are exposed to changes in fair value are dependent upon changes in underlying economic or market variables. Specifically, with respect to credit risk, an asset or liability is eligible for fair value hedging according to SFAS 133 if:

The hedged item is a financial asset or liability, a recognized loan servicing right, or a nonfinancial firm commitment with financial components, the designated risk being hedged is (1) the risk of changes in overall fair value of the entire hedged item; (2) the risk of changes of fair value attributable to changes in designated benchmark risk; (3) the risk of changes in its fair value attributable to changes in related foreign currency exchange rates; or (4) the risk of changes in fair value attributable to both changes in the obligor's creditworthiness and changes in the spread over the benchmark interest rate with respect to the hedged item's credit sector at the inception of the hedge (referred to as credit risk).[6]

This definition of assets or liabilities eligible for credit risk hedging recognizes that credit erosion can be creditor specific (changes in the obligor's creditworthiness) as well as erosion of the general credit sector. For instance, if credit spreads were to widen in general across the spectrum of BBB credit ratings, a credit derivative used to hedge this general credit spectrum risk would be eligible for fair value hedging.

Under SFAS 133, both the derivative instrument designated as a fair value hedge and the hedged item must be marked to fair value each reporting period. The change in value of both the derivative instrument and asset or liability being hedged must also be recorded in the income statement. To the extent the changes in value of the credit derivative exactly offset the change in value of the credit-risky asset or liability, there will be no impact on net income.

Let's use an example of an investor hedging the fair value of a credit-risky asset contained in his portfolio. At $t = 0$ the investor purchases a high-yield bond and a credit put option to hedge against the decline in value of a high-yield bond in his portfolio. The bond has a current price of $1,000, the put option is struck at the money, the maturity of the option is one year, and the investor sells the high-yield bond at the end of one year.

To start with, we assume that the cost of the option is zero. We acknowledge that this assumption is unrealistic, but it will help to demonstrate the application of SFAS 133. We will relax the assumption of a costless option in a moment.

At the end of one year, assume that the high-yield bond has declined by $100, and the value of the option at maturity is $100. The change in the value of the option exactly offsets the change in value of the high-yield bond. At the end of one year, the investor settles the credit put

---

[6] See Paragraph 21(f) of SFAS 133. This paragraph was amended by the July 2002 amendment to SFAS 133.

option and sells the bond. The put option must be debited by $100 to reflect an increase in value with a credit to earnings to reflect this change in value. Conversely, the high-yield bond must be credited by $100 to reflect a decline in value with a corresponding charge to earnings. These accounting entries are reflected in the general ledger demonstrated in Exhibit 12.6.

Notice, first, that all of the debits and credits within each general ledger category balance out. For example, at the bottom of the Cash columns there is a total debit of $1,000 and a total credit of $1,000. The debit and the credit are equal. The same is found across the general ledger categories of Put Option, High-Yield Bond, and Earnings. In each case, the debits equal the credits. This ensures that we have our accounting house in order, there are no lose ends.

Last, in Exhibit 12.6, notice that the debit and credit amounts are equal in the Earnings ledger. This is because the gain on the put option exactly offset the loss on the high-yield bond. As a consequence, there is no impact on earnings. The put option hedge is 100% effective.

How would this change if the put option was not completely effective in hedging the change in value of the high-yield bond? This is known as "hedge ineffectiveness" under SFAS 133, and must be recorded in current income. Another example will help to demonstrate this concept.

Let's take the same circumstances as described above, except now, the put option cost $25 to purchase. All other details remain the same. Exhibit 12.7 shows the accounting entries for this new example.

First, note that at time $t = 0$ there is an accounting entry to recognize the purchase of the put option for $25. The put option is purchased with a strike price equal to the cost of the high-yield bond, or $1,000. The option strike price is set at the money. Although the option has no current intrinsic value (option strike price minus the current value of the bond), it does have a time value premium. The cost of $25 represents the cost of insurance over the one-year holding period of the high-yield bond. This is known as the *time value of the option*. The cost of the option is credited to cash and debited to the put option as a short-term asset.

At the end of the year, the high-yield bond has declined in value to $900. Now, the intrinsic value of the option has increased to $100 (strike price minus the current value of the high-yield bond). However, the time value of the option has gone to zero because the option has matured. The decline in time value of the option of –$25 and the increase in intrinsic value of the option of +$100 leads to a change in value of $75. This amount is credited to earnings to reflect the change in value of a fair value hedge.

EXHIBIT 12.6 Application of SFAS 133 to a Fair Value Hedge of a High-Yield Bond

Transaction	Cash		Put Option		High-Yield Bond		Earnings	
	Debit	Credit	Debit	Credit	Debit	Credit	Debit	Credit
t = 0								
Cash		$1,000						
High-Yield Bond					$1,000			
To record purchase of bond								
(Note that the cost of the put option is $0)								
t = 1								
Credit Put Option			$100					$100
To record change in value								
High-Yield Bond						$100	$100	
To record change in value								
Sale of High-Yield Bond	$900					$900		
Settle Credit Put Option	$100			$100				
Totals	$1,000	$1,000	$100	$100	$1,000	$1,000	$100	$100

288

EXHIBIT 12.7 Application of SFAS 133 with a Costly Fair Value Hedge

Transaction	Cash Debit	Cash Credit	Put Option Debit	Put Option Credit	High-Yield Bond Debit	High-Yield Bond Credit	Earnings Debit	Earnings Credit
t = 0								
Cash		$1,000						
High-Yield Bond					$1,000			
To record purchase of bond								
Cash		$25						
Put Option			$25					
To record purchase of option								
t = 1								
Credit Put Option			$75					
To record change in value								$75
High-Yield Bond						$100	$100	
To record change in value								
Sale of High-Yield Bond	$900					$900		
Settle Credit Put Option	$100			$100				
Totals	$1,000	$1,025	$100	$100	$1,000	$1,000	$100	$75

289

Concurrently, the change in value of the high-yield bond, as the hedged item, must be recorded as a charge to earnings. Therefore, Earnings is debited by $100 to record this decline in value while the High-Yield Bond ledger is credited by $100 to also reflect the decline in value.

Looking across the totals at the bottom of Exhibit 12.7, we can now see that not every general ledger category balances out. For instance, there is a total debit to Cash of $1,000, and a total credit of $1,025. This reflects a net outflow of cash—the cost of the credit put option. Also, the Earnings category is out of balance; there is a total debit of $100 and a total credit of $75. This nets to a net charge to Earnings of $25 which reflects the cash outflow to purchase the credit put option. Even though individual general ledger categories may be out of balance, the whole general ledger does balance as the net credit of $25 from Cash balances the net debit of $25 in Earnings.

As a final example, suppose that the credit put option costs $25 and the high-yield bond increases in value by $10. Exhibit 12.8 reflects the general ledger entries for this situation. At maturity of the credit put option, its value will be zero because the value of the high-yield bond exceeds the strike price. Therefore, the change in value of the option is –$25. However, the change in value of the high-yield bond is +$10. Both changes in value must be reflected in Earnings, with the net change equaling –$15. This is the amount of hedge ineffectiveness, and it must be recorded in current income. At the bottom of Exhibit 12.8, there is a net credit to Cash of $15 and a net debit to Earnings of $15. These two amounts offset each other. All other general ledge accounts balance out.

Notice what FASB calls "hedge ineffectiveness" is simply a plug figure to reflect the fact that the total debits and credits across the general ledger accounts must balance at the end of the day. The application of a fair value hedge does not guarantee a perfect offset between the derivative instrument and the hedged item. Basis risk, option premia, differences in calculation methods can all lead to an imperfect match between the hedging derivative and the hedged item. Any difference must be recorded in income. Also, hedge ineffectiveness does not necessarily mean that there will be a charge (debit) to earnings. It could be the case that the change in value with respect to the derivative instrument is greater than the change in value of the hedged item. In this case there would be a positive credit to earnings.

Embedded Derivatives

One of the thornier issues with respect to SFAS 133 is how to account for credit derivatives that are embedded within a security. In some cases, the derivative instrument must be separated from the "host contract" and recorded separately. This process is known as *bifurcation*.

EXHIBIT 12.8 Application of SFAS 133 with a Costly Fair Value Hedge

Transaction	Cash Debit	Cash Credit	Put Option Debit	Put Option Credit	High-Yield Bond Debit	High-Yield Bond Credit	Earnings Debit	Earnings Credit
t = 0								
Cash		$1,000						
High-Yield Bond					$1,000			
To record purchase of bond								
Cash		$25						
Put Option			$25					
To record purchase of option								
t = 1								
Credit Put Option				$25			$25	
To record change in value								
High-Yield Bond					$10			$10
To record change in value								
Sale of High-Yield Bond	$1,010					$1,010		
Settle Credit Put Option	$0			$0				
Totals	$1,010	$1,025	$25	$25	$1,010	$1,010	$25	$10

If the credit derivative must be bifurcated, then it must be marked to market each quarter with changes in fair value recorded in net income as demonstrated in Exhibit 12.5. Alternatively, in some cases, the credit derivative does not need to be separated from the host contract and does not require separate accounting treatment.

The specific rule requires bifurcation of a host contract and its embedded derivative instruments if all of the following criteria are met:

1. The economic characteristics and risks of the embedded derivative instruments are not clearly and closely related to the economic characteristics and risks of the host contract.
2. The hybrid instrument that embodies both the embedded derivative instrument and the host contract is not remeasured at fair value under other GAAP requirements with changes in fair value reflected in income.
3. A separate instrument with the same terms and conditions as the embedded derivative instrument would be a derivative instrument subject to the requirements of SFAS 133.[7]

This is a long-winded test. Fortunately, most issues of bifurcation come down to the first requirement: whether the embedded derivative instrument is clearly and closely related to the host contract. We examine three cases of embedded credit derivatives: (1) those where the coupon of the bond is reset upon some credit event; (2) those derivatives that allow the bond to be put or called upon a credit event; and (3) credit derivatives that are attached to a bond after it is issued.

1. Credit Derivatives that Reset the Coupon Rate

This is the simplest type of embedded derivative to account for under SFAS 133. FASB provides specific guidance with respect to certain embedded credit derivatives that apply to a reset of coupon payments:

> The creditworthiness of a debtor and the interest rate on a debt instrument are considered to be clearly and closely related to the host contract. Thus for debt instruments that have an interest rate reset in the event (1) default (such as the violation of a credit-risk related covenant); (2) a change in the debtor's published credit rating; or (3) a change in the debtor's creditworthiness as indicated by a change in its spread over Treasury bonds; the related embedded derivative would not be separated from the host contract.[8]

---

[7] Paragraph 12, SFAS 133.
[8] Paragraph 61(c), SFAS 133.

EXHIBIT 12.9   IFCT Embedded Credit Call Options

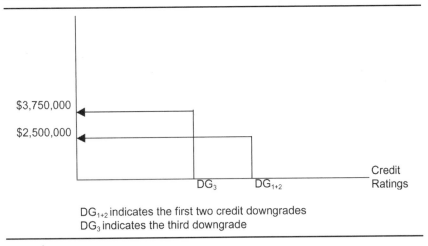

DG$_{1+2}$ indicates the first two credit downgrades
DG$_3$ indicates the third downgrade

Let's review an example of this. Consider the example of a $500 million bond issue in 1997 by the International Finance Corporation of Thailand (IFCT), a Thai government bank. The bonds were issued at par value with a stated condition that investors would receive 50 bps in additional coupon income should the creditworthiness of Thailand fall by two credit-rating levels. Further, bondholders would receive another 25 bps of coupon income for every further credit downgrade after that.

The investors who purchased these bonds bought a debt security plus a basket of credit call options. If the government of Thailand's credit rating declined by two credit levels, investors had the right to call for an additional 50 bps of coupon income. Every additional decline in credit rating level resulted in an additional credit call option worth 25 bps. Exhibit 12.9 displays these credit call options.

The IFCT bonds were backed by the credit of Thailand. Therefore, the credit call options were exercised specifically as a result of a change in the debtor's creditworthiness and, consequently, were clearly and closely related to the host contract. These options do not need to be recorded separately.[9]

2. Embedded Credit Derivatives that Allow the Bond to be Called or Put

In addition to the credit call options, the IFCT bonds also contained an embedded put option. Investors had the right to put the bonds back to

---

[9] See also Paragraph 190, SFAS 133.

the IFCT at par value if the credit rating of Thailand declined below investment grade. For embedded derivatives that can accelerate the prepayment of debt, SFAS 133 has another rule. Embedded call and put options that can accelerate the payment of a debt instrument are considered to be clearly and closely related to the host contract (and therefore, do not require bifurcation) *unless* both of the following conditions apply:

1. The debt involves a substantial premium or discount (for example, zero-coupon bonds involve a substantial discount); *and*
2. The embedded derivative is only contingently exercisable.[10]

In addition, there is a carve-out exception even if a credit option is contingently exercisable. Such embedded credit options will be considered clearly and closely related to the host contract, if they are indexed only to interest rates or credit risk, and not to some extraneous factor. A picture may help to explain this convoluted process.

These steps are complicated, but FASB attempted to address the creative minds of the financial markets. They can be presented in the decision matrix form that is presented in Exhibit 12.10. We demonstrate how this matrix works for the IFCT bond as well as two other contingently exercisable options. Although the IFCT embedded credit put option is contingently exercisable (the put may only be exercised if the credit rating of Thailand declined below investment grade), the put option does not need to be bifurcated because the bonds were issued at par value.

In our second example in Exhibit 12.10, we demonstrate a put option that is contingent on the credit rating of a second, unrelated company. Although it would seem that this option is not clearly and closely related to the debt of Company A, it does not need to be bifurcated because the bond was issued at par value. This seems to be a loophole in SFAS 133 that has not been closed by either SFAS 138 or the July 2002 amendment to SFAS 133. When SFAS was drafted, FASB was most concerned with equity-linked bonds. That is, bonds that included an embedded derivative whose payoff was tied to some equity return component. What SFAS 133 did not consider is a bond with an embedded derivative whose payoff is determined by the creditworthiness of an entity other than the bond's issuer. Note that if the put option embedded within the bond issued by Company A could be exercised based on the value of Company B's stock (instead of Company B's credit rating), the option would be bifurcated.

---

[10] Paragraph 61(d), SFAS 133.

EXHIBIT 12.10 Demonstration of the Decision Tree for Embedded Credit Options

Example	Indexed Payoff?	Substantial Discount or Premium?	Contingently Exercisable?	Accounting under SFAS 133
1. IFCT Bonds issued at par.	No	No	Yes	No need for bifurcation because there was not a substantial premium or discount.
2. Debt issued at par by Company A is putable if the credit rating of Company B declines by two steps. Company B is an unrelated company.	No	No	Yes	The put option does not need to be bifurcated because the bonds were not issued at a substantial discount or premium.
3. Debt issued by Company A is putable by the investor if the S&P 500 increases by 20%. The investor receives the par value of the bonds adjusted for the percentage increase in the S&P 500.	Yes	No	Yes	The put option must be bifurcated because its exercise is contingent on the return of an equity index.

In our last example in Exhibit 12.10, we demonstrate a bond with an embedded derivative tied to an equity market return. Here, the bondholder receives the par value of the bond adjusted for the percentage increase in the S&P 500. Therefore, the embedded contingently exercisable option is not indexed to interest rates or the credit risk of the issuer, and must be bifurcated. As a practical matter, most embedded credit options will be indexed to either interest rates or the credit risk of the underlying issuer, and therefore, in most cases will be clearly and closely related to the host contract.

3. Credit Derivatives that are Added to a Bond after it is Issued

The last case is a credit derivative that is attached to a bond after it has already been issued. Consider the case of the IFCT bonds with the put option. Suppose instead of the option being incorporated into the bonds by IFCT, the dealer who markets the bonds to investors adds the put option to make them more appealing to investors. In this case, investors would put the bonds back to the dealer if the credit rating of Thailand declines below investment grade. According to DIG Implementation Issue B3, a put or call option that is added to a debt instrument by a third party contemporaneously with or subsequent to the issuance of the debt instrument should be accounted for as a derivative under SFAS 133 by the investor. Therefore, it must be marked to market each reporting period with changes in fair value reported in earnings as demonstrated in Exhibit 12.5.

The key to an understanding of this rule is that an option that is added or attached to an existing debt instrument by another party results in the investor having different counterparties (the issuer and the dealer) for the option and the debt instrument. Therefore, the credit derivative should not be considered embedded because the notion of an embedded derivative refers to a single contract that incorporates both the debt component and the derivative component.

What FASB did not explicitly address is the circumstance where the issuer adds a credit dependent option to one of its existing bond issues. For example, what would happen if the IFCT did not initially attach the credit put option when the bonds were issued? Instead, suppose that the IFCT issued the put option to investors at a later date, after the bonds had already been issued. In this instance, there would be only one counterparty for the investor—the issuer would be responsible for both the bond and the put option. Under DIG Implementation Issue B3, this would indicate no bifurcation. Yet, Implementation Issue B3 also states that for bifurcation to not apply, the credit derivative and the debt instrument must be part of the same contract and not separate provisions of separate contracts.

We come down on the side of accounting for the put option separately for two reasons. First, in the circumstances described above, the issuer issued the option separately under a different contract than the bond indenture. Under DIG Implementation Issue B3, this would indicate bifurcation. Also, the standard principle of conservatism, which pervades all GAAP, would support the notion of more disclosure, rather than less.

SUMMARY

In this chapter we tried to condense about 900 pages of derivative accounting rules into about 20 pages of straightforward guidance. A full discussion of SFAS 133 would take a whole book to digest, and even then, there would still be room for a second volume.

For the reader of this book, credit derivatives must be accounted for in three circumstances: (1) when the credit derivative is used to generate capital gain or income enhancement; (2) when credit derivatives are used to hedge the value of a credit-risky asset; and (3) when a credit derivative is embedded within an existing debt instrument. The exhibits provided in this chapter were not meant to exhaust the full scope of SFAS 133, but rather, to narrow the focus of the reader to those accounting rules that are most pertinent to credit derivatives. The adventuresome reader is more than welcome to explore the 900 pages of derivatives accounting rules at his own will (and risk).

CHAPTER 13

Taxation of Credit Derivatives

In this chapter we examine the potential tax treatment of credit derivatives. We admit that the previous chapter presented many complicated accounting rules associated with recording credit derivatives on the balance sheet and the income statement. Unfortunately, it does not get any easier in this chapter.

The tax treatment of credit derivatives in the United States is not precise because, as of this writing, the U.S. Treasury Department and Congress have not established tax laws or regulations that specifically address the transfer of credit risk through a derivative transaction. Some credit derivative transactions resemble closely other products such as guarantees, notional principal contracts, and traditional options such that analogies can be drawn with a high degree of certainty. However, in other cases credit derivatives raise tax issues that cannot be resolved with reasonable certainty. This problem is further exacerbated by the fact that the nomenclature used in credit derivatives may not be synchronized with the tax code. Terms such as "swap" and "option" in credit derivative land can lead to misleading conclusions regarding the tax treatment.

Like the previous chapter, we will strive to keep it simple (that always works for us), breaking down those portions of the tax code that potentially apply to credit derivative transactions. We begin with a review of the constructive sale rules under the tax code and their application to credit derivatives. We then analyze the tax treatment of credit derivatives by type of transaction. We present the analysis for credit default swaps, total return swaps, and credit options. We stick to the basics. Our goal is not to write a tax treatise, but rather to guide the investor and user of credit derivatives through the key provisions of the tax code that impact credit derivatives.

THE TAXPAYER RELIEF ACT OF 1997

The Taxpayer Relief Act of 1997 (the "Act") contained provisions designed to crack down on certain derivative transactions used by large institutions and wealthy individuals to reap economic gains from appreciated financial positions while not recognizing any tax liability. The result is that the tax advantages of many derivative transactions, including credit derivatives, have been eliminated or diminished. However, curiously, the Act carved out certain exemptions that, while not specifically intended to grant relief to credit derivative trades, nevertheless, apply to these transactions.

The Act was signed into law in August 1997 and made several major changes to the U.S. tax code which impacted the way mutual funds operate (elimination of the short-short rule), the way people invest in IRAs, and the way derivative transactions may be taxed. One of those changes pertains to "constructive sales" of assets through derivative transactions that are used to lock in the gain or loss associated with an underlying asset. We begin this section with a brief overview of the Act and its basic provisions. We then discuss when and where it applies to credit derivatives.

Motivation for the Act

The U.S. Congress had become concerned in recent years with respect to numerous financial transactions developed by Wall Street brokerage firms which allowed institutional clients and high net worth individuals to reduce, defer, or eliminate their risk of loss from an underlying instrument without recognizing any taxable disposition. Yet, like most sales of property, these transactions provided the taxpayer with cash, payments, or other property in return for the interest in the underlying investment that the taxpayer had given up. Therefore, the taxpayer was compensated for giving up economic rights to the underlying investment, much the same as a sale of the asset, without recognizing any taxable gain.

To close this tax loophole for wealthy and institutional investors, the Act introduced new Internal Revenue Code ("IRC") Section 1259 of the Internal Revenue.[1] Section 1259 requires a taxpayer to recognize the gain (but not the loss) upon entering into a *constructive sale* of any *appreciated financial position* in an underlying asset as if that investment were sold, assigned, or otherwise terminated at its fair market value on the

---

[1] Actually, this part of the 1997 Act might be more appropriately titled the "The Reduction of Taxpayer Relief."

date of the constructive sale.[2] In sum, taxpayers may no longer use derivative transactions to cheat Uncle Sam. To consider the impact of this rule on the credit derivative market, we need to review its key provisions.

Constructive Sales

Section 1259(c) treats a taxpayer as having made a constructive sale of an appreciated financial position if the taxpayer:

1. Enters into a short sale of the same or substantially identical property.[3]
2. Enters into an offsetting notional principal contract with respect to the same or substantially identical property.
3. Enters into a futures or forward contract to deliver the same or substantially identical property.

A constructive sale can occur if the taxpayer enters into one or more transactions that have substantially the same effect as the three transactions described above. Also, under Section 1259, more than one appreciated financial position and more than one offsetting transaction can be aggregated to determine whether a constructive sale has occurred.

Although not specifically referenced by Section 1259, synthetic derivative positions that accomplish the same economic effect as described in the three positions above would fall under the provisions of the new rule. For example a short call option combined with a long put option position where both options have the same strike price has the same economic consequences as a short futures or forward position. The short call option plus the long put option position forms a synthetic futures contract to deliver an underlying asset. Consequently, it falls within the scope of Section 1259.

Initially, Section 1259 applied only to forward and futures contracts where there was a physical settlement. However, the U.S. Treasury Department has since closed this loophole. Constructive sales rules now

---

[2] In addition to the requirement that capital gain be recognized upon the constructive sale of an appreciated financial position, two other transaction events apply: (1) An adjustment is made to the amount of any gain or loss subsequently taken into account with respect to the position; and (2) the taxpayer's holding period with respect to the position begins anew at the time the constructive sale agreement is initiated. For a full discussion of the Taxpayer Relief Act of 1997, see Mark Anson, "The Impact of the Taxpayer Relief Act of 1997 on Derivative Transactions," *Journal of Derivatives* (Summer 1998).

[3] The Act does not define the term "substantially identical," but the same phrase is used in IRC Section 1091 with respect to wash sales of "substantially identical stock or securities." Under this code section, securities are considered "substantially identical" if they are not substantially different in any material feature or several material features considered together.

apply to futures and forward contracts regardless of whether they are structured to be cash or physical settlement.

Constructive sales are defined by Section 1259 only in terms of "appreciated financial positions"—that is, an existing asset that has increased in value combined with an offsetting derivatives transaction. The converse is not true. Section 1259 makes no reference to the combination of a "depreciated financial position" and an offsetting derivatives position. Consequently, the constructive sales rules do not apply to recognize a tax loss. If taxpayers wish to recognize a capital loss on an asset, they must do it the old fashioned way by selling it.

Appreciated Financial Position

Section 1259(b) defines an appreciated financial position ("AFP") as any position with respect to any stock, partnership interest, or debt instrument where there would be a capital gain if the position were sold, assigned, or otherwise terminated at its fair market value. A position for purposes of an AFP is defined as an investment in the underlying security, a futures or forward contract, a short sale, or an option.

Although Section 1259(b) does not include "swap" in the definition of a position, it is likely that such contracts are considered a "position" because of their economic similarity to futures and forwards contracts. Note that the constructive sales rules apply to either an initial investment in a derivatives contract or an investment in a cash security. Also, an AFP can be a short position in a security that is subsequently closed out through the acquisition of the same or substantially identical property.

Fortunately for credit derivatives, Section 1259(b) carves out an exception to the constructive sales rules for "straight debt." A fixed income obligation is straight debt if:

1. The debt unconditionally entitles the holder to received a specified principal amount;
2. The interest payments with respect to such debt meet the requirements of IRC Section 860G(a)(1)(B)(i) that interest rate payments are payable at a fixed or variable rate; and
3. The debt is not convertible either directly or indirectly into the stock of the issuer or any related entity.

This definition captures much of the leveraged bank loan market as well as credit risk sovereign bonds and also high-yield bonds. However, any high-yield bonds that have an equity kicker or a conversion feature would not fall under this exception. Therefore, a credit derivative instrument combined with straight debt as defined above will not be subject to the constructive sale rules.

EXHIBIT 13.1   Asset Swap on a Credit-Risky Asset

Consider Exhibit 13.1. An investor has a convertible high-yield bond in his portfolio that has appreciated in value. To protect his position, the investor enters into a total return swap with a credit protection seller who wants to obtain credit exposure. This transaction is a constructive sale because the investor has locked in her gain on the high-yield bond through the total return swap. The combination of the high-yield bond and the total return swap form a constructive sale that must be reported for tax purposes. If the high-yield bond was not convertible, the bond would qualify as straight debt, and there would be no constructive sale of the asset.

TAX TREATMENT FOR A TOTAL RETURN SWAP ON A CREDIT-RISKY ASSET

This type of swap is typically used to gain credit exposure to an asset without the need of a capital commitment. Through the examples below, we assume that an investor purchases the total return exposure of a credit-risky asset from a dealer through a total return swap. We also assume the asset underlying the swap agreement is a high-yield bond. We consider the tax perspectives of both the investor and the dealer.

Disposition of the Asset

If the dealer already owns the credit-risky asset, a threshold question is whether the total return swap constitutes a constructive sale of the high-yield bond by the dealer. In effect, it appears that the dealer has sold the high-yield bond to the investor for a series of installment payments by the investor. If so, then the dealer must record the capital gain or loss associated with the constructive sale of the high-yield bond. If the constructive sales rules apply, then the total return swap would not be analyzed as a separate instrument and no tax consequences would be ascribed to the swap. The dealer would be viewed as having sold a credit-risky asset and the investor would be deemed to have purchased a credit-risky asset where the payments made by the investor would constitute his basis in the "acquired" asset and would equal the sales price paid to the dealer.[4]

---

[4] See Bruce Kayle, "Will the Real Lender Please Stand Up? The Federal Income Tax Treatment of Credit Derivative Transactions," *The Tax Lawyer* (Spring 1997).

The dealer would recognize capital gain for the difference between the total swap payments and the current value of the debt.

One interesting loophole within Section 1259 is whether the payments made by the investor to the dealer under the total return swap agreement must be discounted to determine their present value for purposes of calculating the constructive sales price of the credit-risky asset. Although not specified within Section 1259, we believe that the payments made by the investor over the life of the swap agreement should be discounted to determine the proper amount of consideration received by the dealer in determining his capital gain.

However, if the high-yield bond qualifies as "straight debt," then the constructive sales rules do not apply. Also, remember, the constructive sales rules do not apply if the resulting "sale" results in a loss. The constructive sales rules apply only when there is a potential gain from the constructive sale.

Integration of the Credit Derivative and Underlying Asset

If the total return swap does not constitute a constructive sale, then the next issue that must be addressed is whether the total return swap should be integrated into the underlying credit-risky asset. Section 1.1275-6 of the IRC deals with the integration of qualifying debt instruments. This section provides for the integration of a qualifying hedging instrument with an underlying debt instrument if the two combined are substantially equivalent to the cash flows of either a fixed or variable rate debt instrument.

There are two key provisions of Section 1.1275-6. First, Integration only applies if the term of the swap is equal to the maturity of the debt. Any mismatch in tenor of the swap and maturity of the debt, and integration is not allowed. Second, the combined cash flows of the total return swap and the underlying debt instrument must permit the calculation of a yield to maturity. This second condition means that the payments under the swap agreement must be either fixed or floating periodic payments such that a yield to maturity may be calculated.

Under integration, the underlying credit-risky asset and the total return swap are not treated separately, they are treated as a single integrated transaction. The timing of cash flows are then governed by the integration rules of Section 1.1275-6. If the investor's payments to the dealer are fixed or based on a floating reference interest rate and that term of the total return swap coincides with the maturity of the underlying debt instrument, then the combined cash flows will allow the dealer to calculate a yield to maturity.

If integration is allowed, the dealer would account for the combined debt/credit swap position as a single debt position. The dealer would be

EXHIBIT 13.2   Integration of a Total Return Credit Swap

treated as continuing to own the underlying credit-risky asset but with its yield adjusted to that promised by the payments made by the investor. To expand our example, suppose that a dealer owns a high-yield bond with a market value of $1,000,000 that matures in two years. The dealer and the investor enter into a total return swap with a tenor of two years. The dealer promises to pay the total return of the high-yield bond (coupons plus capital appreciation/depreciation) to the investor, and the investor promises pays to the dealer a fixed amount of 8% times the notional amount of the swap ($80,000). This example is demonstrated in Exhibit 13.2.

In effect, the dealer has transformed a credit-risky asset with uncertain cash flows into an asset with certain cash flows of 8% per year.[5] In fact, the yield to maturity for the dealer is now the 8% promised by the investor under the total return swap. Because the tenor of the total return swap and the maturity of the high-yield bond are synchronized, the dealer will account for the high-yield bond and credit swap as one integrated instrument with an annual coupon income of 8%.

From the investor's perspective, he must recognize each swap payment separately for tax purposes. We discuss this next.

No Integration of the Total Return Swap and the Underlying Asset

If integration is not allowed, both the dealer and the investor must account for the swap payments separately. In this case, IRC Section 1.446-3 applies. This code section addresses the tax treatment of "notional principal contracts."

A notional principal contract is a financial instrument that provides for the payment of amounts by one party to another at specified intervals calculated by reference to a specified index upon a notional principal amount in exchange for specified consideration or a promise to pay similar amounts. IRC Section 1.446-3(c)(1)(ii) includes among the definition of notional principal contracts: interest rate swaps, basis swaps, caps, floors, commodity swaps, equity swaps, total return swaps, equity index swaps, and similar agreements. Although credit derivatives are not spe-

---

[5] The credit risk to the dealer is no longer the underlying high-yield bond. Instead, the dealer accepts counterparty credit risk—the risk that the investor may not make good on its swap payments.

cifically identified, total return swaps would include total return swaps on credit-risky assets. In this chapter we use the term "total return swap" to be consistent with IRC rules. This is the same type of asset swap on a credit-risky asset as described in earlier chapters. In addition, a specified index can be a single security or a basket of securities.[6]

Under Section 1.446-3, all payments under a notional principal contract will be treated as ordinary income or deductions. Specifically, the net payment or inflow must be recorded for tax purposes as a net expense or net income. All taxpayers must recognize the ratable daily portion of a total return swap payment for the taxable portion of a year to which a credit swap applies. An example should help to clarify these provisions.

Let's continue with our example of a dealer that owns a high-yield bond. The dealer and the investor enter into a swap agreement on May 1, 2003 where the dealer promises to pay the total return of the high-yield bond to the investor and the investor will pay the current 6-month LIBOR. Payments by both parties will be made every six months and the notional value of the swap is $1,000,000. The high yield bond has a face value of $1,000,000, a current market value of $980,000, two years to maturity, and a coupon of 8%. Both the dealer and the investor are on a calendar year tax basis.

On May 1, 6-month LIBOR is 7% and on November 1, 6-month LIBOR is 7.5%. On November 1, the market value of the bond is still $980,000, but on December 31, the market value is $985,000.

For the investor his cash and ratable payments for calendar year 2003 will be

$$7\% \times 0.5 \times \$1,000,000 + 7.5\% \times (61/365) \times \$1,000,000 = \$47,534$$

Note that under the IRC, partial year payments for a notional principal contract are calculated on an actual/365 day count convention. The investor must include in his swap payment calculation the ratable portion of his swap obligation for the period November 1 to December 31.

The dealer's cash and ratable payments for calendar year 2003 are

$$8\% \times 0.5 \times \$1,000,000 + 8\% \times (61/365) \times \$1,000,000$$
$$+ \$5,000 \times (61/365) = \$54,205$$

The difference between the dealer and the investor is that the dealer must recognize the ratable portion of the bond coupon as well as the

---

[6] We note that the tax rules for notional principal contracts can apply to credit forward transactions. A credit forward transaction can be viewed as a single period total return swap.

appreciated value of the high yield bond in determining its ratable payment for 2003.

Netting these two payments ($54,205 − $47,534) equals net taxable income to the investor of $6,671. Symmetrically, this results in a taxable deduction to the dealer of $6,671.

Things get a bit more complicated in the second year. Assume that on May 1, 2004 6-month LIBOR is 7.75% and at November 1, it is 8%. Also assume that on May 1, 2004, the market value of the high-yield bond is $985,000, and on November 1, 2004, it is $990,000, and on December 31, 2004, the market value of the high-yield bond is $1,000,000.

For the investor, the cash and ratable payments for the year are

$$7.5\% \times (120/365) \times \$1{,}000{,}000 + 7.75\% \times 0.5 \times \$1{,}000{,}000$$
$$+ 8\% \times (61/365) \times \$1{,}000{,}000 = \$76{,}777$$

In words, the investor's recognized payment consists of three components:

1. The remaining swap payment for the period of January through April 2004 based on LIBOR set on November 1, 2003.
2. The 6-month LIBOR payment at 7.75% from May 1, 2004 through October 31, 2004.
3. Ratable portion of 6-month LIBOR at 8% for the months of November and December 2004.

For the dealer, his cash and ratable payments are[7]

$$\$4{,}165 + 8\% \times (120/365) \times \$1{,}000{,}000 + 8\% \times 0.5$$
$$\times \$1{,}000{,}000 + 8\% \times (61/365) \times \$1{,}000{,}000 + \$5{,}000$$
$$+ (61/365) \times \$10{,}000 = \$90{,}836$$

The dealer's payments consist of:

1. The remaining $5,000 capital appreciation of the high-yield bond over the period January 1, 2004 to April 30, 2004.
2. The remaining coupon payment of 8% over the period January 1, 2004 to April 30, 2004.
3. The coupon payment of 8% from May 1, 2004 to October 31, 2004.
4. The capital appreciation of the high-yield bond between May 1, 2004 and Oct. 31, 2004.

---

[7] Note that we round the portion of the 8% coupon from January 1 to April 30 to be equal to $26,630, the remaining amount of the $40,000 semi-annual coupon payment.

EXHIBIT 13.3   Tax Treatment for a Total Return Swap

Year 2003: Investor

7% 6-month LIBOR payment, May 1 to Oct. 31	$35,000
Ratable portion of 7.5% 6-month LIBOR payment, Nov. 1 to Dec. 31	$12,534
Total payment recognized for taxes	$47,534

Year 2003: Dealer

8% semiannual coupon, May 1 to Oct. 31	$40,000
Ratable portion of semi-annual coupon, Nov. 1 to Dec. 31	$13,370
Ratable portion of bond appreciation, Nov. 1 to Dec. 31	$835
Total payment recognized for taxes	$54,205
2003 Net Income to Investor (Net deduction to Dealer)	$6,671

Year 2004: Investor

7.5% 6-month LIBOR payment, Jan. 1 to April 30	$24,657
7.75% 6-month LIBOR payment, May 1 to Oct. 31	$38,750
Ratable portion of 8% 6-month LIBOR payment, Nov. 1 to Dec. 31	$13,370
Total payment recognized for taxes	$76,777

Year 2004: Dealer

Remaining bond appreciation, Jan. 1 to April 30	$4,165
Remaining 8% coupon, Jan. 1 to April 30	$26,630
8% Semiannual coupon, May 1 to Oct. 31	$40,000
Capital appreciation of bond, May 1 to Oct. 31	$5,000
Ratable portion of 8% semi-annual coupon, Nov. 1 to Dec. 31	$13,370
Ratable portion of bond appreciation, Nov. 1 to Dec. 31	$1,671
Total payment recognized for taxes	$90,836
2004 Net Income to Investor (Net deduction to Dealer)	$14,059

5. The ratable portion of the 8% coupon for November and December 2004.
6. The ratable portion of the $10,000 capital appreciation for the period of November and December 2004.

The net of the cash and ratable payments for 2004 is $90,836 − $76,777 = $14,059. This is net income to the investor and a net deduction to the dealer. We summarize all of this information in Exhibit 13.3. As a summary of a total return swap, we provide Exhibit 13.4. This exhibit summarizes the decision tree to determine whether a total return

EXHIBIT 13.4   Decision Tree for the Tax Treatment of a Total Return Swap

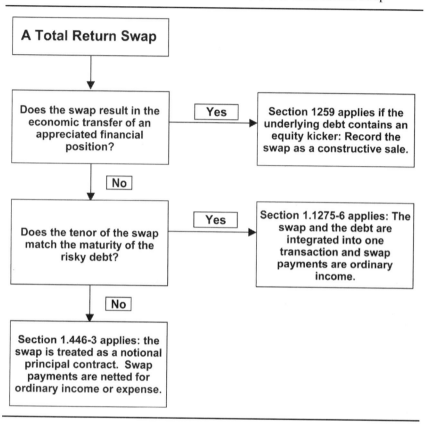

swap should be recognized as a constructive sale, an integration into a single debt instrument, or to be treated as a notional principal contract.

TAX TREATMENT OF A CREDIT DEFAULT SWAP

A credit default swap is the simplest of credit derivative trades to understand. The credit protection buyer makes periodic payments to the credit protection seller in return for a lump sum payment should the underlying debtor default on the credit-risky asset. Yet, the tax treatment for this type of transaction is even more complicated than that for total return swaps. We work through the same issues as those for total return swaps.

A Constructive Sale under Section 1259

With a credit default swap, the credit protection buyer essentially has a put option to sell the credit-risky asset to the credit protection seller after a default occurs. Section 1259 does not consider at-the-money or out-of-the money put options to be constructive sales. However, deep in-the-money put options may be subject to the constructive sales rules. With a deep in-the-money put option, the taxpayer has locked in a gain up to the strike price of the put option. Based on examples in the tax code, the Treasury Department will not consider an in-the-money put option to be a constructive sale unless the put option strike price is at least 20% in the money. Otherwise, there is no constructive sale. Similarly, unless the credit default swap is set so that it has significant initial value to the credit protection buyer at the outset, it is unlikely that a credit default swap will fall within the requirements of Section 1259.

Integration with the Underlying Credit-Risky Asset.

Integration is unlikely to be allowed with a credit default swap. Recall form our discussion above that there are two key conditions for integration to apply under Section 1.1275-6. First, the tenor of the credit default swap must match the maturity of the credit-risky asset upon which it is written. If there is a mismatch of tenor and maturity, the underlying asset, integration will not be allowed. Second the combined cash flows associated with the credit default swap and the underlying credit-risky asset must be sufficiently clear to permit the calculation of the yield to maturity.

While matching the tenor of the credit default swap with the maturity of the credit-risky asset should is not problematic, the second condition of calculating a yield to maturity does present a problem. The payment the dealer makes to the investor upon the occurrence of a default is not known with certainty. In fact, the dealer may never have to make a payment because default may never occur. More to the point, the dealer's payment is based on the market value of the credit-risky asset at the point of default and not on any set of periodic fixed or floating payments. Consequently, a yield to maturity cannot be calculated by the investor for the credit-risky asset, and the integration rules do not apply.

Treating a Credit Default Swap as a Notional Principal Contract

Consider a dealer and an investor who enter into a credit default swap where the investor purchases the swap as credit protection against a credit-risky asset that it owns. The investor promises to make periodic payments to the dealer and the dealer promises to make a payment upon the occurrence of default. If a default occurs, the investor is no longer obligated to continue to make payments to the dealer. The dealer makes a lump sum payment to the investor to insure against the loss of value of the credit-risky asset and the credit default swap terminates. There are several problems with treating a credit default swap as a notional principal contract.

First, the dealer does not make period payments to the investor; the dealer's payment is triggered by an event of default. Therefore, the dealer's payment is considered "nonperiodic" for purposes of Section 1.446-3. Nonperiodic payments must be included in income by the investor and deducted by the dealer over the life of the notional principal contract.[8] This creates the first problem, since the life of the credit default swap cannot be known with certainty. The dealer's payment expressly terminates the swap agreement, truncating the term of the swap agreement. Second, the amount of payment that the dealer must make is also not known with certainty. In fact, the dealer's payment may be zero if no default occurs. Therefore, the dealer and the investor are left to guess what might be the tenor of the swap and what might be the dealer's payment upon an event of default. It is quite likely that the dealer and the investor will have a difference of opinion as to the tenor of the swap and the size of the dealer's payment in the event of default.

Perhaps the biggest problem associated with classifying a credit default swap as a notional principal contract is the character of income and gain and loss with respect to the underlying asset. As discussed above, under Section 1.446-3, notional principal contract payments are treated as ordinary income and expense, not capital gain or loss. However, consider the situation where there is a default on the underlying asset and the dealer makes a lump sum payment to the investor. Under the notional principal contract rules, the investor must treat the lump sum payment as ordinary income even though it has incurred a capital loss on the value of the underlying asset. Therefore, the investor is subject to a mismatch in tax character between the loss on a capital asset and the ordinary income it receives as a result of that loss. Further, to the extent that the investor has capital gains in her portfolio that could be shielded by a capital loss, the lost value on the underlying credit-risky asset will not be available to shield these gains.

Tax Treatment if the Credit Default Swap is a Guarantee

Another way to view a credit default swap is that it is a guarantee by the dealer to pay the investor in the event of the Default. First, the dealer

---

[8] Specifically, a nonperiodic payment must be recognized over the term of the contract by allocating it in accordance with the values of a series of cash-settled forward contracts that reflect the risk of the underlying index or asset and the notional principal amount. See IRC 1.446-3(e)(3).

promises that the investor will be made whole. This is similar to a guarantee in that the dealer protects the investor from any harm resulting from the debtor's default. In addition, the payment made by the dealer is specifically contingent on the underlying debtor's nonperformance.

If a credit default swap is treated as a guarantee, the investor's payments to the dealer will be ordinary deductions to income. For the dealer, its payment upon the event of default will be treated as an expense and payments received from the investor will be treated as ordinary income.

However, there are several problems with treating a credit default swap as a guarantee. First, the dealer's payment is related to the change in market value of the underlying credit-risky asset but not necessarily the debtor's specific default. The change in the market value of the credit-risky asset will not measure the debtor's nonperformance—this could be a missed payment or some other breach of a debt covenant. In other words, the dealer does not step into the shoes of the Debtor to perform the debt covenant that the debtor breached. Instead, the dealer makes a payment to the investor to make up any lost value as a consequence of the debtor's breach.

Also, the dealer has no right of subrogation, that is, the ability to step into the shoes of the Debtor and cure the default. Last, the investor may not own the underlying credit-risky asset. The investor might have used the credit default swap to make a bet on the creditworthiness of the underlying debtor. In sum, while treating a credit default swap as a guarantee has convenient tax consequences, it may not be the best characterization of a credit default swap.

Treating a Credit Default Swap as a Put Option

Most credit default swaps call for a single payment to made to the credit protection buyer in the event of default. The payment equals the difference between the price of the credit-risky asset at the time the swap agreement is made and current market value of the asset at the moment of default. The payout to the credit protection buyer may be described as

$$\text{Payout to investor} = \begin{cases} \text{Asset value at time of swap} - \text{Asset market value;} \\ \quad \text{if default} \\ 0; \text{ if no default} \end{cases}$$

The above expression describes a put option. More specifically, it describes a binary put option based on only two states of the world: default or no default.

If the credit default swap is treated as an option, then it becomes a capital asset under Section 1234. For the investor, the payments it makes to the dealer are considered capital payment to acquire an asset: the put option. Therefore, the investor is not allowed to deduct these payments as an expense. If the credit default swap expires worthless (there is no default during its term), the investor will have a capital loss equal to the payments it has made to the dealer. If there is a default and the credit-risky asset declines in value, then the investor will have a capital gain or loss depending upon whether there is a net inflow or outflow of cash to the investor after it receives the lump sum payment from the dealer.

With respect to the dealer it should be noted that for brokers, banks, and dealers who regularly deal in option transactions, there is no capital gain or loss from the option, it is all ordinary income or expense. The reason is that such transactions are conducted in the ordinary course of their business, and therefore should be treated as income or expense items. If the dealer is not in the business of transacting in options (unlikely, but possible) then it will recognize capital gain or loss similar to the investor, subject to its capital gain rates.

In summary, credit default swaps are economically easy to describe and understand. However, with respect to the tax code, they are more like the square peg in the round hole. There is no direct guidance as to where to put these transactions for tax purposes. In Exhibit 13.5 we summarize the decision matrix for the tax treatment for credit default swaps. We conclude that they are best classified as credit options for tax purposes.

AN OPTION ON A CREDIT-RISKY ASSET

Credit options face many of the same issues and much of the same analysis as total return swaps and credit default swaps discussed above. Rather than go through a repetitive discussion of the tax rules, we focus on the tax treatment most likely to affect these transactions.

Integration of the OCRA with the Credit-Risky Asset

An option on a credit-risky asset (OCRA) is similar to our discussion of a credit default swap discussed above. Consider a dealer who promises to pay to an investor the decline in value of a credit-risky asset over the term of the credit option while the investor makes either a lump sum payment or periodic payments to the dealer to pay for the credit protection. The investor gets credit protection similar to the credit default swap. However, a key difference compared to a credit default swap is

EXHIBIT 13.5   Decision Tree for the Tax Treatment of a Credit Default Swap

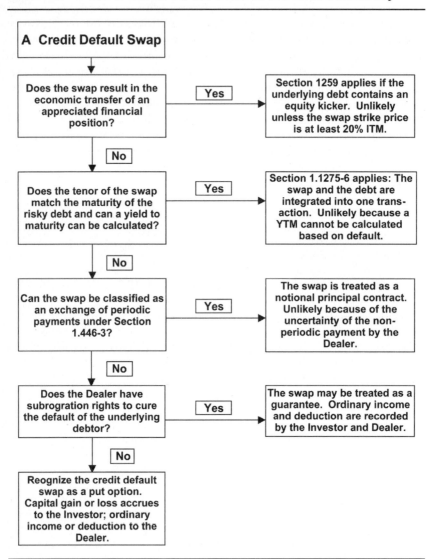

that there does not need to be a default to collect a payment. The dealer's payment to the investor is not contingent on any event. This is important because it may allow the investor to integrate the option and the underlying risky asset.

If the investor owns the underlying credit-risky asset, then it would be entitled to integrate the credit put option with the asset into one debt instrument, subject to the two conditions discussed above. It can be argued that the payment by the dealer replaces any loss of value on the credit-risky asset. Therefore, the investor can calculate the yield to maturity as the coupon on the underlying credit-risky asset less the payments made to the dealer. Under these circumstances, IRC Section 1.1275-6 applies and the investor will record ordinary income from the integrated transaction of the credit-risky debt and the credit option. The dealer will record ordinary income from the investor's payments and ordinary deduction for any amount paid out as loss of value on the asset.

Treating the OCRA as a Put Option

Suppose, however, that the investor does not own the underlying asset, and simply wishes to make a credit bet on the potential deterioration of the creditworthiness of the credit-risky debt. The payout to the investor at the maturity of the OCRA may be described as

Payout = [Strike price of the credit option – Market value of asset; 0]

This is simply a put option, and the investor has acquired an asset subject to the rules that govern capital gains and losses. The investor will not be able to deduct the payments for the OCRA. Instead, it will record these payments as the basis for a capital asset. If the OCRA expires worthless, the investor has a capital loss. If the OCRA expires in the money, the investor will net the option payment with the option premium to determine the net capital gain or loss. The dealer will recognize ordinary income or expense from the cash flows associated with the option.

Exhibit 13.6 summarizes this decision matrix.

OPTION ON A CREDIT SPREAD

Options on a credit spread (OCS) are typically tied to a reference riskless asset such as U.S. Treasury bonds. It is important to note that these types of assets are *not* written on an underlying credit-risky asset. Because a OCS is written on a credit spread and not an underlying asset, they cannot be viewed as a constructive sale under Section 1259. Further, since they do not compensate the investor for a loss in market value of an underlying asset, OCS are not financial guarantees. Also, integration does not apply because there is no underlying credit-risky asset to integrate. As a result, the tax treatment for an OCS is a bit more straightforward.

EXHIBIT 13.6   Tax Treatment for an Option on a Credit-Risky Asset

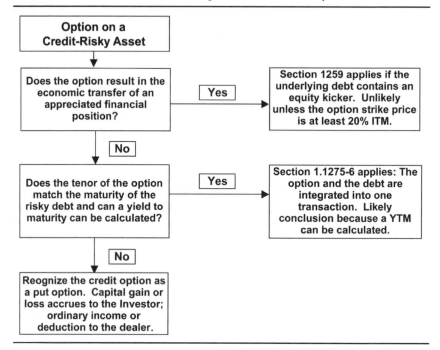

Treating OCS as Notional Principal Contracts for Tax Purposes

IRC Section 1.446-3 does not address options on a credit spread. However, it does include within its definition of a notional principal contract, interest rate caps, collars, and floors. An option on a credit spread performs a similar function to that of an interest rate cap or floor: the payment at a future date equal to the product of a notional principal amount and the excess of a specified index over an interest rate (the cap rate). The similarity of these transactions lends itself to arguing that an OCS can be accounted for as a notional principal contract. If this election is made, then all cash flows associated with this option would be ordinary income as demonstrated in Exhibit 13.3.

Treating OCS as Options for Tax Purposes

An OCS can be a call or put option that is used to hedge a widening of credit spreads or to simply express a view about the direction of credit spreads. For example a call option on a credit spread may be expressed as

EXHIBIT 13.7 Tax Treatment for an Option on a Credit Spread

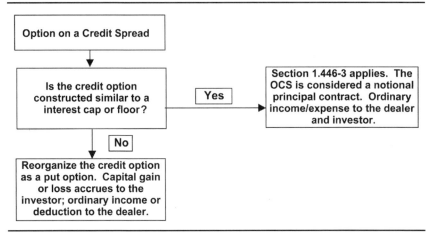

Call option payout
= [Credit spread at maturity – Strike credit spread; 0]
× Risk factor × Notional amount of the option

The above credit derivative can be treated as an option. This means that the premium paid by the investor to hedge credit risk is a nondeductible capital expenditure. If the OCS expires worthless, the investor will have a capital loss equal to the payments it has made. If the OCS is exercised in the money, the investor will net the payments made to and from the dealer to determine the net capital gain or loss. Once again, for a dealer transacting in these type of credit derivatives, all payments are either ordinary income or expenses.

Exhibit 13.7 demonstrates the choices associated with an option on a credit spread.

SUMMARY

Once again, we have digested hundreds of pages of tax regulations into a shorter format. It is important to reiterate that there is no specific tax guidance on credit derivatives as of this writing. The application of the tax rules must be done by analogy to existing regulations for other types of derivative transactions. We admit that we are not infallible. However, we have presented a discussion of tax treatment that is consistent with similar derivative transactions for which there are tax rules. As a result, this chapter provides a rigorous framework for analyzing the tax consequences of credit derivatives.

Index